Racial Purity and Dangerous Bodies

Racial Purity and Dangerous Bodies

Moral Pollution, Black Lives, and the Struggle for Justice

Rima Vesely-Flad

Fortress Press
Minneapolis

RACIAL PURITY AND DANGEROUS BODIES

Moral Pollution, Black Lives, and the Struggle for Justice

Cover image: Black Lives Matter, by Alex Nabaum (2015); from the private collection of Roderic Southall. Exhibited at United Theological Seminary in 2015.

Cover design: Alisha Lofgren

Print ISBN: 978-1-5064-2049-3

eBook ISBN: 978-1-5064-2050-9

The paper used in this publication meets the minimum requirements of American National Standard for Information Sciences — Permanence of Paper for Printed Library Materials, ANSI Z329.48-1984.

Manufactured in the U.S.A.

This book was produced using Pressbooks.com, and PDF rendering was done by PrinceXML.

For my family.
And for racial justice activists worldwide.

But we can surely accept the general proposition that, in our societies, the systems of punishment are to be situated in a certain "political economy" of the body: even if they do not make use of violent or bloody punishment, even when they use "lenient" methods involving confinement or correction, it is always the body that is at issue—the body and its forces, their utility and their docility, their distribution and their submission.

—Michel Foucault, *Discipline and Punish*

***

Get away [garbled] . . . for what? Every time you see me, you want to mess with me. I'm tired of it. It stops today. Why would you . . . ? Everyone standing here will tell you I didn't do nothing. I did not sell nothing. Because every time you see me, you want to harass me. You want to stop me [garbled] selling cigarettes. I'm minding my business, officer, I'm minding my business. Please just leave me alone. I told you the last time, please just leave me alone. Please, please, don't touch me. Do not touch me.

Video of the arrest shows four officers wrestling Eric Garner to the ground and restraining him.

I can't breathe. I can't breathe. I can't breathe. I can't breathe. I can't breathe. I can't breathe. I can't breathe. I can't breathe.

The video shows officers restraining him.[1]

1. Eric Garner's last words on July 17, 2014. Susanna Capelouto, "Transcript: Eric Garner's Last Words," WQAD.com, December 4, 2014, http://tinyurl.com/h59qqem.

***

The voice of an officer shouts: Hands up!

Immediately, Rakeyia Scott says: Don't shoot him.

She begins walking closer to the officers and Mr. Scott's vehicle:
Don't shoot him. He has no weapon. He has no weapon. Don't shoot him.

Ms. Scott pleads, her voice becoming louder and more anxious: Don't shoot him, don't shoot him. He didn't do anything.

Fifty seconds into Ms. Scott's video, four shots ring out.[2]

---

2. Transcript of the death of Keith Lamont Scott on September 21, 2016. "VIDEO: NBC Releases Wife's Cellphone Footage of Police Shooting of Keith Lamont Scott in Charlotte," *Democracy Now!*, September 23, 2016, http://tinyurl.com/jgqeabn.

Contents

Acknowledgments

I have relied upon the encouragement and support of numerous individuals over the years of initiating and completing this project. The students in my Sociology of Religious Communities class at Sing Sing Prison during the 2004–2005 academic year inspired me to return to graduate school for a doctorate. Week after week, I pondered how they—as intelligent, self-reflective, persevering community leaders—had ended up in lockdown for so many years. I am grateful to Tai-Chi, KB, Shabaka, Brain, Tony, David, Wai, Frank, Messer, Anthony, and Mik for helping me think through questions of individual culpability and social responsibility in the phenomenon of mass imprisonment.

I also gained much inspiration and insight from my colleagues in the New York criminal justice community. The dedicated activists who live out their commitments to justice always propel me to work harder toward the end goal of dismantling mass incarceration. Thank you especially to members of the policy committee of the Interfaith Coalition of Advocates for Reentry and Employment: Susan Antos, Judith Brink, Juan Cartegena, Annette Warren Dickerson, Paul Keefe, Kirsten Levingston, Glenn E. Martin, Demi McGuire, Vivian Nixon, Sue Porter, Alan Rosenthal, Kate Rubin, McGregor Smythe, Gabriel Torres-Rivera, and Willie Thomas.

I am grateful to my students and colleagues at Warren Wilson College, where I have taught since 2013. Upon my arrival, I encountered a community of warm and engaged students and supportive colleagues, all of whom celebrate cross-disciplinary research, teaching, and community-based work. In this small, nurturing academic setting, my colleagues have provided numerous opportunities to converse in depth about methodologies for engaging undergraduates in the study of social justice. I especially thank Ben Feinberg, division chair of the social sciences; as well as Julie Wilson, Brooke Millsaps, and Catina Bacote, my co-coordinators in establishing an Inside-Out college prison program at the Swannanoa Correctional Center for Women. And I am grateful to college administrators who supported two trips to Ferguson and a trip to Charlotte to participate in Black Lives Matter protests and organizing.

Faculty participants at the Wabash Center for Teaching and Learning in Theology and Religion were particularly inspirational. I participated in a teaching workshop for pre-tenure faculty of African descent during the 2015–2016 academic year. Indeed, the intellectual excitement I felt during each of our gatherings inspired me to turn my dissertation into a book. I am especially grateful to each member of the extraordinary group of scholars who gathered each time. I thank the leadership: Carolyn Medine, Willie Jennings, Ralph Watkins, Melanie Harris, and Tim Lake, along with my fellow participants: Trina Armstrong, Adam Bond, Stephanie Crumpton, Elise Edwards, Joseph Flipper, Tamara Henry, Tamara Lewis, Michael McCormack, Donyelle McCray, Monique Moultrie, Richard Newton, Aliou Niang, and Joseph Winters.

I am also grateful to readers at various stages of this project: my dissertation committee members: Gary Dorrien, James H. Cone, Euan Cameron, and James Samuel Logan. I am especially grateful to Dr. Logan for the extensive mentoring that he offered throughout the duration of the writing and job search process, and to Dr. Cone for challenging me to think deeply about Black people's agency in the face of systemic oppression. I am also grateful to friends who read different chapters: Catina Bacote, Geoffrey Habron, Rebecca Gordon, Jermaine McDonald, and Patrisia Macias-Rojas.

I thank my editor at Fortress Press, Neil Elliott, who understood *exactly* what I was trying to say in this book as I engaged in cross-disciplinary research and worked intensively with concepts of purity and pollution. I am grateful that he believed in a project that draws from so many different disciplines.

I am thankful to mentors I encountered along the way, including Tracey Hucks, Sandy Barkan, Shahnaz Rouse, Gina Sharpe, and Venerable UJotika Bhivamsa, and to friends near and far who provided an important emotional support system during this lengthy project: Letitia Campbell, Kitty Ufford-Chase, Eleanor Harrison, Kari Henquinet, Jermaine McDonald, Dawn Chávez, Idoia Gkikas, and Julie Wilson.

I also received significant support from the Episcopal Church Foundation (ECF), which provided a three-year fellowship during my doctoral program, and from the Fund for Theological Education (FTE), which granted me fellowships over two years during my doctoral program. I am especially grateful to my grant officers, Anne Ditzler at ECF and Matthew Wesley Williams at FTE, for celebrating successes.

Last but certainly not least, I could not have completed this book project without my family. I am deeply grateful to my mother, Jude Wrzesinski, and my stepfather, John Wrzesinski, who provided countless hours of childcare to both of my children. I thank my godmother, Judi, who worked as a college professor for many years, and my brother, Laurent, who recently completed a doctoral program; we frequently commiserated about the pressures of teaching and writing at the same time. I am grateful to my sons, Matai and Jaxson, who kept me laughing and made sure that I got outside to play almost every day. Finally, to my husband, Ethan, who went beyond the call of duty as he took our children out of the house when I needed a quiet environment, made sure we ate healthy, home-cooked meals, and put down his own work time and again so that I could write. He endured many weekends where I spent long hours in front of the computer, he embarked upon countless errands, and he offered skillful copyediting advice. He believed in this project from beginning to end. I couldn't have done it without him.

Introduction

Charlotte, North Carolina, September 23, 2016

Protesters marched over a highway, followed by police officers. A heli-copter circled overhead. The protesters chanted repeatedly: "Hands up! Don't shoot!" They walked en masse under a bridge. Spotlights from the helicopters illuminated their signs. "The people, united, can never be defeated." As they passed through the uptown streets of Char-lotte, North Carolina's largest city, National Guard officers stood facing them. "No justice, no peace! No racist po-lice!" "You can't stop the rev-olution!" "Black lives matter. Black lives matter. Black lives matter."

Outraged protestors are taking to the streets, demanding police accountability and an end to the war on Black people.[1] State vio-lence—police aggression, militarized responses to demonstrations, mass incarceration, post-imprisonment reentry barriers, cyclical poverty, and failing social institutions—defines the parameters of daily life for most impoverished Black people. These material conditions arise from the racist edifice of symbolic constructs of Black people as polluted: immoral, slothful, and dangerous.

The criminalization of Black men who have been killed by police since 2013 highlights the salience of symbolic constructs. Trayvon Mar-tin, 17, assassinated while walking in his father's apartment complex, was wearing a hoodie. Michael Brown, 18, executed while walking down the street, was deemed "no angel." Tamir Rice, 12, shot in a playground while playing with a toy gun, was considered threatening. Freddie Gray, 25, handcuffed and suffering from a snapped spinal cord

---

1. "End the War on Black People," The Movement for Black Lives, accessed September 20, 2016, http://tinyurl.com/zk2rg3y.

after police officers failed to strap him into a police van, lived in a symbolically polluted neighborhood: an impoverished neighborhood in Baltimore. His crime: making eye contact with a police officer.

Even when the actions of Black people appear nonthreatening, the bodies of Black people are deemed dangerous. Eric Garner, 43, killed by a police officer who performed an illegal choke hold, was standing outside of a bodega on Staten Island. Philando Castile, 32, shot to death through an open window by a police officer, had reached for his identification upon the officer's request. Alton Sterling, 37, tackled to the ground by two police officers and executed at close range, was standing outside of a convenience store where he sometimes sold DVDs. Terence Crutcher, 40, shot in the back while he held up his hands, was pulled over on the side of the road. Keith Lamont Scott, 43, surrounded and murdered by police, was sitting in his car at his apartment complex, waiting for his son to step out of a school bus.

These Black men are killed because their dark skin symbolizes moral and physical danger. Several centuries of discourse on Black bodies as morally polluting entities has resulted in perpetual subjugation and harassment by government officials. The result is the erection of symbolic boundaries between white bodies and Black bodies, between white neighborhoods and Black neighborhoods, between those who are protected by law and those who are violently subjugated to the whims of police officials.

Policing and the interlocking spheres of the US penal system, then, perform a particular function: to intimidate and control the bodies of Black people who are constructed as polluted, threatening, and dangerous. This book argues that the institution of policing operates as a complex, sophisticated system focused on keeping the threatening elements of society—people of African descent—in a constant state of harassment and tension so that Blackness cannot pollute the morals of mainstream society. Policing, along with incarceration and post-imprisonment reentry barriers, sequesters and restrains polluted Black bodies.

The US penal system functions on two symbiotic levels: the material and the symbolic. The French sociologist Loïc Wacquant states: "in historical reality penal institutions and policies can and do shoulder [two] tasks at once: they simultaneously act to enforce hierarchy and control contentious categories, at one level, and to communicate norms and shape collective representations and subjectivities, at another."[2] Indeed, there are material considerations for disproportionate policing and mass imprisonment in US society: these systems function as methods to consolidate political power, as engines of economic development in rural communities, and as intimidating forces in urban communities that perpetuate poverty and social isolation. However, there is a symbolic dimension that perpetuates the penal system as well. This book argues that symbolic constructs of racialized, polluted bodies sustain violence against Black people, even when the material systems, such as prisons, become too costly for state governments to maintain.

***

The interlocking spheres of race, impoverishment, incarceration, and political representation have resulted in the largest prison system in the world; the United States, with less than 5 percent of the world's population, now contains 25 percent of the world's prison population. While material gains are garnered through the political economy of penality, we might further understand the US penal system—including policing, imprisonment, and post-incarceration reentry barriers—as indicative of a society rife with enduring racialized pollution boundaries.

Social pollution is a phenomenon theorized in religious studies, particularly the subfields of biblical studies, anthropology of religion, and religious ethics. Christian ethics, in particular, draws upon biblical interpretations as well as contemporary social sciences for analyses and argument. Consequently, I argue that religious frameworks offer important lenses for understanding contemporary US policing, imprisonment, and post-incarceration reentry practices. New Testament biblical narratives contain stories about Jesus of Nazareth, a "pure" Jew who challenged boundaries of social pollution in Jewish society, in which purity was the "premier structuring value."[3] Jesus of Nazareth embraced those who were deemed polluted in first-century Palestine: demon-possessed persons, lepers, blind men, bleeding women, and tax collectors.[4] He applied spittle to a blind man's eyes. He ate unclean foods with unclean people. His disciples did not wash their hands.

In short, Jesus of Nazareth and his followers transgressed boundaries

2. Loïc Wacquant, *Punishing the Poor: The Neoliberal Government of Social Insecurity* (Durham, NC: Duke University Press, 2009), xiv.
3. Jerome H. Neyrey, "The Idea of Purity in Mark's Gospel," *Semeia* 35 (1986): 91–128.
4. Ibid.; see also Louis William Countryman, *Dirt, Greed, and Sex: Sexual Ethics in the New Testament and Their Implications for Today* (Minneapolis, MN: Fortress, 1989) and David A. deSilva, *Honor, Patronage, Kinship and Purity: Unlocking New Testament Culture* (Downers Grove, IL: InterVarsity, 2000).

of purity and pollution, and in so doing, demonstrated an ethical approach in a highly regulated society. Contemporary religious ethicists argue that pollution boundaries exist in contemporary US society as well. Those whose identities are marginalized in mainstream society—poor persons, drug-addicted persons, and people with criminal convictions, to name a few—threaten to pollute the morals of the mainstream social order. They are constructed as inherently immoral and therefore ethically incompetent. Moreover, in contemporary US society, moral pollution is associated with dark skin, hair, and phenotype: Black bodies in Black communities. Therefore, Black bodies are held in check to prevent moral transgression upon racialized pollution boundaries.

Disproportionate policing, mass imprisonment, and post-incarceration systems initiate as well as reinforce racialized pollution boundaries in the United States. Alongside scholars who identify the historical roots of the contemporary penal system in institutions of slavery, convict leasing, penal farms, and Jim Crow segregation in the United States, I argue that these racialized pollution boundaries originated with the arrival of the first African slaves. Boundaries between "pure whites" and "immoral Blacks" were maintained by legal statute until 1964, upon passage of the Civil Rights Act. Thereafter, racialized pollution boundaries have been perpetuated by the system of mass imprisonment, which depends upon disproportionate policing fueled by the War on Drugs, unprecedented prison building, and a series of reentry barriers that lock people with felony convictions into permanent second-class citizenship.

Thus, a primary argument made in this book is that racialized pollution boundaries are maintained by the contemporary penal system. A second, related theme of this book examines how anti-police-brutality activists challenge racialized pollution boundaries and, in so doing, reconstruct the meaning of pollution and the meaning of the Black body. I argue that these activists, while lacking institutional mechanisms to dismantle pollution boundaries, nonetheless have effectively shifted the prevailing crime-and-punishment paradigm in the court of public opinion. Social media and street demonstrations illuminate the practices of unwarranted police violence against Black bodies and refute the dominant narrative that justifies disproportionate force against, arrest of, and incarceration of Black people. In so doing, protestors humanize and legitimize the Black body: they create a new narrative.

A third, final argument made by this book is that by focusing on disproportionate policing and police brutality, the challenge articulated by Black Lives Matter activists makes visible only one part of the penal system: that of policing. In protesting police brutality against Black people, activists' broader demand to "end the war against Black people"[5] is for the most part obscured. I anticipate that the protests will extend further to more invisible reaches of the US penal system and thus begin to dismantle the multiple symbolic constructs that uphold mass imprisonment and societal reentry barriers. The Black Lives Matter movement, in its fierce critique of racism, has a platform to illuminate how the image of the formerly incarcerated person is constructed and racialized. It continues to be necessary to deconstruct the image of the ex-felon and the barriers that render formerly incarcerated people second-class citizens. In sum, there exists great potential to tackle yet another symbolic pillar that upholds the US penal system.

An Explanation of Pollution Boundaries: Douglas and Durkheim

Anthropologist Mary Douglas explains how societies respond to people associated with social pollution. She theorizes that "dirt" is the byproduct of producing order, and that individuals and societies reject anything and anyone that is considered defiled. In an effort to impose order, societies separate, purify, demarcate, and punish those who transgress boundaries or are associated with pollution. Dirt offends against order, and eliminating it is not a negative movement—in the eyes of those who undertake such rituals—but rather a positive effort to organize the environment.[6]

Chasing dirt, Douglas argues, makes the environment conform to an idea. Rather than evidence of irrationality, chasing dirt is, in fact, a creative movement, an attempt to relate form to function, to make unity of experience.[7] Pollution ideas work in the life of society at different levels: on one level, they are used as instruments to influence and correct people. Social elites articulate admonitions regarding danger. Influential leaders of society urge members to stay away from that which is physically unkempt. Warning protects society from danger.

On another level, beliefs in the dangers posed by dirt and disorder

5. "End the War on Black People," The Movement for Black Lives, accessed September 20, 2016, http://tinyurl.com/zk2rg3y.
6. Mary Douglas, *Purity and Danger: An Analysis of Concepts of Pollution and Taboo* (New York: Routledge, 2000 [1966]), 2.
7. Ibid.

are expressed as threats and mutual exhortation. At this level, the exhorters may invoke the laws of nature to bolster the moral code: There could be natural disaster if people do not abide in right relationship.

Morally upright individuals avoid, then, dangerous persons.

> [Because a] polluting person is always in the wrong. He has developed some wrong condition or simply crossed some line which should not have been crossed and this displacement unleashes danger for someone. . . . Pollution can be committed unintentionally, but intention is irrelevant to its effect—it is more likely to happen inadvertently.[8]

Pollution can be corporally and non-corporally symbolic. For example, contact with sexual fluids can be considered dangerous. Certain behaviors, particularly if they involve transmission of sexual fluids, are considered polluting. Fluids are an important symbol because they can transgress boundaries. Blood, semen, and pus all flow and change shape—they are not rigid or fixed. As unstable elements, they symbolize that which is suspicious, potentially dangerous, and untrustworthy.[9]

The contrast between symbols that identify danger and symbols that identify wholesomeness pervades society. Societies set themselves apart from symbols of defilement and orient themselves towards symbols of purity. The idea of holiness is given an external, physical expression in the symbol of the healthy, whole, properly regulated body, as well as in larger society.[10] The symbol of the degraded, immoral, and dangerous body, by contrast, is set against the idea and image of the holy, pure body.

Deviance is set against order. In response to differences within a society, as well as to external pressures, a society will exaggerate differences. The only way in which order is created is to starkly distinguish between what is within and without, above and below, male and female.[11] In the US context, social order is created by starkly distinguishing between dark and light skin color.

Indeed, in a social sphere deeply affected by the European transat-

---

8. Ibid., 114.
9. Ibid., 3.
10. Douglas notes that, for example, in Leviticus, the animals offered in sacrifice must be physically perfect; the priests must be physically perfect; women must be purified after childbirth; all bodily discharges are defiling; anyone who exhibits bodily discharge is disqualified from approaching the temple; and the high priest may never have contact with death. See *Purity and Danger*, 52.
11. Douglas, *Purity and Danger*, 4.

lantic slave trade and colonialism, Douglas's theories illumine how Western societies distinguish between dark and light skin color, and consequently penalize dark skin. There are, to be sure, numerous critiques of Douglas: she does not address systems of power, such as economic systems, colonialism, slavery, or dominant cultures and institutions within a nation-state context. Yet her ideas are critical for understanding how bodies that are associated with pollution come to be excluded from mainstream social institutions.

Douglas conceptualized her theories of purity and danger in non-Western contexts, even as she argued that Western nations fostered pollution boundaries as well. Douglas's ideas of purity and danger are further illuminated by Émile Durkehim's theories of criminal law and systems of punishment.[12] Indeed, Durkheim's description of collective consciousness and criminal law illustrates how ideas of social pollution manifest in the US penal system. Durkheim suggests that in modernity, moral ideas are encoded in society's criminal laws. Penal codes reveal social arrangements. Furthermore, criminal laws not only reflect religious and secular ideals of morality—criminal laws also reinforce them.

For Durkheim, morality is the common basis of society, which is established to protect collective life. Thus when an act, regardless of its gravity, provokes a collective punitive reaction, it is because that act has infringed upon the collective's idea of the good. This offensive act, known as a "crime," depicts a kind of antagonism between the individual and the interests of larger society; thus members of society morally condemn criminal acts as threats to the collective.[13] Universal condemnation springs from a collective consciousness, "the totality of beliefs and sentiments common to the average members of society [which] forms a determinate system with a life of its own."[14] Durkheim argues that every society possesses moral collective consciousness; that such consciousness does not change from generation to generation; and that while only realized in individuals, collective consciousness is completely distinct from the consciousness of individuals. Thus, he argues, "an act is criminal when it offends the strong, well-defined states of the collective consciousness."[15]

12. Douglas identified her intellectual work as rooted in Durkheim's theories of society.
13. Emile Durkheim, *The Division of Labor in Society*, trans. W.D. Halls (New York: The Free Press, 1984 [1893]), 33. Durkheim also believed that there are numerous acts that are regarded as criminal that are not, in themselves, harmful to society, and, further, there are acts that can be disastrous for society without suffering the slightest repression. See pp. 32–33.
14. Ibid., 38–39.

Because criminal acts offend against collective moral consciousness, such acts are equated with immorality. Durkheim identifies the precise definition of immorality, "particularly that special form of immorality which society represses by an organized system of punishment, and which constitutes criminality."[16] In parsing the definition, Durkheim explains:

> We should not say that an act offends the common consciousness because it is criminal, but it is criminal because it offends the consciousness. We do not condemn it because it is a crime, but it is a crime because we condemn it.[17]

For Durkheim, an action becomes a crime when society condemns and punishes it. He believes that generally, punishment "constitutes essentially a reaction of passionate feeling, graduated in intensity, which society exerts through the mediation of an organized body over those of its members who have violated certain rules of conduct."[18] Indeed the collective consciousness defines crime; it also unites in opposition to crime. Offensive acts, then, strengthen previously established collective moral sentiments.

At the heart of the reaction to breaches in morality, Durkheim tells us, is a vengeful spirit that seeks to redress harm enacted upon a cherished belief. Durkheim believes that penal law is essentially religious in origin, and even in the context of modernity, it continues to bear a certain stamp of religiosity.[19] Collective revenge evokes this sense of the sacred; it creates solidarity and social cohesion, and furthermore buttresses the collective consciousness. "Indeed the acts which such law forbids and stigmatizes as crimes are of two kinds: either they manifest directly a too violent dissimilarity between the one who commits them and the collective type; or they offend the organ of the common consciousness."[20]

Durkheim believes that punishment does not serve to correct a guilty person, and that its real function is to maintain the cohesion of society by sustaining the common consciousness. He thus insists that punishment should be not only consistent but also conspicuously and publicly reinforced. Such visible enactment indicates that the senti-

15. Ibid., 39.
16. Ibid., 40.
17. Ibid.
18. Ibid.
19. Ibid., 56.
20. Ibid., 61.

ments of the collectivity are still unchanged, that the communion of minds sharing the same beliefs remains absolute, and in this way the injury that the crime has inflicted upon society is made good.[21]

That goodness, or positive function, underscores Durkheim's analysis of the primary purpose of punishment: above all, it is intended to have its effect on "honest" people. It is to unite and to buttress collective moral sentiments and to strengthen social bonds.

Durkheim's theories provide useful tools for explicating the social function of punishment. While many scholars agree that there are gaps in his theory,[22] I argue that his theories remain salient.[23] Durkheim helps us to understand how moral constructs operate in cultural consciousness. At the same time, it is important to emphasize that Durkheim's emphasis on criminal acts ignores the reality of criminalized *bodies*.[24] His social theories ignore racial classification and systems of power, and do not address the ways in which criminal law functions as a system of coercion and force against peoples whose mere physical *appearance*—apart from their actions—renders them deviant.

Nevertheless, Durkheim illuminates how historical constructions of Black immorality have shaped contemporary collective consciousness and why jails and prisons in the United States contain disproportionate members of young Black men. In the United States, criminal law and institutions of punishment control and contain Black bodies that threaten to pollute society's moral boundaries. Indeed, codes provide symbolic notions of morality that are fundamental to the institutional function of the prison: laws and systems of punishment furnish bifurcated notions of good versus evil, purity versus danger, white versus Black, citizen versus outcast.[25]

The Politics of Black Immorality

The idea that people of African descent pose a physical and cultural threat has become a staple of conservative discourse. In the moral politics of crime policy, Republican law-and-order politics have exploited fears of integration exhibited by white, working-class voters. In the

21. Ibid.
22. See, for example, Garland, 23–42.
23. Wacquant, *Punishing the Poor*.
24. Although he developed his social theories in the late nineteenth century, Durkheim ignored racial classification and colonialism, instead focusing on "primitive" and "modern" societies that developed mechanical or organic solidarity.
25. Chapter 4 illuminates this fact in the particular case study of Stop and Frisk policing in New York City.

1960s, Republicans aimed to dismantle the New Deal coalition and the gains made in the movement for civil rights.[26]

The explanation for the disproportionate and vastly increased incarceration of Black people is generally articulated in the following way: the Republican strategy shifted the emphasis from economic issues to values and, in doing so, elevated race as a subtext within political discourse.[27] In 1962 and 1963, many conservatives feared that the social bonds of family, neighborhood, and "civility" were coming apart.[28] Much of the protest on the part of white voters coalesced around increased rates of individuals receiving public assistance. "Welfare cheats" and their dangerous offspring were heightened in media outlets. Inevitably, these images promoted the idea that African Americans were undeserving, violent beneficiaries of the welfare state—that they were morally polluting, lazy, and vicious.[29]

Indeed, the conservative view that the causes of crime lie in the human "propensity towards evil" became a hallmark of political discourse.[30] This argument elevated images of dangerous Black men, in particular, and fueled fears that racial integration would lead to moral pollution.[31] The *National Review*, a conservative magazine, argued that support for segregation and the backlash against civil rights were essential to reviving the conservative agenda.[32] Republican Party elites took advantage of white disaffection with the Democratic Party, particularly in light of its alliances with African Americans, and devised a "Southern Strategy" with the idea of joining the "Negrophobe" South and the West in a conservative coalition.[33] In 1964, white working-class voters rallied behind the Arizona Republican presidential nominee, Barry Goldwater, who promoted a law-and-order message. Goldwater's platform was quickly interpreted as a racist subtext in the Deep

26. Michael W. Flamm, *Law and Order: Street Crime, Civil Unrest, and the Crisis of Liberalism in the 1960s* (New York: Columbia University Press, 2005); Katherine Beckett, *Making Crime Pay: Law and Order in Contemporary American Politics* (New York: Oxford University Press, 1997); Vesla Mae Weaver, "Frontlash: Race and the Development of Punitive Crime Strategy," *Studies in American Political Development* 21, no. 2 (Fall 2007): 230–65.
27. Thomas Byrne Edsall and Mary D. Edsall, *Chain Reaction: The Impact of Race, Rights, and Taxes on American Politics* (New York: W. W. Norton, 1992).
28. James Q. Wilson, *Thinking about Crime* (New York: Basic Books,1983), 20.
29. Beckett, *Making Crime Pay*, 36.
30. Ibid., 10–11.
31. Flamm, *Law and Order*, 34–35.
32. Joseph Lowndes, *From the New Deal to the New Right: Race and the Southern Origins of Modern Conservatism* (New Haven, CT: Yale University Press, 2008), 49–54.
33. Kevin Phillips, *The Emerging Republican Majority* (Garden City, NY: Anchor, 1970), 232. The GOP elected ten new governors in 1966, seven of whom were in the South and West. See also M. Stanton Evans, *The Future of Conservatism: From Taft to Reagan and Beyond* (New York: Holt, Rinehart & Winston, 1968), 51.

South vein. His racially conservative agenda "gained so much credence that he swung the Deep South into the Republican column."[34] Goldwater blamed the "welfare state" for the breakdown in civic order and referred to urban riots, political demonstrations, and street crime as an overall threat to society.[35]

The passage of the 1964 Civil Rights Act and the 1965 Voting Rights Act, known as the "Second Reconstruction," was seen as popularizing civil disobedience and promoting disrespect for law and authority. White Americans overwhelmingly associated street crime—and thus social pollution—with African Americans, who were seventeen times as likely as white men to be arrested for robbery.[36] As riots unfolded in Watts in 1965 and in Detroit and Newark—amongst one hundred other cities—in the "long, hot summer" of 1967, fears and outrage in white America swelled. Vietnam protestors also sparked a residual antipathy in white working-class voters. All demonstrators, regardless of intent, represented lawlessness, disorder, and enemies of the state.

In 1968, white voters flocked to Alabama Governor George Wallace, a strident segregationist, and former California Senator Richard Nixon as the 1968 Republican presidential contenders.[37] After Nixon received the nomination, he adopted numerous tactics from Wallace's campaign.[38] With explicit, detailed promises of law and order, Nixon promised tough responses to liberalism, blaming the Democratic Party for rising rates of crime. Law and order became the vehicle by which whites transmitted their antipathy to integration and fear of racial violence. Nixon won narrowly against Hubert Humphrey and proceeded to address crime rates through a federally mandated War on Drugs that promised to alleviate disorder and fear of violent attacks.[39]

Nixon's law-and-order presidential administration influenced the election of Republican gubernatorial candidates on the state level, which in turn directly affected a massive campaign of prison building.[40]

---

34. Phillips, *Emerging Republican Majority*, 204.
35. Ibid.
36. Flamm, *Law and Order*, 5.
37. John C. Green, "Seeking a Place," in *Toward an Evangelical Public Policy: Political Strategies for the Health of the Nation*, ed. Ronald J. Sider and Diane Knippers (Grand Rapids: Baker Books, 2005), 24.
38. Lowndes, *From the New Deal*, 100.
39. Lyndon Johnson was actually the first president to give a presidential address specifically on crime. Under his administration, the Law Enforcement Assistance Act (LEAA) provided the first federal program to assist states and localities for the purpose of providing training programs and experimental projects to strengthen their local law enforcement. See Weaver, "Frontlash," 243.
40. Sarah Lawrence and Jeremy Travis, "The New Landscape of Imprisonment: Mapping America's Prison Expansion," The Urban Institute, April 29, 2004. Governors are responsible for state budgets and also appoint members of the parole board.

Indeed, the success of law-and-order rhetoric prompted Democrats as well as Republicans to adopt increasingly harsh stances on crime.[41]

The Reagan administration appealed to conservatives by adopting strategies similar to Nixon's War on Drugs and by arguing that crime derives from human vice rather than socioeconomic conditions:

> Choosing a career in crime is not the result of poverty or of an unhappy childhood or of a misunderstood adolescence; it is the result of a conscious, willful choice made by some who consider themselves above the law, who seek to exploit the hard work and, sometimes, the very lives of their fellow citizens.[42]

Shortly after his election to the presidency, Reagan announced:

> We can begin by acknowledging some absolute truths. . . . Two of those truths are: men are basically good but prone to evil; some men are very prone to evil—and society has a right to be protected from them. . . . The war on crime will only be won when an attitude of mind and a change of heart takes place in America—when certain truths take hold again . . . truths like: right and wrong matters; individuals are responsible for their actions; retribution should be swift and sure for those who prey on the innocent.[43]

In October 1982, Reagan officially announced his administration's War on Drugs with the overt purpose of controlling predatory, morally polluting individuals. George H. W. Bush followed Reagan's lead and signed extensive crime bills into law. In August 1989, Bush characterized drug use as "the most pressing problem facing the nation."[44] He used catch phrases such as "user accountability," "zero tolerance," and "get tough."[45]

As the actions and rhetoric of the Nixon, Reagan, and Bush administrations demonstrate, conservatives have fought fiercely against the perceived sloth and corresponding violence that, in their eyes, is the inevitable result of social welfare programs. They argue that the base problem lies in the morally polluting men and women whose low character hastens the decline of *Pax Americana*.

---

41. David F. Greenberg and Valerie West, "State Prison Populations and Their Growth, 1971–1991," *Criminology* 39, no. 3 (August 2001): 11. See also Weaver, "Frontlash," 251, who argues that as early as 1968, Democrats were desperately trying to mimic Republican law-and-order programs.
42. Ronald Reagan, quoted in Beckett, *Making Crime Pay*, 49.
43. Ibid.
44. Ibid., 44.
45. Ibid.

Conservatives blame bad behavior on a lack of "family governance" —that is, the absence of a strong patriarchal father who imposes corporal punishment upon his children.[46] Indeed, much of the animosity toward welfare derives from the fact that female-headed households are perceived to contribute to generations of laziness and criminality—to moral decay—because fathers are strict whereas mothers are soft, fathers discipline where mothers excuse. A household without a father is destined to breed idleness and intemperance. Furthermore, sex outside of marriage exhibits a lack of self-control, yet another trait of an immoral character. Thus, unmarried women with "illegitimate" children, especially those on welfare, perpetuate a social decline that will rot American society from the inside. Finally, family degeneration is linked to drug use and violence, which perpetuate a downward spiral that will morally pollute a cohesive society.

The authors of *Body Count*—William Bennett (former "drug czar" under George H. W. Bush), John P. Walters (former "drug czar" under George W. Bush), and John DiIulio (director of faith-based initiatives under George W. Bush)—assert that the penal system is designed to address a widespread drug and crime problem that is rooted in "moral poverty." They suggest that children under the age of nine have the potential to avoid criminal behavior but that adolescents and adults in "criminogenic" communities of color are irretrievably mired in cultural pathologies.

These authors acknowledge the fact of historical racism but argue that contemporary racism is an unpersuasive explanation for disproportionate Black imprisonment in the present day: "Tragically, it is true that until the second half of this century, America's criminal justice institutions, like many other American institutions, were guilty of discrimination based on race. Fortunately, however, the justice system,

---

46. George Lakoff, *Moral Politics: How Liberals and Conservatives Think* (Chicago: University of Chicago Press, 2002). Lakoff unpacks the argument for orphanages that is invoked repeatedly in cultural conservatives' writings. How does it serve family values to take children away from the only family they have ever known? If the family values are "strict father" values, the answer is clear. To conservatives, the problem is the lack of strict father values, beginning with self-discipline. They see welfare mothers as not having those values themselves and not raising their children to have those values. They see orphanages as institutions that will inculcate those values. They believe that if the children of welfare mothers are raised to have strict father values, then the cycle of dependency, immorality, and lawlessness will stop, and that this will help solve the problems of crime and drugs as well. As to the observation that orphanages impose hardships on children and that the children would be denied their mother's love, the conservative reply is clear: these children need to learn the discipline to overcome hardships, and they need to learn strict father values more than they need the love of a mother who does not teach those values. Orphanages may cost the taxpayer more, but if they contribute to a moral society, they are worth paying for. See Lakoff, *Moral Politics*, 186.

like the rest of American society, has come a long way."[47] Thus, in their eyes, race is not a significant variable in determining whether a convicted adult offender is sentenced to probation or prison, the length of the term imposed, or how prisoners are disciplined. Disproportionate penalization of Black men is solely due to criminal proclivities resulting from the lack of male figures in the home and a culture of moral poverty.

> What, then, is one to make of the widely reported reality that a third of black men in their twenties are under some form of correctional supervision today (about one-third of them in prison or jail, the rest on probation or parole)? The same, we think, that one should make of the fact that blacks are about 50 times more likely to commit violent crimes against whites than whites are to commit violent crimes against blacks. Both sad statistics originate largely in the fact that young black males commit crime at higher rates than do young white males. . . . Blacks have been "responsible for a disproportionate amount of serious violent crime."[48]

Despite evidence that incarceration rates have risen dramatically as a result of the War on Drugs, Bennett, Walters, and DiIulio insist that "virtually all convicted criminals who do go to prison are violent offenders, repeat offenders, or violent repeat offenders."[49] The authors advocate for long sentences and intensive parole and probation supervision.[50] Indeed, in the eyes of some scholars, these influential advisors in Republican administrations have fed the moral panics that led to severe crime laws and, consequently, mass imprisonment. Legal scholar Michael Tonry describes a "moral panic" as what occurs

> when the official reaction to a person, group of persons, or series of events is out of all proportion to the actual threat offered, when "experts" perceive the threat in all but identical terms, and appear to talk "with one voice" of rates, diagnoses, prognoses, and solutions, when the media representations universally stress "sudden and dramatic" increases (in numbers involved or events) and "novelty," above and beyond that which a sober, realistic appraisal could sustain.[51]

47. William J. Bennett, John DiIulio, and John P. Walters, *Body Count: Moral Poverty . . . and How to Win America's War Against Crime and Drugs* (New York: Simon & Schuster, 1996), 43.
48. Ibid., 45.
49. Ibid., 94.
50. Ibid., 109–36.
51. Michael Tonry, *Thinking about Crime: Sense and Sensibilities in American Penal Culture* (New York: Oxford University Press, 2004), 85.

Indeed, Tonry argues, the drug-related moral panic drove three decades of harsh crime policies, such as three-strikes laws, zero-tolerance policing, and expansions of the death penalty. Despite the fact that crime began to drop in 1979 and 1980, the harshest drug laws enacted at the federal level under the guidance of the presidential administration's "drug czar" took place ten years later, largely because the moral panic surrounding drug use had not abated. In the 1980s and 1990s, the moral panic about drugs operated as a backdrop to the legal institutions, which enacted unprecedented, harsh criminal laws: mandatory minimum sentences for simple possession of crack cocaine and the death penalty for some drug offenses.

As in past moral panics, the political response to drugs has escalated even as usage has fallen.[52] In the most recent moral panic about drugs, the legislation enacted at the height of the drug scare has permanently reshaped the political sphere.[53] More than forty years after the first mandatory minimum drug laws were put into place, 2.3 million individuals are in local, state, and federal carceral facilities. An economic crisis minimally impacted the trends. The war on terror has not detracted from the phenomenon of mass imprisonment. Racialized images of immoral criminals are as prevalent and powerful as ever.

Moral panics are fueled by images of sloth and violence that project people of color as socially polluting. For example, the popular representation of the "welfare queen" is Black.[54] Images of internal enemies of color who reject dominant cultural values reinforce moral discourses in public policy debates. Welfare queens and drug dealers represent these stark images of evil: the people who are selling drugs to children, living off the government, having sex—sometimes interracial sex—out of marriage, and perpetuating the social pollution that leads to decline.

Sociological analyses of images of Blackness illumine the extent to

52. James A. Morone, *Hellfire Nation: The Politics of Sin in American History* (New Haven, CT: Yale University Press, 2003). Morone identifies several moral panics (also mentioned in the introduction)—such as movements to apprehend white female prostitutes, alcohol users, Chinese opium users, and Mexican American marijuana users—in the late nineteenth and early twentieth century that permanently reshaped political institutions.
53. Ibid., 477.
54. Jill Quadagno, *The Color of Welfare: How Racism Undermined the War on Poverty* (New York: Oxford University Press, 1994). In 2000, the largest percentage of Temporary Assistance for Needy Families (TANF) recipients were Black. The distribution has changed, however, perhaps because the recession drove more white families onto welfare, and perhaps because some Black families had reached the five-year lifetime limit. In 2010, Black and white women each made up 32 percent of the total of those receiving TANF. See "Characteristics and Financial Circumstances of TANF Recipients, Fiscal Year 2010," Office of Family Assistance, August 8, 2012, http://tinyurl.com/hlxvb9u.

which the Black body is linked to violence and laziness.[55] Loïc Wacquant argues that "the reigning public image of the criminal is not just that of 'a monstruum—a being whose features are inherently different from [whites]'—but that of a Black monster, as young African-American men from the 'inner city' have come to personify the explosive mix of moral degeneracy and mayhem."[56] David Garland concurs that "the recurrent image of the offender ceased to be that of the needy delinquent or the feckless misfit and became much more threatening—a matter of career criminals, crackheads, thugs, and predators—and at the same time much more racialized."[57]

> In its standard tropes and rhetorical invocations, this political discourse relies upon an archaic criminology of the criminal type, the alien other. Sometimes explicitly, more often in coded references, the problem is traced to the wanton, amoral behavior of dangerous offenders, who typically belong to racial and cultural groups bearing little resemblance to "us."[58]

"The blockbuster political images are so easily at hand: fatherless kids with high-power weapons," James Morone notes.[59] Nearly a half-century after the initiation of harsh crime laws, the desire for mass imprisonment has not retreated as other moral panics have in the face of other grave dangers such as the terror acts of September 2001 and the financial crisis of 2008. There has been virtual silence among political elites on the costs and implications of mass imprisonment. Even with hundreds of advocacy groups working to end mass imprisonment, there is widespread complacency about locking up 3 percent of the US population—a policy that costs billions, directly affects millions of individuals and families, and permanently strips more than five million people of political participation.

The partisan politics of crime policy fail to challenge how contemporary ideas about those who are associated with social pollution are deeply rooted in historical beliefs about divine purposes, holy bodies, moral societies, and the color of one's skin.

55. See, for example, Erica R. Meiners, *Right to Be Hostile: Schools, Prisons, and the Making of Public Enemies* (New York: Routledge, 2007); David Garland, *Culture of Control: Crime and Social Order in Contemporary Society* (Chicago: University of Chicago Press, 2001).
56. Loïc Wacquant, "Deadly Symbiosis: When Ghetto and Prison Meet and Mesh," *Punishment & Society* 3, no. 1 (January 2001): 118.
57. Garland, *Culture of Control*, 102.
58. Ibid., 135.
59. Morone, *Hellfire Nation*, 487.

Theories of Biological and Social Causes of Black Criminality

The US penal system, as an institution that punishes those who deviate from the dominant culture, exaggerates the distinctions made between normal and deviant, sacred and profane, white and Black bodies.[60] Dominant discourse defines Blacks in terms of bodily characteristics and constructs those bodies as ugly, dirty, defiled, impure, contaminated, or sick.[61] Media agencies, particularly since the 1960s, have emphasized representations of the irrational, violent Black male.[62] These popular moral discourses, as well as practices of punishment, have focused upon controlling dark-skinned males who threaten to pollute society from within.

In short, the Black body functions as both a symbol of and an explanation for crime. Several influential conservative intellectuals—who have worked closely with the aforementioned conservative policy makers—appeal to the explanatory power of individual proclivities or genetics. James Q. Wilson acknowledges that there is no "crime gene," yet he asserts that there are genes that affect our personality (especially the tendency to be impulsive) and our intelligence, and these, combining in poorly understood ways, can make people more vulnerable to familial and social factors that reduce rather than strengthen impulse control or lessen rather than heighten human willingness to take into account the well-being of others.[63] In his text *Crime and Human Nature*, coauthored with Richard Herrnstein in 1985, Wilson argues that biological factors induce proclivities toward crime. "The biological factors whose traces we see in faces, physiques, and correlations with the behavior of parents and siblings are predispositions toward crime that are expressed as psychological traits and activated by circumstances. . . . Crime cannot be understood without taking into account individual predispositions and their biological roots."[64]

While Wilson and Herrnstein cannot identify the particular physiological factor or factors responsible for what they consider disproportionate Black criminality, they refer to a particular body type common

60. This assertion is influenced by Michel Foucault, *Discipline and Punish: The Birth of the Prison*, trans. Alan Sheridan (New York: Random House, 1995).
61. Iris Marion Young, *Justice and the Politics of Difference* (Princeton, NJ: Princeton University Press, 1990), 123.
62. John M. Sloop, *The Cultural Prison: Discourse, Prisoners, and Punishment* (Tuscaloosa: University of Alabama Press, 1996), 117–18, 123, 136.
63. James Q. Wilson, *On Character: Essays* (Washington, DC: AEI Press, 1991), 4.
64. James Q. Wilson and Richard J. Herrnstein, *Crime and Human Nature* (New York: Simon & Schuster, 1985), 103.

to Black men that is associated with criminality, as well as to cognitive inferiorities amongst Blacks that are commonly found in identified criminals. *Crime and Human Nature* asserts: "Even allowing for the existence of discrimination in the criminal justice system, the higher rates of crime among black Americans cannot be denied."[65] Wilson and Herrnstein identify four major theories that purport to account for racial differences in the prevalence of crime, including (1) constitutional factors such as intelligence and temperament that may or may not be genetic, (2) economic deprivation, (3) a "culture of poverty" amongst Blacks, and (4) a peculiarly Black inability to take into account distinct rewards.[66] They suggest that all of these theories are accurate in some way but assert that none of them fully explains disproportionate violence amongst Blacks. They insist, however, that "the one factor that seems clearly associated with offending and appears disproportionately among blacks is a low intelligence score."[67] They further conclude: "If lowered measured intelligence is associated with crime independently of socioeconomic status, and if blacks, on average, have lower such scores, than these facts may help explain some of the black-white differences in crime rates."[68]

This assertion is further explored in *The Bell Curve*, coauthored by Herrnstein and Charles Murray eleven years later. The authors unearth a half-century of data arguing that differences in intelligence are intractable and significantly heritable, and that the average IQs of various socioeconomic and ethnic groups differ significantly.[69] While they distance themselves from theories that argue for innate criminality, they point to scientific literature that identifies an average IQ score of about 92 for white offenders—eight points below the mean.[70] Herrnstein and Murray further peg the average IQ score of Blacks at 85—even further below the mean for white offenders. Thus, in their view, the average Black person is substantially inferior in cognitive ability than the average white criminal. The research of sociologist Robert Gordon, who has analyzed Black-white differences in crime, supports their view. Gordon argues that "virtually all of the difference in the preva-

---

65. Ibid., 461.
66. Ibid., 466–67.
67. Ibid., 470.
68. Ibid., 471.
69. Richard J. Herrnstein and Charles Murray, *The Bell Curve: Intelligence and Class Structure in American Life* (New York: Free Press, 1994), 9.
70. Ibid., 235.

lence of black and white juvenile delinquents is explained by IQ differ-ence, independent of the effect of socioeconomic status."[71]

The findings of Wilson, Murray, and Herrnstein have been widely discredited by scholars. Yet the continuation of the War on Drugs, along with crime policies such as Stop and Frisk, Truth in Sentencing, and mandatory minimums, suggests that their theories continue to affect crime policy. Indeed, Wilson and Murray have played prominent roles in conservative think tanks, and Wilson served on federal drug policy commissions during Republican administrations.

In another ideological camp, there exists a body of scholarship that identifies racial differences in criminal behavior but points to socioeco-nomic conditions as the primary cause for violent crime committed by Black youth. Legal theorists Franklin E. Zimring and Gordon Hawkins offer statistics on US crime rates that suggest not only how dispropor-tionate rates of incarceration in the United States appear when com-pared to those of other Western nations but furthermore how dispro-portionate rates of Black imprisonment are. They suggest that Black crime in the United States garners widespread attention not because of drug deals, as is commonly believed, but rather due to incidences of lethal violence.[72] In the midnineties, Blacks were five times as likely to be homicide *victims* as whites but eight times as likely to be *arrested* for homicide, typically in "slum neighborhoods" of big cities that exclu-sively house impoverished Black residents.[73]

> Every aspect of serious violence in the United States is linked with statis-tical and policy questions involving race. And very few of the important aspects of race relations are not connected to concerns about violence: its incidence, its consequences, and attitudes toward it. . . . The average con-centration of violence arrests among black offenders is more than twice as high as the concentration in nonviolent offenses. Blacks are more than seven times as likely as whites to be arrested for offenses of violence. Yet even this 7-to-1 ratio understates the extent of black offenses of violence. The aggregate national arrest picture tells us that blacks are slightly more than four times as likely as whites to be arrested for serious assault, but more than eight times as likely to be arrested for killing someone.[74]

71. Ibid., 338.
72. Franklin E. Zimring and Gordon Hawkins, *Crime Is Not the Problem: Lethal Violence in America* (New York: Oxford University Press, 1997).
73. Homicide is the tenth leading cause of death for the US population as a whole, but intentional homicide is the leading cause of death among young Black males in the United States, and the death rate for young Black males ages fifteen to twenty-nine per 1000 population is over forty times as great as for white females of all ages (US Department of Health and Human Services 1991). See ibid., 65.

Zimring and Hawkins attribute high rates of Black violence not to character malformation or genetic predisposition but to the social structure of society. Similarly, legal scholar Michael Tonry argues that structural poverty and discrimination lead to higher rates of violent crime by Blacks. Like Zimring and Hawkins, he suggests that racial difference in patterns of offending, not racial bias by police and other officials, is the principal reason that such greater proportions of Blacks than whites are arrested, prosecuted, convicted, and imprisoned.[75] Since the midseventies, approximately 45 percent of those arrested for murder, rape, robbery, and aggravated assault have been Black.[76] But Tonry also asserts that disproportionate punishment of Blacks became much worse after 1980 as a consequence of deliberate, politically motivated policies under Republican presidential administrations that exploited the subtext of race to buttress policy decisions. Thus, the high rates of incarceration are due not solely to increased violent proclivities of Black people but rather to the politicization of crime.

The analyses put forth by Zimring and Hawkins, as well as Tonry, suggest that higher rates of Black violent crime factor significantly into higher rates of incarceration—in short, that immoral behavior drives disproportionate Black imprisonment. While Tonry offers a more nuanced analysis, in that he points to the politics of crime as a factor for high rates of Black imprisonment, the subtext in Zimring and Hawkins's work is that images of Black criminals are in fact accurate, thus warranting excessive surveillance and disproportionate Black imprisonment.[77]

In sum, despite the varying emphases on the role of environment, both conservative and liberal scholars of crime policy exaggerate racial difference between Black and white violent crime in society, thereby exaggerating *moral* difference in the broader politics of crime policy. Proponents of both ideological traditions seek to explain what they describe as disproportionate Black *criminality*. Whether they locate the causes in genes or social structures, they never question the basic premise that disproportionate arrests and incarcerations suggest genuinely moral differences between Blacks and whites. Although studies

74. Ibid., 73.
75. Michael Tonry, *Malign Neglect: Race, Crime, and Punishment in America* (New York: Oxford University Press, 1995). He also notes that cynical policies of the Bush and Reagan administrations, and not racial differences in patterns of offending, are the principal reason that racial disparities in the justice system steadily worsened after 1980.
76. Ibid., 4.
77. Tonry acknowledges this but still concludes that racial differences in patterns of offense and not racial bias by police officials drives disproportionate Black incarceration.

have shown that police target economically depressed neighborhoods and infrequently examine criminal activity in affluent communities, these authors assert that Blacks commit more crime. Therefore they are more criminal. In the focus on the criminal Black body and violent Black crime, these authors isolate a larger phenomenon without adequately problematizing it. Consequently, their theoretical work provides clear examples of how the Black body has been constructed by influential thinkers as representative of degraded character and social pollution.

The Cultural Symbol of the Immoral Black Body

The construct of the Black criminal pervades US culture to such a large extent that, for the most part, it remains unchallenged. Whereas scholars of politics emphasize the ways in which elites employ symbols of Black degradation, and whereas theorists of crime discuss the numerical significance of Black criminality, religious ethicists analyze the historical significance and reconstruction of Black images. Analysis of the symbolic construction of the criminalized Black body initiates inquiry into how conquest, colonization, enslavement, and nation-building provided material and intellectual justifications for Black degradation. Charles Long, in *Significations*, argues that the racial theories and forms of symbolism that justified conquest simultaneously brought forth new interpretations of Black bodies. People and realities were othered, objectified, and named as colonizers formed new concepts and reinterpreted existing symbols. In the process of conquest, religious symbols were racialized. This is important, Long argues, in that

> religious symbols, precisely because of their intrinsic power, radiate and deploy meanings; the spread of these meanings creates an arena and field of power relationships which, though having their origin in symbols and symbolic clusters, are best defined in terms of significations and signs.[78]

Long's argument is elaborated in Willie Jennings's *The Christian Imagination*, a text that elucidates the racial hierarchies articulated in the fifteenth century, as Spanish and Portuguese colonizers observed "fair" and "ugly" bodies sold in the marketplace. Skin, phenotype, and hair

---

78. Charles Long, *Significations, Signs, Symbols, and Images in the Interpretation of Religion* (Aurora, CO: Davies, 1995), 2, 4.

texture were assigned value—with the European standard of beauty deemed most desirable—and consequently associated with Christian imagery.[79] Those with European bodies symbolized closeness to divinity, while bodies with dark skin, African phenotypes, and tightly curled hair symbolized heathenness and degradation. Religious symbolism and signs perpetuated enduring dichotomous associations between white purity and Black pollution.

The historical religious symbol of the degraded Black body has perpetuated a notion that physical differences represent moral and intellectual differences, which in the contemporary period are conflated with *cultural* differences.[80] Etienne Balibar writes:

> Racism—a true "total social phenomenon" inscribes itself in practices (forms of violence, contempt, intolerance, humiliation and exploitation), in discourses and representations which are so many intellectual elaborations of the phantasm of prophylaxis or segregation (the need to purify the social body, to preserve "one's own" or "our" identity from all forms of mixing, interbreeding or invasion) and which are articulated around stigmata of otherness (name, skin colour, religious practices). It therefore organizes affects (the psychological study of these has concentrated upon describing their obsessive character and also their "irrational" ambivalence) by conferring upon them a stereotyped form, as regards both their "objects" and their "subjects".[81]

It is in discourses and representations, symbols and signs, that the desire to "purify the social body" is most apparent. Such discursive practices are fully oriented towards preserving the "pure" social center in contrast to polluting forces that are identified as threateningly invasive, akin to weeds that take over a cultivated garden or a virus that threatens to corrupt and kill an individual's healthy body. In the context of a social body, polluted elements are constructed as "other" according to geography (such local neighborhoods and national origin), skin color (identified from historical racial hierarchies), and cultural practices (including linguistic inflection and religious practices). Thus pervasive stereotypes denigrate the physical bodies, practices, and cultural affects of the members of the "impure" social groups.

79. Willie Jennings, *The Christian Imagination: Theology and the Origins of Race* (New Haven, CT: Yale University Press, 2010).

80. A significant early twentieth-century sociological initiative to explain the cultural defects of African Americans emerged at the University of Chicago. See Muhammad's chapter "Incriminating Culture: The Limits of Racial Liberalism in the Progressive Era," 88–145.

81. Etienne Balibar, "Is there a Neo-Racism?," *Race, Nation, Class: Ambiguous Identities* (New York: Verso Books, 1988), 17–18.

The constructed stereotypes of those who are "polluted" allows for the construction of an "us" over and against the identification of "them." This is inseparable from race, for in practice, the notion of "us" versus "them" depends upon racial hierarchy. Thus, Balibar notes, symbolic representations functionally do more than simply denigrate or disparage: symbolic representations create a parallel, oppositional, racialized symbolic "community."[82] Members who seek to self-identify as "pure" or upright—that is, who seek to be "white"—often reject those who embrace cultural practices that are identified with Blackness, that is, impurity. In turn, those who embrace Blackness reject assimilationist practices that are associated with a constructed, false, white purity. Balibar concludes:

> It is a racism whose dominant theme is not biological heredity but the insurmountable ability of cultural differences, a racism which, at first sight, does not postulate the superiority of certain groups or peoples in relation to others but "only" the harmfulness of abolishing frontiers, the incompatibility of life-styles and traditions. . . . It is granted from the outset that races do not constitute isolable biological units and that in reality there are no "human races". It may also be admitted that the behaviour of individuals and their "aptitudes" cannot be explained in terms of their blood or even their genes, but are the result of their belonging to historical "cultures".[83]

Culture is collapsed with race, which becomes a central identifying mark of purity or impurity. Although race signifies an interpretation of the body, Balibar argues that contemporary racism functions not by parsing biological differences between different types of bodies (as was done in the early eighteenth century by scientists such as Carl von Linné and Comte de Buffon) but rather by parsing *cultural* differences.

Thus cultural symbols are highlighted and explained to justify relegating certain groups to marginalized positions; furthermore, cultural references that replace biological determinism function similarly. Indeed, Balibar states: "culture can also function like a nature, and it can in particular function as a way of locking individuals and groups *a priori* into a genealogy, into a determination that is immutable and intangible in origin."[84]

In the US, the shifts in racial constructs can be seen as a shift

82. Consequently, Balibar argues, those persons and communities that are racially denigrated struggle to see themselves as a community.
83. Ibid., 21.
84. Ibid., 22.

between biological racism and "laissez faire" racism. Sociologist Lawrence Bobo states: "Jim Crow racism was premised on notions of black biological inferiority; laissez faire racism is based on notions of black cultural inferiority."[85] In a national 1990 survey, white Americans rated blacks, Hispanics, and Asians as less intelligent, more prone to violence, lazier, less patriotic, and more likely than whites to prefer living on welfare.[86]

Even as cultural symbols replace biological determinism as explanation for Black immorality, the contemporary discourse on Black cultural inferiority finds expression in material institutions. Anthony Pinn's *Embodiment and the New Shape of Black Theological Thought* argues that the Black body has a "presence as a discursive construction, and it is monitored with regard to its development, (re)presentation, and control."[87]

> The construction of black bodies through discursive means, in relationship to mechanism of power results in fixed "things"—black bodies that are rigid, truncated realities not to be viewed, understood, and appreciated in diverse ways. Rather, to draw from the quantum physicist David Bohm, they are the result of a unified and unique truth. This truth is built for the benefit of white supremacy, to limit the scope of black bodies. The dilemma for those possessing bodies so formed is that there is little "space" for a diverse range of opinions and perspectives on these discursive bodies. Their meaning is fixed—incoherent (again to borrow from Bohm), and dialogue concerning them is also fixed and limited to the "truth" of these bodies provided by those with the power to control the means of their production. The discursive black body, formed as a matter of power dynamics and white supremacy, is a fragmented "something." This body is a mutation, a matter of warped reality representing a piece of black meaning that has lost its integrity and relationship to a more robust depiction of humanity. This discursive black body, then, is perceived as having no positive relationship to intelligence, civil liberties, privileged social spaces, and the like. And, the black material body, likewise, is believed, as a matter of social truth, to be understood as having no core relationship to beauty, privileged social spaces, and so on.[88]

The discursive, material Black body is inseparable from the construct

85. Ibid., 186.

86. Lawrence Bobo, James R. Kluegel, and Ryan A. Smith, "Laissez-Faire Racism: The Crystallization of a 'Kinder, Gentler' Anti Black Ideology," in *Racial Attitudes in the 1990s: Continuity and Change*, eds. Steven A. Tuch and Jack K. Martin (Westport, CT: Praeger, 1997), 15–43 (199).

87. Anthony Pinn, *Embodiment and the New Shape of Black Theological Thought* (New York: New York University Press, 2010), 6.

88. Ibid.

of the Black criminal, for the same symbolic and material power structures are at work in the penal system. Wacquant argues that materiality and symbolism form the bedrock upon which structures of penal power are erected. "The prison symbolizes material divisions and materializes relations of symbolic power; its operation ties together inequality and identity, fuses domination and signification, and welds the passions and the interests that traverse and roil society."[89]

Indeed, Wacquant's arguments can be seen in Michel Foucault's *Discipline and Punish*, in which an argument for the meaning of signs as discursive power is made. "The art of punishing, then, must rest on a whole technology of representation. . . . The complex of signs must engage with the mechanics of forces."[90]

Penal power in the US context rests upon cultural symbols, signs, and representations alongside material forces. Moreover, penal power in the US rests upon *racialized* symbols, signs, and representations, primarily the constructed symbol of the polluted Black body. Thus, criminalization of Black people cannot be understood apart from a discursive dimension that functions primarily in cultural symbols and signs. Indeed, it is on the discursive level that scholars of religion, theologians, and ethicists contribute significantly to scholarly and political analyses of Black criminalization.

Religious Symbols as Resistance

While numerous scholars critique Black and womanist theologies as insufficiently addressing the nature of power,[91] liberation theologians play an important part of illuminating the material dimensions of Black criminalization as well as constructing new symbols of Blackness. James H. Cone, in *The Cross and the Lynching Tree*, argues that a new kind of "lynching" is taking place in the penal system of the United States,[92] as Black people are far more disproportionately stopped, frisked, arrested, beaten, detained, incarcerated, and killed by police officers. Yet, Cone argues, the suffering wrought by the penal system is not the last word: Christian symbols serve to reignite the potential and beauty of those symbolic Black bodies that have been materially oppressed. Indeed, Black skin, phenotype, and hair assume new significance in the

---

89. Wacquant, *Punishing the Poor*, 173–77.
90. Foucault, *Discipline and Punish*, 104, 106.
91. For example, see Pinn, *Embodiment*.
92. James H. Cone, *The Cross and the Lynching Tree* (Maryknoll, NY: Orbis, 2011), 163.

eyes of God *because* Black people have been oppressed, for the down-trodden are claimed and privileged in the arms of a liberating God.

Contemporary theological ethicists have similarly emphasized seemingly contradictory signs in Christian faith that result in a symbolic reconstruction of Black bodies. Mark Lewis Taylor's *The Executed God* argues that the same Jesus that is worshiped in predominantly white churches on Sunday mornings was a prisoner of the Roman Empire and executed on death row. Following the analysis of Mumia Abu-Jamal, a Black man currently serving a life sentence, Taylor states: "Not only was Jesus, the 'Lord' and 'founder' of what came to be called Christianity, executed (after arrest, flogging, torture, and a forced march), but Christians' first prophet, John the Baptist, was also imprisoned and executed."[93]

Thus, Taylor argues, remembering the symbols of the executed Christian God and his comrades is crucial for resisting complicity in a racist society. Christian symbols serve to facilitate active resistance to racial oppression. Similarly, James Samuel Logan in his book *Good Punishment?* argues that as Black bodies have been constructed as degraded and criminal for centuries, believers in Christ must engage in "ontological intimacy"[94] and, in so doing, must engage liturgical symbols of a degraded, criminalized God:

> Clues about what such an [ontological] intimacy entails for Christians can be discerned in God's self-unveiling as the lowly-born, tortured, spat-upon, beaten, and crucified Jesus Christ of Nazareth. . . . The Jesus of the Good Friday story provides Christians with one of history's most profoundly radical displays of the place of criminals within a politics of ontological intimacy: *They crucified him with criminals, one on either side* (Luke 23:33).[95]

Logan and Taylor, as theological ethicists, highlight the images of a

---

93. Mark Lewis Taylor, *The Executed God: The Way of the Cross in Lockdown America* (Minneapolis: Fortress, 2001), xii.

94. James Samuel Logan, *Good Punishment? Christian Moral Practice and U.S. Imprisonment* (Grand Rapids: Eerdmans, 2008), 203. Logan draws from theologian Stanley Hauerwas to discuss "ontological intimacy." He states (ibid., 202): "The name I give to the ultimate restorative relationship in support of which 'good punishment' aims is the politics of ontological intimacy. Recall Hauerwas's suggestion that 'ontological intimacy' refers to the Christian understanding that literally nothing exists outside God since God makes the entirety of the finite realm *ex nihilo*, through an act of purest and gentlest generosity. Therefore all of creation should be understood as participating in the power of God's being. This means that all that is related through bonds of ontological intimacy should aim to exist in communion because all that is is rooted in a more primordial communion with God as modeled in history by Jesus Christ."

95. Ibid., 203–4.

criminalized, beaten, executed God whose first-century existence eerily parallels contemporary US society. Indeed, the function of punishment—in every period, in every society—serves to contain and remove polluted persons whose bodies threaten the purity of society. Thus, contemporary Christian practitioners employ the image of a crucified Jesus in liturgical symbols and worship practices.

The image of an executed Jesus has particular salience in an era of social media, through which police brutality is quickly known and grassroots activism is quickly mobilized. Kelly Brown Douglas argues that contemporary Stand Your Ground laws—the pieces of legislation that were employed to shield the killer of Trayvon Martin—comprise legislation that perpetuates the symbolism of threatening Black bodies.[96] Indeed, for Douglas, as for Taylor and Logan, the symbolic Black body is scorned, despised, and crucified. Yet, in Douglas's theological construction, this rejected Black body also represents hope for God's presence and deliverance in a paradoxical world.

The symbolism of the Black body in religious ethics, then, is paramount for claiming two intertwining narratives: one that emphasizes the long, historical construction of an immoral Black body, and a second narrative that maps images of a crucified Jesus, the savior of the world, onto all oppressed Black bodies. In sum, the first narrative highlights humanistic research into historical theology, Enlightenment philosophy, and contemporary criticisms of disproportionate policing and mass imprisonment, while the second narrative is lived out in the liberation theologies that take seriously the material plight in impoverished, disproportionately policed Black communities.

Indeed, *Racial Purity and Dangerous Bodies: Moral Pollution, Black Lives, and the Struggle for Justice* is located at this intellectual intersection: the scholarly deconstruction of the dominant narrative of Black immorality and the communal construction that envisions Black bodies as salvific and chosen by God. This book employs multiple methodologies to examine its claims.

Methodology

This book is an analytical text. I support the claims in *Racial Purity and Dangerous Bodies* through a careful study of primary texts in theology, philosophy, sociology, political science, and critical race theory.

96. Kelly Brown Douglas, *Stand Your Ground: Black Bodies and the Justice of God* (Maryknoll, NY: Orbis, 2015).

I investigate primary writings on race and criminality, from the fifteenth century to the nineteenth century, as well as contemporary policy documents, news reports, and sermons. Furthermore, I employ qualitative interviews with activists, advocates, and clergy to illuminate policy reports and grassroots activism.

While this book does not propose constructive theological ethics, I devote chapter 6 to clerical interpretations of the Gospels in the early twenty-first century. To this end, *Racial Purity and Dangerous Bodies* examines liberation theology in the context of Ferguson's uprising and the intellectual bridge that clergy provide to well-educated elites in mainstream institutions and to grassroots youth activists.

Finally, the methodological approaches in this book are inspired by the Movement for Black Lives, which is visibly and forcefully challenging racialized pollution boundaries in twenty-first-century US society. I have personally engaged in the method of participatory action research by attending anti-police-brutality protests, church services, and strategy meetings.[97] Indeed, the inspiration for this book has been sustained by the relentless outrage, struggle, and optimism of grassroots racial justice activists.

Outline of the Book

As a book that weaves together theological and philosophical treatises, sociohistorical theory, and contemporary public policy, *Racial Purity and Dangerous Bodies* contends that societies institutionalize pollution boundaries on micro and macro levels. Furthermore, the book argues that those who are deemed polluted are precisely the most vocal and effective agents for redrawing pollution boundaries. I examine racialized pollution boundaries in the United States at three levels: in official discourse, in institutional policies and practices, and in anti-police-brutality movements.

Part 1, "Race and Moral Pollution," explains the historical and contemporary contexts in which racialized pollution boundaries have been constructed and exploited. In chapter 1, I review constructions of race and morality, and argue that social pollution is primarily discussed in moral terms. I examine theological, philosophical, and scientific ideas during the Age of Exploration and the Enlightenment, periods which promoted a multifaceted argument that physical appear-

---

97. Michelle Fine, Maria Elena Torre, Kathy Boudin et al., "Changing Minds: The Impact of College in a Maximum-Security Prison," January 2001, PDF, http://tinyurl.com/ze9hu6p.

ance represented internal morality. That is, the color of one's skin depicted an individual's moral capacity; it also revealed the moral capacity of one's racial group. Finally, I argue that Black people were constructed as internal enemies that threatened the moral foundations of white, Christian, capitalist nations.

Chapter 2 traces the religious and philosophical constructions of dark-skinned people in the nineteenth-century US as intellectually and morally degraded, and thus in need of authority figures who could assert control. As northern states abolished slavery, elites exhibited deep-seated anxieties about the presence of free Black people in the new republic and advocated building penitentiaries. In the South, at the conclusion of the Civil War, elites developed state penal systems and private convict leasing schemes in which Black people were rounded up, falsely charged, and forced to serve long sentences. White authority figures used the postbellum penal system to control the bodies of free Black people who threatened to pollute the purity of southern culture.

Chapter 3 investigates contemporary policing systems that function to corral and control bodies associated with moral pollution. Disproportionate surveillance occurs in racially- and class-segregated communities, with sophisticated technologies bolstered by the War on Drugs. In the early decades of the twenty-first century, there are 2.3 million people in US prisons—nearly half of whom are Black—and little recognition of the devastation wrought by drug task forces and sophisticated policing systems; mandatory minimum sentences; the expansion of carceral institutions across rural America; and finally, the process of permanently locking "felons" out of employment, housing, and voting opportunities. I argue that present-day policing practices, incarceration in jails and prisons, and post-reentry barriers operate as the primary social instruments for containing bodies associated with moral pollution.

Part 2 of *Racial Purity and Dangerous Bodies* examines two contemporary racial justice movements: anti-Stop and Frisk in New York City and the Black Lives Matter movement in Ferguson, Missouri. Chapter 4 analyzes the anti-Stop and Frisk coalitions that challenged policing practices in New York City from 1993 until 2013. Grassroots resistance to stereotyping Black people as immoral, polluted bodies arose in New York City in the early 1990s. High-profile incidents of police brutality and routine police practices sparked organizing, campaigns, and court cases. Sustained outrage led to favorable court rulings and the passage of citywide legislation, which in turn led to changes in policing practices. This chapter argues that the anti-Stop and Frisk movement facilitated important organizing and consciousness building, but due to the movement's strategic reliance on court cases and legislation, it did not lead to a mass uprising that confronted the construction of Black people as polluted.

In chapter 5, I examine how the Black Lives Matter movement nationally, and particularly in Ferguson, has challenged racialized pollution boundaries by constructing a new narrative on Blackness. Protestors have focused on the criminalization of Black bodies, and in so doing have shifted a dominant narrative that equates Blackness with criminality. Groups of young Black activists, joined by liberal clergypersons, have employed social media and planned mass demonstrations to reframe the image of the polluted, Black criminal body, beginning with Trayvon Martin and culminating in street demonstrations protesting the murders of numerous Black men and women. In bypassing mainstream media and uplifting a newly constructed meaning of the Black body, these activists demonstrate that they are less interested in incremental legal change and more focused on visible outrage against dominant cultural messages that undergird police brutality.

Chapter 6 explores important symbolic constructs of Blackness in the liberation theology that emerged in Ferguson after the killing of Michael Brown. Liberationist clergypersons challenge historical images of Blackness as physical representations of inner immorality and pollution. For clergy in the Black Lives Matter movement, the criminalized body of Michael Brown and the crucified body of Jesus convey a theological assertion: criminalized Black people, who are associated with moral pollution, are crucified as Jesus was two thousand years ago. Furthermore, as followers of Jesus, clergypersons are called to challenge racial injustice. Several clergypersons in the St. Louis area identify Michael Brown as a contemporary Jesus of Nazareth: born in desperate conditions, living among oppressed peoples, murdered by state violence, and resurrected in the Social Gospel.

Racial Purity and Dangerous Bodies concludes with an analysis of the achievements of the Black Lives Matter movements in their challenge to the symbol of the morally polluting Black criminal. Much has been accomplished, and there is still much work to be done. I argue that in order to effectively redraw racialized pollution boundaries, there must be a broad challenge to the symbolic, racialized constructs of the "felon" and the "ex-felon," which uphold mass imprisonment and post-incarceration reentry barriers. In short, there must be multiple challenges to the overlapping penal systems which function to control Black lives that are deemed immoral, dangerous, and polluted.

PART I

Race and Moral Pollution

1

A Socio-Historical Review of
Race and Morality

Without a theory of how Blackness has been constructed as a specific and enduring feature of social pollution, we cannot hope to comprehensively understand the emergence and perpetuation of disproportionate Black imprisonment in contemporary US society. In this chapter, I make three specific arguments about the nature of social pollution in Western societies. First, in the democratic structure of Western societies, in which individuals must be socialized into complying with norms, laws, and capitalist economy, *social pollution is primarily discussed in moral terms.* Second, theological, philosophical, and scientific ideas during the age of exploration and the Enlightenment promoted a multifaceted argument that *physical appearance represents individual and social morality.* That is, the color of one's skin depicts one's moral capacity; it also exhibits the moral capacity of one's racial group. Third, while there are multiple dimensions of social pollution (now reframed as moral pollution) in Western societies, *Black people are constructed as internal enemies that threaten the moral foundations of white, Christian, democratic, capitalist nations.*

Race and Morality in Western Societies

In challenging the US penal system, it is necessary to make explicit the dynamics of moral pollution in Western contexts, particularly the link between moral constructs and racism. This chapter outlines historical constructs of Blackness as immoral and degraded. Indeed, the contemporary context has arisen from a long historical backdrop: Black people have been constructed as spiritually degenerate, intellectual inferior, and inherently violent for many centuries. During the transatlantic slave trade, colonization, and the emergence of democratically ruled societies, Black people were subjugated as slaves and servants and excluded from political participation. The following sections illuminate the origins of racialized constructions of morality.

Race and Morality in Catholic Theology

Enduring images of dark-skinned savages emerged in thirteenth-century scholastic centers in the Latin West.[1] Albertus, the most influential philosopher of nature of his time,[2] incorporated Aristotle's philosophy of natural hierarchies into a theological framework to discern divine truths and prescribe moral guidelines.[3] Aristotle identified hierarchies in all dimensions of life: in the household and the *polis*, in the heavens and the natural world. He exaggerated difference; in every category of phenomenon, he saw some members as superior to others.[4]

---

1. Nicolás Wey Gómez, *The Tropics of Empire: Why Columbus Sailed South to the Indies* (Cambridge, MA: MIT Press, 2008). It is important to note that whites encountered Blacks in antiquity. Frank Snowden writes that the encounter of Mediterranean whites and African Blacks constitutes the oldest chapter in the annals of Black-white relations. He further contends that Mediterranean whites did not discriminate against Blacks because of their color. See Frank M. Snowden Jr., *Blacks in Antiquity: Ethiopians in the Greco-Roman Experience* (Cambridge, MA: Harvard University Press, 1970); Frank M. Snowden Jr., *Before Color Prejudice: The Ancient View of Blacks* (Cambridge, MA: Harvard University Press, 1991).

2. Alberto Magnus (1193–1280), also known as "Albertus" and "Albert the Great," was the founder of the high scholastic theology of the middle and late thirteenth century.

3. Over the course of about twenty years (1250–70), Albertus rewrote all of Aristotle's known philosophy, including his works on logic, natural and moral philosophies, and metaphysics. Albertus's paraphrases to the Aristotelian corpus would come to reflect Aristotle's works—both authentic and spurious. See Wey Gómez, *Tropics of Empire*, 240.

4. In Aristotle's philosophy, the relationships within the household and community exist for the greater society. Members of a society—ruler and subordinate—must follow "natural" patterns of superiority and inferiority for the happiness of the superior people. Aristotle's first analysis of the member parts of society regards the union of male and female, so that "the race may continue." He emphasizes hierarchy in this initial relationship as he justifies the "natural" dynamic of ruler and ruled: "The male is by nature superior, and the female inferior; and the one rules, and the other is ruled; this principle, of necessity, extends to all of mankind." In addition to the male-female union, a household consists of master and slave, one disposed to the intellectual workings of the mind, the other a "living possession" to carry out physical tasks, "so that both may be pre-

4

Albertus both utilized Aristotle's concept of hierarchy and also departed from Aristotle in his theory of nature. Albertus believed everything in creation owed its qualities to its particular geographical location. This was true for humans, beasts, and plants as well as for elements and inanimate compounds.[5] Albertus's logic led him to conclude that people who inhabited "temperate" places were ruled by the soul, whereas people who originated from hot or cold climates were ruled by the body. This deduction shaped Albertus's moral philosophy: because geography affected blood flow and the body interfered with the immediate operations of the human soul, Ethiopians and northern Europeans possessed inferior souls, while people of southern Europe and the Mediterranean, who lived in temperate climates, possessed superior souls.[6]

Later, Albertus would read a Latin translation of Aristotle's *Politics* and establish a direct connection between nature, place, and the condition of slavery.[7] Indeed, Aristotle's hierarchies were foundational for emerging Catholic doctrines supporting European expansion into Africa and the Americas. The combination of the Aristotelian notion of slavery as natural and Albertus's view of geography as proximate cause in shaping nature undergirded the basic ideas that supported European conquest and enslavement in the fifteenth century. By the beginning of the Portuguese and Spanish expeditions, explorers were thoroughly steeped in the natural and moral philosophies of Aristotle and Albertus. In 1493, Pope Alexander VI literally divided the world into spheres of influence for the nascent Portuguese and Spanish Empires.[8] Their expeditions would affirm, and in fact cement, the natural philosophies

served." Indeed, Aristotle's arguments for household hierarchy were rooted in his concept of a "natural" order in which the state is, by nature, prior to the family. Consequently, the units of a household ultimately function to maintain the proper operations of a state that commits to promoting the self-sufficiency and the greatest happiness of its members. The slave is an "instrument for maintaining life" within the household. His inferior state of servitude can be discerned both in body and soul. The relationship between master and slave is natural, "for that which can foresee by the exercise of mind is by nature intended to be lord and master, and that which can with its body give effect to such foresight is a subject, and by nature a slave." Aristotle expounded at some length about the relationship between the master and slave, in order to clarify the purpose of such an arrangement as well as to refute contesting arguments. See Aristotle, *Politics*, in *The Basic Works of Aristotle*, ed. Richard McKeon (New York: Modern Library, 2001).

5. Wey Gómez, *Tropics of Empire*, 252–53.

6. It is worth noting that at this time, the concept of "Europe" was not established and thus Albertus saw stark distinctions between northern people who would later become generally identified as "European" and southern people.

7. Wey Gómez, *Tropics of Empire*, 282.

8. The pope, as monarch, directed the mission of bringing the world to Christ. See R. N. Swanson, "The Pre-Reformation Church," in *The Reformation World*, ed. Andrew Pettegree (London: Routledge, 2000).

of the era. Indeed, Columbus wrote in his chronicles: "The inhabitants of the north and south are unfit for exercising power."[9]

Columbus was only one representative of the racial imagination that had taken hold in Portugal and Spain in the fifteenth century. Approximately half a century prior to Columbus's expedition, the royal chronicler of Prince Henry the Navigator of Portugal, Gomes Eannes de Azurara, reflected on the various colors (and relative beauty) of a group of African captives:

> On the next day, which was the 8th of the month of August, very early in the morning, by reason of the heat, the seamen began to make ready their boats, and to take out those captives, and carry them on shore, as they were commanded. And these, placed all together in that field, were a marvelous sight; for amongst them were some white enough, fair to look upon, and well proportioned; others were less white like mulattoes; others again were black as Ethiops, and so ugly, both in features and in body, as almost to appear (to those who saw them) the images of the lower hemisphere.[10]

The native peoples of the "lower hemisphere" were labeled "barbarians" and "like talking animals"[11] who were both depraved and natural servants. Thus their enslavement was rationalized. The Aristotelian humanist scholar Ginés de Sepúlveda justified conquest and forced servitude using Aristotle's thesis on the differing natures of free humans and servants. He wrote:

> Therefore, the difference between those who are free by nature and servants by nature, is the same that should exist between government applied to the Spaniards and that which is applied to those barbarians by natural law. The empire, therefore, should be shaped in such a way that the barbarians, in part by fear and force, in part by benevolence and

---

9. Quoted in Wey Gómez, *Tropics of Empire*, 291.

10. Gomes Eannes de Azurara, *The Chronicle of the Discovery and Conquest of Guinea*, vol. 1 (London: The Hakluyt Society, 1896), 81. Religion scholar Willie James Jennings notes that Azurara's description is not the first time the words *white* and *Black* indicate something like identity. Their anthropological use in the Iberian and North African regions has an episodic history that extends well before Azurara's utterances. Azurara, however, exhibits an aesthetic that was growing in power and reach as the Portuguese and Spanish began to join the world they imagined with the world they encountered through travel and discovery. Thus, while terms like "race" were not yet used, an aesthetic that furthers distinctions based upon skin color was becoming an authoritative tool for demarcation between peoples. See Willie James Jennings, *The Christian Imagination: Theology and the Origins of Race* (New Haven, CT: Yale University Press, 2010), 23.

11. Luis N. Rivera, *A Violent Evangelism: The Political and Religious Conquest of the Americas* (Louisville, KY: Westminster John Knox, 1992), 134.

equity, would be within the limits of duty in such a way that they would not or could not plot uprisings against Spanish domination.[12]

The multiple levels of subjection that were enacted upon the indigenous peoples of the Americas and Africa emphasized their difference from Europeans in appearance and behavior, body and spirit, simultaneously. On his encounter with indigenous people in the Americas, Columbus reflected, "[The natives] lack arms, go naked, and are very cowardly."[13] Dr. Diego Alvarez Chanca, who accompanied Columbus on his second journey, stated, "Their bestiality surpasses that of any other beast in the world."[14]

The Spanish and Portuguese subjected Amerindian people to brutal torture; as a result of being enslaved, indigenous people died at alarming rates, so much so that the sixteenth-century Jesuit theologian Bartolomé de las Casas proposed to King Charles that Negro slaves be imported directly from Spain or Africa to the islands.[15] An entire body of legislation was created to protect the Indians from colonizing exploitation while colonizers exploited the labor of Africans. Juliana Beatriz Almeida de Souza, a scholar of this period, writes that impediments to indigenous slavery contributed to the growth of the demand for Black slaves. "Discrimination against blacks and Indians involved two different weights and led to an understanding that blacks were born to be slaves and were essentially inferior to both whites and Indians."[16]

Las Casas, who advocated for the importation of African slaves over decades, and only toward the end of his life admitted that Black slavery was as tyrannical as enslavement of Indians, was one prominent person who viewed Blacks as more fitting than Amerindians for slavery. Other bishops, such as Diego de Landa of New Spain, also defended Black slavery. The missionary Alonso de Sandoval raised the question of whether the torrid zones could be inhabited and related the Black color of Africans to their descent from Ham. In the Scriptures, Sandoval found an argument to link Black slavery to the Word of God, eternal truth, and natural evil.[17] For these theologians, the image constructed

12. Ibid., 135.
13. Ibid., 95.
14. Ibid., 136.
15. King Charles was born in Flanders and arrived in Spain in September 1517. He was the grandson of Ferdinand and Isabella.
16. Juliana Beatriz Almeida de Souza, "Las Casas, Alonso de Sandoval and the Defense of Black Slavery," trans. Eoin O'Neil, TOPOI—Revista de Historia 2, no. 6 (2006): 12. See http://socialsciences.scielo.org/pdf/s_topoi/v2nse/scs_a04.pdf.

in sixteenth-century America of an idyllic world inhabited by natural man differed from that of Africa. Although these men had not visited Africa, they regarded Africans as having rejected the Catholic faith. Thus Africans could not be innocent, as Amerindians were.[18]

There was, then, a staunch effort to convert Africans to the Catholic faith. The Spanish Jesuit theologian Luis de Molina concluded his apology with the following: "by being among us in this way, [the African slaves] are converted to Christianity and also enjoy a better material life than what they had before, where they were naked and had to be content with miserable servitude."[19] The influential sixteenth-century Jesuit Alessandro Valignano, a prominent authority in the church's missionary endeavors, noted that Africans, like other reprobates, exhibited degenerate characteristics: they went around half naked, they had dirty food, they practiced polygamy, they showed avarice, and they displayed "marked stupidity."[20] Valignano wrote of the people of Monomotapa of Mozambique:

> They are a very untalented race . . . incapable of grasping our holy religion or practicing it; because of their naturally low intelligence they cannot rise above the level of the senses . . . ; they lack any culture and are given to savage ways and vices, and as a consequence they live like brute beasts. . . . In fine, they are a race born to serve, with no natural aptitude for governing.[21]

The sense of racial superiority articulated in this European-versus-African polarity was inseparable from the religious arrogance of the Spaniards.[22] Referencing Christian texts on slavery and sin, the conquerors surmised that enslavement of heathen native peoples was justified and, indeed, blessed by God. When Europeans seized or purchased infidels, they saw themselves as dealing a blow to infidelity in general as well as procuring new souls for the church.[23] They believed that the native peoples possessed souls, albeit inferior ones, and that conversion to Christianity need have no effect on social status.[24]

17. Ibid.
18. Ibid.
19. Ibid., 182.
20. Quoted in Jennings, *Christian Imagination*, 35.
21. Ibid., 34.
22. Rivera, *Violent Evangelism*, 51.
23. David Brion Davis, *The Problem of Slavery in Western Culture* (Ithaca, NY: Cornell University Press, 1966), 100–101. See also Jennings, *Christian Imagination*, 26. In the bull *Romanus Pontifex* of January 8, 1455, Pope Nicholas V awarded regions of the known world to Portugal. The papal claim to space rested on an ecclesiastical principle: the church was seen to exist for the sake of the world; thus, the pope lays claim to the entire world, for the sake of Christ and through Christ.

In the analysis of religion scholar Willie James Jennings, white Europeans thought of themselves as embodying holy effects and saving grace, while also possessing a unique capacity to detect their presence (or absence) in others.[25] The logical deduction was that Black people were incapable of achieving election due to their inferior nature and thus were inherently degenerate. The Catholic classification of dark-skinned people as inferior, and European Christians as superior, influenced Enlightenment philosophers who wrote after the Reformation, as well as Protestant theologians who sought to establish a "city on a hill."

Race and Morality in Post-Reformation Protestant Europe

The concept of "race" did not come into common parlance until the late eighteenth century. When the scholar deemed "the father of race"—Immanuel Kant—first wrote on race in the 1770s and 1780s, the modern pseudobiological theory of race did not yet exist.[26] None of the accepted systems of natural history used the concept of race. The prevalent theory was of a single humanity divided into varieties that were explained by referencing differences in climate, customs, and government. But these theories were discarded by new discoveries in the West Indies and by the explanations of Carl Linnaeus and Georges-Louis Leclerc, Comte de Buffon.

24. Davis, *Problem of Slavery*, 101–2. Similarly, the notion of racial superiority fed a burgeoning supersessionist world view taking root in Spain's Catholic Church, in which believers in Christ supplanted Jews as God's chosen people. In supersessionist thinking, the church replaces Israel in the mind and heart of God. The Spanish monarchs understood Jews as racial aliens who were a potential contagion to the body politic, for the Jewish people, through the exodus narrative in which they set themselves against Pharaoh, had created for themselves a historical narrative counter to the hegemonic narrative told by the oppressor. The struggle between Jews and others was conceived in terms of race struggle. In 1478, Spain persecuted Jews in the inquisition; in 1492, the monarchs expelled Iberian Jews who had not converted. Correspondingly, in the same year that Spain expelled its Jews, Spain concluded a holy war against Islam and approved Columbus's expedition. Jennings (*Christian Imagination*, 32–33) explains: "This [supersessionist] effect begins with positioning Christian identity fully with European (white) identity and fully outside the identities of Jews and Muslims. . . . Such suspicion and fear, though common in Christian Spain and Portugal as well as in other parts of medieval Europe, indicated a profound theological distortion. Here was a process of discerning Christian identity that, because it had jettisoned Israel from its calculus of the formation of Christian life, created a conceptual vacuum that was filled by the European. But not simply qua European; rather the very process of becoming Christian took on new ontic markers. Those markers of being were aesthetic and racial." For more on supersessionist thinking, see J. Kameron Carter, *Race: A Theological Account* (New York: Oxford University Press, 2008), 42–77.
25. Jennings, *Christian Imagination*, 33–34.
26. Mark Larrimore, "Sublime Waste: Kant on the Destiny of the 'Races,'" in *Civilization and Oppression*, ed. Cheryl Misak (Calgary: University of Calgary Press, 1999), 101. Larrimore explains that the word *race* had only recently entered the German language from the French, and when not used for animals (especially horses), it was used interchangeably with words like *Geschlecht*, *Gattung*, and *Art* to denote kind or lineage. In England and France, it was also used inconsistently.

Linnaeus and Buffon published in the mid-eighteenth century, when the authority of science promoted the activities of observing, comparing, measuring, and ordering the physical characteristics of human bodies.[27] Linnaeus was Aristotelian in his approach to classification: he sought to discern the properties of living things. Regarded as the father of modern taxonomy, his books are considered the beginning of modern botanical and zoological nomenclature: he drew up rules for assigning names to plants and animals. He was the first the use binomial nomenclature (such as *Homo sapiens*) consistently and was the first to author the racial division of humankind in 1735. He argued that species were fixed in number and kind—they were immutable prototypes—but that varieties were members of a species that might change in appearance. Races were a prime example.

Mammalia
Order I. Primates
Foreteeth cutting: upper 4; parallel teats 2, pectoral

HOMO
Sapiens. Diurnal; varying by education and situation

1. Four footed, mute, hairy. *Wild man.*
2. Copper-coloured, choleric, erect. *American. Hair* black, straight, thick; *nostrils* wide; *face* harsh; *beard* scanty; obstinate, content, free. *Paints* himself with fine red lines. *Regulated* by customs.
3. Fair, sanguine, brawny. *European. Hair* yellow, brown, flowing; *eyes* blue; gentle, acute, inventive. *Covered* with close vestments. *Governed* by laws.
4. Sooty, melancholy, rigid. *Hair* black; *eyes* dark; *fevere*, haughty, covetous. *Covered* with loose garments. *Governed* by opinions.
5. Black, phlegmatic, relaxed. *Hair* black, frizzled; *skin* silky; *nose* flat; *lips* tumid; crafty, indolent, negligent. *Anoints* himself with grease. *Governed* by caprice.[28]

For Linnaeus, then, despite the absence of a taxonomy that formally placed Europeans at the top of a hierarchy, the characteristics associated with the European body indicated superior European character. The European was "sanguine" (cheerfully optimistic, hopeful, and confident), whereas the American was "choleric" (easily irritable and

27. Cornel West, *Prophesy Deliverance! An Afro-American Revolutionary Christianity* (Philadelphia: Westminster, 1982), 48.
28. Carl von Linné, "The God-Given Order of Nature," in *The System of Nature*, excerpted in *Race and the Enlightenment: A Reader*, ed. Emmanuel Chukwudi Eze (Malden, MA: Blackwell, 1997), 13.

angered) and the African "phlegmatic" and "indolent" (apathetic, slug-gish, and lazy). The European obeyed laws, which indicated collective decision making after thoughtful reflection, whereas the American was governed by customs (that is, thoughtless group-think), and the African was governed by "caprice" (whimsical, sudden, unpredictable moods)—the very opposite of reflective, lawful determination. The European wore clothing ("close vestments"), whereas the American painted himself with red lines and the African covered himself with grease. Indeed, Linnaeus's taxonomy demonstrated a racial scale in which inner character was represented by physical appearance. Lighter-skinned people were more beautiful, intelligent, and likely to wear clothing. Darker-skinned people, on the other hand, were more lazy, unpredictable, and greasily naked.

Upon publishing *The System of Nature* in 1735, Linnaeus became one of the most influential scientists in eighteenth-century Europe. His col-league Comte de Buffon, who achieved prominence for mathematics and scientific investigation in France in the mid-eighteenth century, similarly published reflections on the racial scale in his *Natural History of Man.* Buffon argued that all races have a single origin, a concept known as "monogenism." Moreover, color was caused by environmen-tal conditions: "Nothing can prove more clearly that the climate is the principal cause of the varieties of mankind, than this colour of the Hot-tentots, whose blackness could not be diminished but the temperature of the climate."[29] Hot climate, then, produced dark skin. For Buffon, the ideal climate was temperate, which "lies between the 40th and 50th degree of latitude, and it produces the most handsome and beautiful men."

It is from this climate that the ideas of the genuine colour of mankind, and of the various degrees of beauty, ought to be derived. The two extremes are equally remote from truth and from beauty. The civilized countries situated under this zone, are Georgia, Circassia, the Ukraine, Turkey in Europe, Hungary, the south of Germany, Italy, Switzerland, France, and the northern part of Spain. The natives of these territories are the most handsome and the most beautiful people in the world.[30]

Buffon proposed the "degeneration theory," which argued that people of darker hues degenerated from an original white color. Since climate

29. Comte de Buffon, "The Geographical and Cultural Distribution of Mankind," in *A Natural History, General and Particular*, excerpted in Eze, *Race and the Enlightenment*, 22.
30. Ibid., 26.

(and quality of food, to a lesser extent) was the origin of "ugly and ill-made" bodies,[31] he argued that authorities should control climate in order to revert dark skin to whiteness.

Although Buffon found similarities between apes and humans, he rejected the idea of common descent. He was later considered the "father of evolution," even though he rejected the idea that his theory was a theory of evolution. Rather, he argued, the division of living beings into orders, classes, and species represented the variety of nature.

Buffon published at the same time that the authority of scientific observation and the elevation of human reason gained new adherents. He published his multivolume *A Natural History, General and Particular,* between 1748 and 1804. He was thus a contemporary of the Prussian-born moral theorist Immanuel Kant, who later became known as "the father of race."

Kant's first essay on race, "Von den verschiedenen Racen der Menschen," was one of three treatises published in 1775 to argue for human personhood by means of a concept of race.[32] Kant argued for a natural system based on lineages, rather than an "artificial" system based on classes.

> Among the deviations, that is, among the hereditary dissimilarities that we find in animals that belong to a single line of descent, are those called races. Races are deviations that are constantly preserved over many generations and come about as a consequence of migration (dislocation to other regions) or through interbreeding with other deviations of the same line of descent, which always produces half-breed off-spring. Those deviate forms that always preserve the distinction of their deviation are called variations. Variations resemble each other, but they do not necessarily produce half-breeds when they mix with others. Those deviations which often, but not always, resemble one another may, on the other hand, be called varieties. Conversely, the deviation which produces half-breed off-spring with others, but which gradually dies out through migration, may be called a special stock. Proceeding this way, Negroes and whites are clearly not different species of human beings (since they presumably belong to one line of descent), but they do comprise two different races. This is because each of them perpetuate themselves in all regions of the

31. Ibid., 27.
32. Larrimore, "Sublime Waste," 102. Kant was, in part, arguing against Henry Home, also known as Lord Kames, who proposed a polygenist theory in an influential essay translated into German. This first essay was actually an advertisement for a lecture course in physical geography. It was revised and republished in 1777.

earth and because they both, when they interbreed, necessarily produce half-breed children, or blends (Mulattoes).[33]

Kant argued for four different races of the human genus: (1) the white race, (2) the Negro race, (3) the Hun race (Mongol or Kalmuck), and (4) the Hindu or Hindustani race.[34] Kant was not only interested in classifying races, however. He primarily sought to provide a teleological explanation for the reality of different races; in other words, he sought to explain *why* there were different races rather than simply providing mechanical explanations.[35] Scholars agree that his desire to provide a teleological explanation for racial difference provided the foundation for his later text, *Critique of Judgment*.[36] Indeed, Kant insisted that nothing happens by chance, that everything in nature has a purpose:

> This principle, which is at the same time a definition, is as follows: *An organized product of nature is one in which every part is reciprocally purpose, [end] and means.* In it nothing is vain, without purpose, or to be ascribed to a blind mechanism of nature. . . . It is an acknowledged fact that the dissectors of plants and animals, in order to investigate their structure and to find out the reasons, why and for what end such parts, such a disposition and combination of parts, and just such an internal form have been given them, assume as indisputably necessary the maxim that nothing in such a creature is *vain;* just as they lay down as the fundamental proposition of the universal science of nature, that *nothing* happens *by chance.* In fact, they can as little free themselves from this teleological proposition as from the universal physical proposition. . . . For example it may be that in an animal body many parts can be conceived as concretions according to mere mechanical laws (as the hide, the bones, the hair). And yet the cause which brings together the required matter, modifies it, forms it, and puts it in its appropriate place, must always be judged of teleologically; so that here everything must be considered as organized, and everything again in a certain relation to the thing itself is an organ.[37]

Kant argued that the four races were the products of seeds (*Keime*) and natural predispositions (*Anlagen*) rather than the result of chance or mechanical laws alone. Thus, the seeds of all the races were latent from the start in everyone, and the appropriate seed was actualized to serve

33. Immanuel Kant, "Of the Different Human Races," in *The Idea of Race*, ed. Robert Bernasconi and Tommy L. Lott (Indianapolis: Hackett, 2000), 9.
34. Ibid., 11.
35. Robert Bernasconi, "Who Invented the Concept of Race? Kant's Role in the Enlightenment Construction of Race," in *Race*, ed. Robert Bernasconi (Malden, MA: Blackwell, 2001), 24.
36. Ibid., 2, 15, 27.
37. Immanuel Kant, *Critique of Judgment* (Mineola, NY: Dover, 2005), 166–67.

a purpose that arose from the circumstances.[38] The seeds or predispositions, then, could not be undone by differences in climate; they must be permanent. Transpiration of elements is the most important bodily response to climate, and so the skin is the most important organ. Kant focused exclusively on color as a racial marker—"the race of the *whites*, the *yellow*, Indian, the negro and the *copper-red* American."[39]

Kant's lecture notes on Anthropology included extended discussions such as the following:

1. The American people are uneducable [*nimmt keine Bildung an*]: for they lack affect and passion. They are not amorous, and so are not fertile. They speak hardly at all . . . care for nothing and are lazy.
2. The race of Negroes, one could say, is entirely the opposite . . . : they are full of affect and passion, very lively, chatty and vain. It can be educated, but only the education of servants, i.e. they can be trained. They have many motives [*Triebfedern*], are sensitive, fear blows and do much out of concern for honor.
3. The Hindus have incentives, but have a strong degree of calm, and all look like philosophers. That notwithstanding, they are much inclined to anger and love. They are thus educable in the highest degree, but only to arts and not to sciences. They will never achieve abstract concepts.[40] . . . The Hindus will always stay as they are, they will never go farther, even they started educating themselves much earlier.
4. The race of the whites contains all motives and talents in itself: and so one must observe it more carefully. To the white race belongs all of Europe, the Turks, and the Kalmucks. If ever a revolution occurred, it was brought about by the whites, and the Hindus, Americans, Negroes never had any part in it.[41]

Clearly, for Kant, each of the four "races" had its own meaning, with whites setting the standard to which every other should, but could not, aspire to. The dark skin of non-Europeans had particular meaning, over and above the very aspect of complexion. For Kant, as for other Europeans at the time, it was not only the color of Africans but the hues of various peoples encountered by explorers that needed to be accounted for.[42] Nonetheless, Kant was particularly challenged by the darkness of

38. Bernasconi, "Who Invented?," 23–26.
39. Larrimore, "Sublime Waste," 106–7.
40. Larrimore notes that Kant repeats this statement many times in his writings on India.
41. Quoted in Larrimore, "Sublime Waste," from Kant's unpublished notes (xxv.2 1187–88), 111–12.
42. It is important to note that Kant wrote and lectured on many different peoples, not just Africans, and often placed Americans far below Africans in the hierarchies of peoples he acknowledged.

14

Africans, whom he considered a "base race" along with whites.[43] Skin, iron content in skin, and humid warmth produced a "thick, turned-up nose and thick, fatty lips. . . . In short, all of these factors account for the origin of the Negro, who is well-suited to his climate, namely, strong, fleshy, and agile. However, because he is so amply supplied by his motherland, he is also lazy, indolent, and dawdling."[44] He referred to Black people as "born slaves"[45] and in the same notes a few lines later wrote: "Americans and Blacks cannot govern themselves. They thus serve only for slaves."[46] Indeed, seeds inherent to all peoples meant that Black people could never achieve civilization, for Kant wrote: "The Negro can be disciplined and cultivated, but is never genuinely civilized. He falls of his own accord into savagery."[47]

Indeed, physical geography, for Kant, also bore upon "moral" or "cultural" geography. For example, Kant lectured on the "moral geography" of Africans who permitted theft, Chinese who deserted children, Brazilians who buried children alive, and Eskimos who strangled them.[48] As a moral philosopher, he concluded that such actions were based upon unreflective mores and customs that resulted from an "inclination to evil." Those who lacked the ethical principles spelled out in Kant's moral philosophy could not be properly human. Kant concluded that non-Europeans not only lacked proper manners, but also, they were predisposed to natural impulses that limited the development of moral character, the essential seed for radical autonomy and inner freedom.

The perfect race, then, was the European race:

> The greatest riches of earth's creation are found in this region [between 31 and 52 degrees latitude] and this is also where human beings must diverge least from their original form, since the human beings living in this region were already well-prepared to be transplanted into every other region of the earth. We certainly find in this region white, indeed, brunette inhabitants. We want, therefore, to assume that this form is that of the lineal root genus. The nearest northern deviation to develop from this original form appears to be the noble blond form. This form is char-

43. Kant, "Different Human Races," 12.
44. Ibid., 17.
45. Robert Bernasconi, "Kant as an Unfamiliar Source of Racism," in *Philosophers on Race: Critical Essays*, ed. Julie K. Ward and Tommy L. Lott (Oxford: Blackwell, 2002), 152, quoting from Kant's unpublished notes (AA, XV/2, p. 878).
46. Ibid.
47. Ibid., 158; see also Larrimore, "Sublime Waste," 111.
48. Eze, *Race and the Enlightenment*, 200.

acterized by its tender white skin, reddish hair, and pale blue eyes. This form inhabited the northern regions of Germany.[49]

Scholar J. Kameron Carter argues that for Kant, at this point, whites are no longer described as a race (even if they are thought of as one). They are simply "white, indeed, brunette inhabitants." They are a group apart. Whites "are a 'race' that is not quite a race, the race that transcends race."[50] Carter notes an unpublished quote from Kant in which Kant wrote: whites "contain all the impulses [*Triebfedern*] of nature in affects and passions, all talents, all dispositions to culture and civilization and can as readily obey as govern. They are the only ones who always advance to perfection."[51]

Whites can advance toward perfection because they are able to embody moderation, the universal ethics of autonomy, and the moral law in a way that Black people, who are trapped in the particularity of their flesh, cannot.[52] Kant opposed race mixing; his published writings reveal that he was vehemently opposed to whites integrating with other races.[53] Kant believed that the white race, which would "always advance to perfection," would otherwise degenerate. His views on race and anthropology, along with his moral philosophy, would have international reverberating effects as the European Enlightenment spread to other shores.

Race and Morality in New England Puritan Society

Ideas of dark bodies as representative of degenerate souls permeated the seventeenth-century British colonies. The first generation of New England theologians expanded the central themes in the Reformed tradition: sin and depravity, moral law and natural law, and faith in the Redeemer; in so doing, they exaggerated differences between themselves and other peoples, distinguished by faith, gender, and color.[54]

The Puritan divines were of striking unanimity as they delineated

---

49. Kant, "Different Human Races," 19–20.
50. Carter, *Race*, 88.
51. Ibid. See also (AA, XV/2, p. 878). This is note number 1,520 in the Adickes edition of Kant's fragments on anthropology. Quoted in Bernasconi, "Kant as an Unfamiliar Source," 147–48.
52. Carter, *Race*, 90.
53. Immanuel Kant, "On the Use of Teleological Principles in Philosophy," in *Race*, ed. Robert Bernasconi. See also Bernasconi, "Kant as an Unfamiliar Source," 154–62.
54. For example, in addition to distinguishing themselves from Jews, New England Puritans set themselves against Antinomians, Arminians, Quakers, and Anglicans who established churches in New England. See Perry Miller, *The New England Mind: The Seventeenth Century* (Cambridge, MA: Harvard University Press, 1939), 182–206, 367–68.

four covenants. The covenant of works (the law) elaborated God's commandments; the covenant of grace (the gospel) extended mercy; the church covenant supported the faithful in communal endeavor; the political covenant structured civil society.[55] In the enactment of their covenants, the New England Puritans exaggerated the differences between the visibly elect and the visibly degenerate. Only the recognizably elect, moral man could participate in civil leadership and thereby exercise visible restraints upon the inhabitants of the colony. These restraints were necessary, because with original sin came the need for police officers, judges, magistrates, jails, and laws to hold accountable human beings who rob, murder, and quarrel amongst themselves.[56] Without a coercive state to restrain evil impulses and administer punishments, life could not be made safe and secure.[57] The magistrates were to have full power to rule over residents for the specifically divine purposes to which the society was dedicated.[58]

The Puritans held a narrow interpretation of divine election. God extended the covenant of grace through Christ. As a "second Adam," Christ served as negotiator and redeemer, advocate and savior.[59] The new covenant mediated by Christ incorporated the covenant of works. The elect were expected to uphold the Ten Commandments as well as exhibit a new state of being as the patriarchs, through Christ, had embodied conviction and humility. "*Abraham* entered into the covenant of grace with God, as the faith of the faithfull [sic] that should believe in Christ, as he did. In *Rom.* 11, he is said to be *the root*, in which all the people of God are graffed [sic]."[60] Grafted into a lineage of faith, the sinful elected into the covenant of grace were offered something new: a clarity of mind, an ease within the heart, a relief from the doubts of the conscience.

Regeneration through the covenant of grace demanded shared commitment, an adaptation to a framework in which God and the faithful conveyed mutual assurance. As God extended mercy, the elect

55. John Witte Jr., "How to Govern a City on a Hill: Puritan Contributions to American Constitutional Law and Liberty," in *God's Joust, God's Justice: Law and Religion in the Western Tradition* (Grand Rapids: Eerdmans, 2006), 150.
56. Perry Miller, "The Theory of the State and of Society," in *The Puritans: A Sourcebook of Their Writings*, ed. Perry Miller and Thomas H. Johnson (Mineola, NY: Dover, 2001), 182.
57. The New England Puritan theory of government mirrors the framework established by John Calvin. See *Institutes of the Christian Religion, Vols. 1 & 2*, ed. John T. McNeill, trans. Ford Lewis Battles (Philadelphia: Westminster, 1960), 4.20.1–32.
58. Witte, "How to Govern," 187.
59. Ibid., 146.
60. Peter Bulkeley, *The Gospel Covenant; Or, The Covenant of Grace Opened* (London: Matthew Simmons, 1651), 38.

responded with faith. Those who did not exhibit the obvious signs of faith—according to the elite—were, with African and native peoples, barred from participating in political life. The elite, like their theological forebears, elevated pious European Christians and cast Jews, Blacks, and Native Americans as outside the sphere of rational personhood and divine election. This racial hierarchy warranted few reflections or remarks in Puritan society. Yet with the presence of native peoples and with the arrival of the first African slaves between 1624 and 1630,[61] Puritan society relegated dark-skinned people to the realm of the inherently reprobate. The covenant tradition, divinely oriented and socially enacted, reiterated a racially inflected hierarchical interpretation of divine rejection versus divine embrace.

The theological interpretation of European Christian election permeated every level of New England consciousness.[62] As the elect race within the kingdom of God in New England, the pilgrims asserted ideological and political rule over the dark-complexioned "subject races." In so doing, they positioned themselves as those conditioning their world rather than being conditioned by it.[63] Racial hierarchy became one norm of the colonial enterprise.[64]

Puritans incorporated into their world view a popular exegesis of Noah's curse in Genesis 9:20–27, in which Ham's ancestry was linked to Africa.[65] A similar understanding depicted native "Indians" as reprobate:

> As for special Relation unto God; whom hath the Lord more signally exalted than his people in this Wilderness? The Name and Interest of God, and Covenant-relation to him, it hath been written upon us in Capital Letters from the beginning. God has his Creatures in this wilderness before we

61. Lorenzo Johnston Greene, *The Negro in Colonial New England: 1620-1776* (New York: Columbia University Press, 1942), 15. Samuel Maverick, apparently New England's first slaveholder, arrived in Massachusetts in 1624.
62. Charles W. Mills, *The Racial Contract* (Ithaca, NY: Cornell University Press, 1997), 21.
63. Jennings, *Christian Imagination*, 60.
64. This statement does not ignore the reality of conquest of Native Americans' land. However, until the eighteenth century, the image of Africa was sharply differentiated from that of peaceful, unspoiled America. Davis (*Problem of Slavery*, 186) writes: "If it was a crime, as many writers asserted, to deprive native Americans of their natural liberty, it was actually an act of liberation to remove Negroes from their harsh world of sin and dark superstition."
65. See Stephen R. Haynes, *Noah's Curse* (New York: Oxford University Press, 2002), 35–37. Haynes describes how Englishman George Best utilized the biblical account of Ham's disobedience to explain Africans' skin color: "as an example for contempt of Almightie God, and disobedience of parents, God would a sonne should bee borne whose name was Chus, who not onely it selfe, but all his posteritie after him should bee so blacke and lothsome, that it might remaine a spectacle of disobedience to all the worlde." Furthermore, Haynes explains, Guillaume de Salluste Sieur Du Bartas, a Calvinist from the south of France who is known for his influence on Milton, depicted Ham as from "amid the sands of Africa," "impudent," and "profane."

came, and his *Rational Creatures* too, a multitude of them; but as to *Sons* and *Children* that are Covenant-born unto God, Are not we the *first* in such a Relation? in this respect we are surely the Lords *first-born* in this Wilderness. Of the poor Natives before we came we may say as *Isa.* 63.19. *They were not called by the Lords Name, he bear not Rule over them:* But we have been from the beginning, and we are the *Lords.*[66]

The distinction between "natural" and "moral," or in this case between "creatures" and covenanted "children," reiterated the theological and political division between nonwhite people and white Christians in the "new world." New England Puritans privileged biblical exegesis and downplayed or ignored the role of colonial conquest and African slavery to depict their settlement as essentially autochthonous.[67] The purification for which Calvinists on the Continent and Puritans in England had striven for three generations was to take place upon virgin soil.[68] Indeed, the very idea of "virgin soil" implied vacant land, unpopulated space, an absence of people. At the same time, European settlers in America described the area beyond the mountains as "Indian country," "the Dark and Bloody Ground . . . a howling wilderness inhabited by savages and wild beasts," or sometimes even "Sodom and Gomorrah."[69]

The dual images of virgin versus dark wilderness nonetheless depicted a scenario in which the arrival of the Puritans brought prosperity and peaceful order to barrenness and chaos. Implicit in the establishment of a covenanted society ruled by the visibly elect were the hierarchical ideals of the Middle Ages.[70] The inherited views of

---

66. William Stroughton, "New England's True Interest," in Miller and Johnson, *The Puritans*, 243.
67. The New England Puritans underwent a process that Mills (*Racial Contract*, 32–33, 41–42) describes as "norming" space: "The norming of space is partially done in terms of *racing* the space, the depiction of space as dominated by individuals (whether persons or subpersons) of a certain race. At the same time, the norming of the individual is partially achieved by *spacing* it, that is, representing it as imprinted with the characteristics of a certain kind of space. . . . Correspondingly, there are rituals of naming which serve to seize the terrain of these 'New' Worlds and incorporate them into *our* world: New England, New Holland, New France—in a word, 'New Europes,' cultural-spatial extensions of Europe." Indeed, the Puritans who colonized Massachusetts Bay envisioned the New Jerusalem as a cultural extension of Europe. Perry Miller (*The New England Mind: From Colony to Province* [Cambridge, MA: Harvard University Press, 1967], 8) writes that the New Englanders believed that "God has peopled New England in order that the reformation of England and Scotland may be hastened, to prove to the 'episcopacy' that true polity and good government may stand together."
68. Miller, *New England Mind*, 8.
69. Mills, *Racial Contract*, 46.
70. Perry Miller (introduction to Miller and Johnson, *The Puritans*, 10) describes Puritans and Anglicans as heirs of the Middle Ages: "They still believed that all knowledge was one, that life was unified, that science, economics, political theory, aesthetic standards, rhetoric and art, all were organized in a hierarchical scale of values that tended upward to the end-all and be-all of creation, the glory of God."

European (white) superiority and African (Black) inferiority were taken for granted by the voyaging Puritans. They believed that God ordained differences in position within society and that the decrees were thoroughly reasonable and just.[71] The racial hierarchy and the slave trade were equated with natural order, for the fixed scale of values evident in the moral universe decreed that some should rule and some should serve.[72] The colony of Massachusetts codified enslavement under the rubric of "just warre" in 1641:[73]

> There shall never be any bond slaverie, willinage or Captivitie amongst us, unless it be lawfull Captives taken in just warres, and such strangers as willingly sell themselves or are sold to us. And these shall have all the liberties and Christian usages which the law of God established in Israell concerning such persons doth morally require. This exempts none from servitude who shall be Judged thereto by Authoritie.[74]

In 1644, Boston merchants began to import slaves directly from Africa.[75] Prominent ministers reasoned that slavery in the English colonies exposed heathens to salvation. They, like their Portuguese and Spanish forebears, believed that contact with Christian doctrine mitigated the horrors of bondage. Whatever suffering the Negro might experience either aboard the slave ship or in slavery was "more than offset by his fortunate delivery from a life of idolatry."[76] After all, Negro and Indian infidels were in an eternal state of misery.[77]

But conversion to Christianity did not shift one's status: Christians of African and Indian heritage continued to be barred from civil rights. Free and enslaved Negroes, regardless of religious identification, remained outside the religiously and racially defined social covenant. There was, in fact, a striking similarity between the medieval position

---

71. Miller, *New England Mind*, 428.
72. Miller, introduction to Miller and Johnson, *The Puritans*, 10.
73. While the transatlantic slave trade was not conducted in a "just war," slavery was nevertheless justified within this interpretation.
74. John Cotton, "A Coppie of the Liberties of the Massachusetts Colonie in New England, Section 91," in *Puritan Political Ideas: 1558-1794*, ed. Edmund S. Morgan (Indianapolis: Bobbs-Merrill, 1965), 196. See also Greene, *Negro in Colonial New England*, 124–25. Prior to codification, slavery existed only by custom. Massachusetts was the first colony to implement perpetual servitude and legal slavery. Greene notes that the traditional enslavement of Black children after 1670 and the elaborate slave codes adopted by all of the New England colonies expanded the legality of slavery initiated in Massachusetts. Connecticut and New Haven colonies used the Massachusetts Code of 1649—including the slave codes—as a model in preparing their legal systems.
75. Greene, *Negro in Colonial New England*, 20–22.
76. Ibid., 62.
77. Cotton Mather, "The Negro Christianized: An Essay to Excite and Assist that Good Work, Instruction of Negro-Servants in Christianity (1706)," in *Against Slavery: An Abolitionist Reader*, ed. Mason Lowance (New York: Penguin, 2000), 20.

regarding infidels and baptism and Puritan advocacy for tutelage in Christian doctrine.[78] In the late seventeenth century, the prominent minister Cotton Mather raised the possibility of African slaves participating in the covenant of grace. His suggestion and efforts to Christianize slaves through a Society of Negroes sparked a backlash from slaveowners, who feared calls for emancipation. Mather in turn enlisted the support of fellow ministers. In 1694, a year after Mather published his *Rules for the Society of Negroes*, a group of clergy collectively affirmed that baptism did not alter the legal position of slaves in the social hierarchy.

Indeed, Mather believed that white slaveowners should convert their Black slaves but echoed the prevailing ideology that such a step would not amend their legal status. He argued that although Africans were the "the most Brutish of Creatures upon Earth" and "the *Blackest* Instances of *Blindness* and *Baseness*," who may be the offspring of Ham,[79] they might be among God's elect.[80] He believed that their souls could be raised from a "dark state" of ignorance to adopt the Christian religion. Indeed, Mather's advocacy included the possibility of slaves who can "by [one's] Instruction be made Wise unto Salvation!"[81] He furthermore stipulated that Christian slaves would be more willing workers and resist insurrection.[82]

> Be assured, Syrs; your Servants will be the *Better Servants*, for being made *Christian Servants*. . . . Were your *Servants* well tinged with the spirit of *Christianity*, it would render them exceeding *Dutiful* unto their *masters*, exceeding *Patient* under their *Masters*, exceeding faithful in their Business, and afraid of speaking or doing any thing that may justly displease you.[83]

Conversion to Christianity, then, ultimately preserved the social order. Even as Mather asserted the presence of souls in African slaves, the theological justification of a racial caste system sanctioned racial slavery. In 1700, the distinguished jurist Samuel Sewall contested slavery on biblical grounds. But even his argument contained references to the inferiority of Africans and abhorrence to integration: "And there is

---

78. Davis, *Problem of Slavery*, 101–2.
79. Ibid., 217.
80. Mather, "The Negro Christianized," 19.
81. Ibid.
82. Davis, *Problem of Slavery*, 205.
83. Mather, "The Negro Christianized," 20. Davis (*Problem of Slavery*, 202–5) describes Mather's project in educating Negroes as a way "that they should be brought up to internalize those precepts of humility, patience, and willing obedience which would allow masters to rule by love instead of force."

such a disparity in their Conditions, Colour & Hair, that they can never embody with us, and grow up into orderly families, to the Peopling of the Land: but still remain in our Body Politick as a kind of extravasat Blood."[84] John Saffin, a slave dealer and trader, refuted his contemporary's essay with biblical passages, spelling out the extent to which Europeans distinguished Africans as a different "degree of men":

> For it was unlawful for the *Israelites* to sell their Brethren upon any account, or pretence whatsoever during life. But it was not unlawful for the Seed of Abraham to have Bond men, and Bond women either born in their House, or bought with their Money, as is written of *Abraham, Gen.* 14.14 & 21.10 & *Exod.* 21.16 & *Levit.* 25.44, 45, 46 v. . . . So God hath set different Orders and Degrees of Men in the World, both in Church and Common weal. . . . This may suffice, that not only the seed of *Cham* or *Canaan*, but any lawful Captives of other Heathen Nations may be made Bond men as hath been proved . . . it is no Evil thing to bring them out of their own Heathenish Country, where they may have the Knowledge of the True God, be Converted and Eternally saved.[85]

Saffin's biblical justification of slavery correctly referenced passages in the Hebrew Bible.[86] And Saffin clearly related the status of slavery to the appearance of Blackness, conveying that dark skin represented an unalterable belonging to a separate nation. He concluded his refutation with a poem called "The Negroes Character":

> *Cowardly and cruel are those* Blacks *innate,*
> *Prone to Revenge, Imp of inveterate hate.*
> *He that exasperates them, soon espies*
> *Mischief and murder in their very eyes.*
> *Libidinous, Deceitful, False and Rude*
> *The Spume Issue of the Ingratitude.*[87]

The associations of Black people with spiritual degeneracy and whites

84. Samuel Sewall, "The Selling of Joseph: A Memorial (1700)," in Lowance, *Against Slavery*, 12. Sewall uses the term "extravasat" to describe an undesirable and unharmonious presence.
85. John Saffin, "A Brief Candid Answer to a Late Printed Sheet, Entitled, *The Selling of Joseph* (1701)," in Lowance, *Against Slavery*, 15–16.
86. Davis (*Problem of Slavery*, 64-65) writes: "These religious connotations of slavery had profound consequences. On Sinai Moses was told that the Hebrews should buy their slaves from neighboring nations, and 'moreover of the children of the strangers that sojourn among you, of them ye shall buy, and of their families that are with you, which they have begotten in your land: and they shall be your possession. And ye shall make them an inheritance for your children after you, to hold for a possession; of them shall ye take your bondmen for ever: but over your brethren the children of Israel shall ye not rule, one over another, with rigor' [Lev 25:44–46]."
87. Saffin, "A Brief Candid Answer," 22.

with Christlike purity conveyed the idea and feeling of *us* against *them*: to be Christian was to be civilized rather than barbarous, English rather than African, white rather than Black.[88] Conversion did not alter these oppositions.

Thus, as the English Puritans established the "New Jerusalem," even baptized Blacks of free status were barred from political participation. Furthermore, free Black people were subjected to the slave codes: they could not walk on the streets after nine o'clock without a pass, nor could they go beyond the limits of the town where they resided. They could use the ferries only under similar conditions. They could not own certain types of property.[89]

Underlying these social restrictions was the pervasive, inherited belief in European rational capacity and African animality that had arisen since the thirteenth century. Protestant theologians believed in the inner freedom of Christians[90] and in individual bodies as temples of God's holy spirit.[91] All human beings, although innately depraved and corrupted, embodied the capacity to reflect and judge; all people embodied a conscience. Jonathan Mitchell asserted:

> That *Maxime* of the *Romans* was and is a Principle of right Reason, *Salus Populi Suprema Lex*, (The welfare of the People is the Supreme Law) and is engraven on the Forehead of the Law and Light of *Nature*. Hence it is owned and confirmed by the *Scriptures*, as we see in the Text; and it is easily deducible from the Law of God: for that that is indeed the Law of Nature, is a part of the Eternal Law of God.[92]

Reason, in the trajectory of Aristotelian scholasticism and sixteenth-century humanism, was a guide and a tool alongside biblical revelation.[93] It was a testimony of conscience.[94] It was ultimately reliant on Christ for its fulfillment, because revelation in Christ supported the fallen rational faculty present in humankind.[95]

---

88. Winthrop D. Jordan, *White over Black: American Attitudes toward the Negro, 1550-1812* (Chapel Hill: University of North Carolina Press, 1968), 94.

89. Greene, *Negro in Colonial New England*, 300–301.

90. Martin Luther, *The Freedom of a Christian* (Philadelphia: Fortress, 1957).

91. Calvin, *Institutes of the Christian Religion*, 3.10.30.

92. Jonathan Mitchell, "Nehemiah on the Wall," in Miller and Johnson, *The Puritans*, 237.

93. E. Brooks Holifield, *Theology in America: Christian Thought from the Age of the Puritans to the Civil War* (New Haven, CT: Yale University Press, 2003), 31–33. He notes the influence of Aristotelian scholasticism and sixteenth-century Ramist humanism, known as *technologia* in seventeenth-century New England. See also Miller, *New England Mind*, 182–206.

94. Calvin, *Institutes*, 4.20.16. See also John T. McNeil's elaborate footnotes in book 2 of the *Institutes*, in which he explicates that natural law in the *Institutes* is usually associated with conscience, also frequently with civil positive law (as will be explored further in this paper) and equity, and the Christian's duties to society.

But those deemed rationally inferior—even converts to Christianity—could not be full human beings. They were not capable of discerning revelation; they could not know the moral law in their hearts. Dark-skinned people did not even possess decayed discernment, much less the spiritual and intellectual capacity to cogently reflect upon their conscience and God's Word. They were not persons capable of intelligent decision-making; they could not play a role in developing lawful society. Africans and Native Americans were associated with animality, superstition, disorder, chaos, and divine rejection. And such associations distinguished the rational person from the subject.

As a result, Africans and Native Americans were ideologically excluded from the intellectual frontiers that would form modern America.[96] Over time, explicit appeals to God for assistance in rational decision-making subsided, but the racial subjugation implicit in European concepts of personhood continued to reinforce concepts of natural hierarchy, even as reason replaced revelation through Christ as the guiding ethos by which to shape society.

Race and Morality in the New Republic

The Puritans bequeathed to the eighteenth-century Founding Fathers an intellectual heritage of political covenant founded upon natural law as well as a society that exaggerated physical differences between people. In the same way that the Puritans believed that a divine creator had implanted rational and moral faculties in human beings, the Founding Fathers promulgated universal natural rights as a manifestation of natural law. Indeed, the Declaration of Independence proclaimed: "We hold these truths to be self-evident: that all men are created equal; that they are endowed by their creator with inherent and inalienable rights; that among these are life, liberty, and the pursuit of happiness."[97] Richard Henry Lee spoke of "those rights which God and nature have given us."[98] Thomas Jefferson insisted upon "those rights which god and the laws have given equally and independently to

95. Miller, *New England Mind*, 184–85. See also Holifield, *Theology in America*, 5.
96. Mills, *Racial Contract*, 56.
97. Thomas Jefferson, "The Declaration of Independence," in *The Papers of Thomas Jefferson*, vol. 1, ed. Julian P. Boyd (Princeton, NJ: Princeton University Press, 1950), 315.
98. Richard Henry Lee, "Letter to John Dickenson [July 25, 1768]," in *The Letters of Richard Henry Lee*, vol. 1, ed. James Curtis Ballagh (New York: Da Capo, 1970).

all."[99] Yet, they contradicted themselves by solely vesting those rights in white men who possessed property.

The Founding Fathers were attentive to the international standards set by their "city on a hill."[100] The empirically derived evidences of the natural world took precedence over the Bible, dogma, and salvation.[101] American natural rights philosophers looked to Enlightenment thinkers such as Locke,[102] Montesquieu,[103] and Blackstone[104] for their

---

99. Thomas Jefferson, "A Summary View [July 1774]," in *The Papers of Thomas Jefferson*, vol. 1, *1760–1776*, vol. 1, ed. Julian P. Boyd (Princeton, NJ: Princeton University Press, 1950), 121.

100. Morone, *Hellfire Nation*, 100–116.

101. Holifield, *Theology in America*, 160.

102. See John Locke, *Two Treatises of Government*, ed. Peter Laslett (New York: Cambridge University Press, 1988). Locke insisted that matter and motion answer to a divine purpose; he inferred that God wills a particular course of action and that it is morally obligatory to follow it. Human beings discerned natural law through the exercise of their faculties. God, "who has given the world to men in common, has also given them reason to make the best use of it to the best advantage of life and convenience." Human beings must act in service of God's ends and further the great design. God was both creator and sustainer; thus, moral obligations must be obedient to God's will rather than the will of a sovereign. Natural law was, in short, a divine command; reason searched for it and confirmed it. But the Scriptures, like convictions and common sense, only confirmed the voice of reason; they did not offer revelation in and of themselves. Furthermore, Locke rejected Adam's fall as the source of irrationality. Indeed, he insisted that human faculties were, in principle, adequate for the discovery of natural law without the assistance of divine grace. See C.B MacPherson, *The Political Theory of Possessive Individualism: Hobbes to Locke* (Oxford: Clarendon, 1962), 10–158, 197–260; Richard Tarnas, *The Passion of the Western Mind* (New York: Ballantine, 1991), 272–74; John W. Shepard, "The European Background of American Freedom," *The Journal of Church and State* 50, no. 4 (Autumn 2008): 647–59; Pierre Manent, *An Intellectual History of Liberalism*, (Princeton: Princeton University Press, 1995), 20–42; and Timothy Stanton, "Hobbes and Locke on Natural Law and Jesus Christ," *History of Political Thought* 29, no. 1 (Spring 2008): 72–75.

103. See Baron de Montesquieu, *Spirit of the Laws*, trans. Thomas Nugent (New York: D. Appleton, 1900). Montesquieu, like Locke, attributed natural law to the creative powers of a deity. The natural law known by God is antecedent to the positive law made by human beings. Individuals know God and the laws of nature as a consequence of their impression upon the human mind. Indeed, Montesquieu argued that "man in a state of nature would have the faculty of knowing, before he had acquired any knowledge." Under the law of nature, men are naturally independent, equal, and have unfettered liberty. Indeed, the principle of equality in the state of nature carried into Montesquieu's proposal for individual freedom under civil law. The liberties that individuals naturally possess as they participate in a social contract are maintained under positive law. Human beings have the right to defend themselves and present evidence on their own behalf. They have the right to marry and divorce. The positive laws governing humans—moral, civil, and political—expand into different forms: the law of nations, general and particular political law, and domestic law. Montesquieu argued for separation of powers in the political sphere. Indeed, historical accounts of the revolutionary era attribute the Founding Fathers' vision for three branches of government to Montesquieu's proposal for executive, legislative, and judicial branches.

104. See William Blackstone, *Analysis of the Laws of England* (Oxford: Clarendon, 1756). Sir William Blackstone was perhaps the most widely read legal scholar prior to and during the American Revolution. His comprehensive articulation of natural law as a basis for absolute rights gained extraordinary credence. He argued that inferiors must obey superiors—but rather than an argument for monarchical rule, he determined that human beings must use their divinely endowed faculties of reason and free will to guide their actions. Blackstone philosophized that the will of the maker, called the law of nature, creates human free will—"but within bounds, for human free will is in some degree regulated and restrained." The creator also gives human beings the faculty of reason to discover the purpose of natural laws. The primary prompt to pursue the "rule of right"—that is, the purpose of natural laws—is self-love, the "universal principle of action." In Blackstone's theory of natural law, the creator "has graciously reduced the rule of obedience to

definitions of natural law and natural rights. Thus, they absorbed scientific methods and concluded that they needed only to observe the natural world and elucidate natural laws for scientific truths, which took precedence over the dictates of a monarchy or the Bible. And in return, Europe looked to the newly formed United States, the first nation to be founded upon principles of natural rights and liberty.

In matters of government, the Declaration of Independence, the Constitution, and the Bill of Rights were positive expressions of an inherent, divinely created natural law.[105] Yet, despite their espousal of universal natural rights, the Founding Fathers, like the Puritans, held a narrow interpretation of citizenship. In addition to excluding white men without property and all white women, the founding patriarchs barred all African and native peoples from participating in political life. Political scientist Rogers M. Smith argues that alongside their adherence to Enlightenment principles and scientific inquiry, the Founding Fathers embraced a myth of Anglo-Saxon purity and freedom. They believed that they had special capacities for liberty that were culturally and providentially definitive of their race.[106] In his treatise "A Summary View of the Rights of British Americans," Jefferson relied on the colonists' "Saxon ancestry" to defend their right to free government and unrestricted trade.[107] Princeton president Samuel Stanhope, in his 1787 *Essay on the Causes of the Variety of Complexion and Figure in the Human Species*, argued that the physical and mental differences in the races resulted from differences in the climates and "habits of society" in which they resided.[108]

That white Americans assumed a connection between shared ancestry, cultural traits, and natural rights meant that they could identify Anglo-Saxons as the *sole* bearers of the providentially favored Anglo-Saxon mission to build a realm of enlightenment and spiritual and political liberty.[109] Smith writes that "even as Pennsylvanians created the most radical of the new state republics, they defended it as a return

this one paternal precept: that man should pursue his own happiness." This quest, for Blackstone, is the foundation of ethics, or natural law.

105. William C. Plouffe, "The Natural Law in the Minds of the Founding Fathers," *Vera Lex* 9, no. 1–2 (2008): 109–22.

106. Rogers M. Smith, *Civic Ideals: Conflicting Visions of Citizenship in U.S. History* (New Haven, CT: Yale University Press, 1997), 73.

107. Thomas Jefferson, "A Summary View of the Rights of British Americans [1774]," in *The Papers of Thomas Jefferson*, vol. 1, 1760–1776, ed. Julian P. Boyd (Princeton, NJ: Princeton University Press, 1950), 132: "Our Saxon ancestors held their lands, as they did their personal property, in absolute dominion, disencumbered with any superior."

108. Smith, *Civic Ideals*, 105.

109. Ibid., 74.

to the 'Genuine Principles' of the 'golden Anglo-Saxon age' before 1066. Such consciousness of themselves as bearers of a superior cultural or racial heritage remained vivid as Congress and the states dealt with various groups they saw as outside the circle of full members of the civic body—British loyalists, blacks, Native Americans, and women."[110]

Identification of Anglo-Saxon heritage with innate natural rights was often articulated in terms of physical superiority and rational supremacy. Indeed, the first public treatise written by a Founding Father on the intellectual inferiority of the Negro was Jefferson's 1781 *Notes on the State of Virginia*. "Blacks," he declared, "whether originally a distinct race, or made distinct by time and circumstances, are inferior to the whites in the endowments both of body and of mind."[111]

> The first difference which strikes us is that of colour. Whether the black of the negro resides in the reticular membrane between the skin and scarf-skin, or in the scarf-skin itself; whether it proceeds from the colour of the blood, the colour of the bile, or from that of some other secretion, the difference is fixed in nature, and is as real as if its seat and cause were better known to us. And is this difference of no importance? Is it not the foundation of a greater or less share of beauty in the two races? Are not the fine mixture of red and white, the expression of every passion by greater or less suffusions of colour in the one, preferable to that eternal monotony, which reigns in all the countenances, that immoveable veil of black which covers all the emotions of the other race?[112]

Notions of Black people's inferior beauty comingled with associations of heightened sexuality. "They are more ardent after their female: but love seems with them to be more an eager desire, than a tender delicate mixture of sentiment and sensation. . . . *In general, their existence appears to participate more of sensation than reflection.*"[113] Jefferson's statement, echoing centuries of Eurocentric moral geography and Christian dichotomies, reiterated a dividing line between body and soul and suggested that Black people were closer to animals than were whites, in that Black people lacked intellectual capacity and rationality.[114]

While Jefferson believed that Black people's inferior intellect might be partially explained by environmental factors, he was not entirely

---

110. Ibid., 101.
111. Thomas Jefferson, *Notes on the State of Virginia* (New York: Penguin, 1998), Query XVII, 150–51.
112. Ibid., 144–45.
113. Ibid.
114. A passage in which Jefferson (*Notes*, 77) describes Black albinos is located in a chapter in which he discusses the "indigenous animals" of Virginia.

convinced that they were actually members of the species Linnaeus had named *Homo sapiens*.[115] Inferior intellectual capacity was innate; it could be improved by training and fine habits but not fundamentally changed. Nature provided whites with the capacity for elevated discourse and problem solving, superior traits that Black people simply did not have. Even as academic discourse on environmental factors gained credence, Jefferson and his contemporaries asserted a notion of Black genetic inferiority.[116]

The perceived lack of rational capacity and artistic skill raised the issue of whether Black people possessed the natural rights of Anglo-Saxons. Jefferson argued that intellectual deficiency did not imply a deficiency in "moral sense" or conscience, because morality was an essential trait for living together.[117] For Jefferson, it was not morality, but the perceived lack of intellectual capacity that raised the question of Black personhood and political participation.

Other elites in the young nation believed that the difference in skin color represented a difference in cognitive ability as well as character; they therefore barred Black people's ability to participate in the social contract.[118] Indeed, they believed that extension of the franchise to free Blacks who were associated with immorality could result in a weakening of the new republic.

By the early nineteenth century, states in the North and South had enacted racially specific labor, voting, vagrancy, and jury laws to encode their beliefs in racial difference. Indeed, regulation grew harsher during the Jeffersonian years as white Americans increasingly depended on slavery and feared the mobility of free Black people. Laws prevented slaves from hiring themselves out for extra work in order to buy their freedom. Free Blacks were denied the right to vote in almost every state. North Carolina compelled free Black people to wear shoulder patches reading "free." Black laborers were refused access to many trades and commercial licenses. Vagrancy laws coerced unemployed Blacks into servitude. The rights of free Black people to obtain jury trials, testify in courts, and obtain counsel were generally denied, and special, brutal criminal penalties for Black convicts were enacted.[119]

The racist attitudes associating Black people with moral pollution in

115. Jefferson, *Notes*, 66.
116. Jordan, *White over Black*, 528. See also Adrienne Koch, *The Philosophy of Thomas Jefferson* (New York: Columbia University Press, 1943), 116.
117. Koch, *Philosophy of Thomas Jefferson*, 116.
118. Smith, *Civic Ideals*, 105.
119. Ibid., 178.

the new republic had reverberating effects on the social institutions that were established, including the prison. Indeed, the first penitentiaries disproportionately incarcerated Black people. Furthermore, associations of Black people with moral degradation perpetuated proslavery discourse. The next chapter explores the evolution of racist constructs, immorality, and crime laws in the nineteenth century.

Conclusion

Since the thirteenth century, constructions of race and constructions of morality have been explicitly linked, leading to assertions that white people were ordained for leadership and Black people for servitude.

Indeed, the association of dark-skinned people with moral pollution has a long history, stretching back to European encounters with people indigenous to Latin America and Africa. The earliest constructions of Black people as physically ugly, spiritually degenerate, and rationally inferior emerged in the religious thought of Spanish and Portuguese explorers, as well as later Enlightenment thinkers. These constructions gained credence in the thought of New England Puritan divines and the Founding Fathers. Blacks were not the only group ostracized from mainstream society, but the construction of Black immorality retained particular cultural salience. To fully understand the function of emerging penal systems in the new republic, we must examine how social constructions of Black immorality fueled white fears of free Blacks recently emancipated from slavery.

2

Constructions of Character and Criminality in Nineteenth-Century US Penal Systems

Introduction

The religious and philosophical constructions of dark-skinned people as intellectually and morally degraded, and thus in need of authority figures who could assert control, emerged as a prominent theme in the fervor of nineteenth-century nation building. As Northern states abolished slavery and simultaneously attempted democratic rule by consent, elites exhibited deep-seated anxieties about the presence of free Black people in the new republic. The penitentiary became one response to widespread concerns and trepidation.

In the early nineteenth century, Southern states also established penitentiaries, yet the institution of chattel slavery controlled the vast majority of Black people in the South; consequently, those sentenced to state confinement were typically white men. At the conclusion of the Civil War, the sentiments of proslavery treatises fueled the development of state penal systems and private convict leasing schemes in which Black people were rounded up, often falsely charged, and forced to serve long sentences. Elites used the postbellum penal system to control the bodies of free Black people who threatened to pollute the purity of Southern culture.

This chapter examines the evolution of the Northern and Southern penal systems as social institutions that protected white society from Black bodies in the aftermath of emancipation.

Northern Penitentiaries

Discourses on Black Degradation in the North

In the late eighteenth and early nineteenth centuries, advocates of free labor successfully fought to emancipate slaves in northeastern states. The reformers identified contradictions between the newly ratified Constitution, which was premised on ideals of liberty, and the institution of chattel slavery. Those who were opposed to racial slavery expressed abhorrence at the conditions of bondage, such as physical abuse, separated families, forced sexual relations, and the belief that one class of people was born to serve an exploitative slaveholding class.[1] Yet emancipation raised concerns about how populations assumed to be deviant—such as freed Black people—should be controlled. Citizens, clergy, and elected officials alike recognized that most whites had an emotional aversion to the idea of Black and white equality, as well as anxieties that Black people would encounter freedom lacking moral clarity and stamina.[2]

The widespread belief that Black people, if freed, would remain an alien and troublesome presence seemed confirmed by the situation of Black men and women who were emancipated after the Revolution: they were seen to have "corrupted characters" whose condition "was fruitful in crime, but rarely productive of happiness."[3] In the early nineteenth century, the New York Manumission Society announced that it viewed "with regret the looseness of manners and depravity of conduct in many of the Persons of Colour in this city."[4] In Massa-

1. See, for example, Horace Bushnell, "A Discourse on the Slavery Questions (1839)," in *Against Slavery: An Abolitionist Reader*, ed. Mason Lowance (New York: Penguin, 2000), 230. Bushnell was not an abolitionist—although he opposed the Fugitive Slave Act and the Compromise of 1850—and he did not participate in the reform movements of his time. But as a leading nineteenth-century theologian and congregational minister, his musings on the evils of slavery reflected widespread views in the North: whites considered Black enslavement morally unjust but did not desire a racially integrated society.
2. George M. Frederickson, *The Black Image in the White Mind: Debates on Afro-American Character and Destiny, 1817-1914* (Hanover, CT: Wesleyan University Press, 1971), 3.
3. Ebenezer Baldwin, *Observations on the Physical, Intellectual, and Moral Qualities of Our Colored Population* (New Haven, CT: L. H. Young, 1834), 41.

chusetts, a state with a very small Black population, a serious concern with free-Negro "depravity" developed in the 1820s. Officials debated whether to restrict Black immigration, in order to protect the physical and moral well being of white citizens.[5]

Those who fretted publicly about widespread numbers of free Black people in the general population debated about how to inculcate Blacks with such middle-class virtues as industrious work habits, temperance, and self-imposed restraint.[6] Black public figures such as David Walker and Frederick Douglass placed the blame for the wretched conditions of enslaved and free Black people squarely on the shoulders of slave-holding and ostensibly liberal whites.[7] They witnessed a rapid development of benevolent societies in the 1820s and 1830s focused on elevating the conditions of free and enslaved Black people—organizations that both fought against the institution of chattel slavery and simultaneously expressed beliefs in Black depravity.

The abolitionist movement drew members who fought vociferously against the "despotism" that upheld a system of racial slavery. Richard Hildreth, one of its most visible proponents, blamed Black immorality on the example set by white slaveholders: "Ferocity of temper, idleness, improvidence, drunkenness, gambling," he wrote, "these are vices for which the masters are distinguished, and these same vices are conspicuous traits in the character and conduct of slaves."[8] But dishonorable whites were not constructed as inherently immoral as Blacks. Hildreth pointed to the general attitude that constructed free Black people as polluted: "The emancipated class is studiously subjected to mortifications and disabilities without number. They are considered as noxious vermin whose extermination is required for the comfort and security of the privileged order."[9]

Polluted Blackness, in the eyes of Hildreth and other critics of slavery, was a result of environment; it did not originate in the innate character of freedmen. Indeed, an intellectual shift away from determinism was sweeping the benevolent societies of the era. An editorial in *The Christian Spectator* noted, "The fact is, that as a class they are branded. . . . Three hundred thousand freemen in this country, are

4. Frederickson, *Black Image*, 4.
5. Ibid., 6.
6. Ibid., 35–42.
7. David Walker, "An Appeal to the Colored Citizens of the World," in Lowance, *Against Slavery*.
8. Richard Hildreth, *Despotism in America: An Inquiry into the Nature, Results, and Legal Basis of the Slave-Holding System in the United States* (Boston: Whipple & Damrell, 1840), 157.
9. Ibid., 72.

freemen only in name, forming only little else than a mass of pauperism and crime. . . . Here the black man is paralyzed and crushed by the constant sense of inferiority."[10]

William Lloyd Garrison, whose impassioned discourses against slavery and colonization alike influenced the growing abolitionist movement,[11] argued that Black people possessed stronger character than whites who encountered the same hostility and social barriers.[12] He and other abolitionists espoused a Christian morality in which whites embraced Black people as equals under God and in society. Christian society, he believed, must strive to perfect an environment inclusive of all classes and races.

Yet even abolitionists exhibited the idea that Black people possessed moral pollution. Garrison, whose belief in racial equality propelled a controversial debate on whether Black people could be socially and politically incorporated into mainstream US society, and who defended Black character to hostile whites, admitted, "It would be absurd to pretend that, as a class, they maintain a high character: it would be equally foolish to deny, that intemperance, indolence, and crime prevail among them to a mournful extent."[13] Abolitionist William Jay, for example, stated in *Miscellaneous Writings on Slavery*, "True it is the free blacks have been rendered by prejudice and persecution an ignorant and degraded class."[14] The leading abolitionist Samuel Gridley Howe, who advocated for the penitentiary system of Pennsylvania, supported the complete separation of convicts, in part because he wanted to keep the races separate. He claimed that a large proportion of the Philadelphia prisoners were mulattoes, "who cannot bear confinement like men of pure Saxon blood," and added that the "colored population when they are drawn is a very degraded one, and addicted to those sexual excesses which lead particularly to cerebral derangement."[15]

Indeed, abolitionists shared with colonizationists—anti-slavery advocates who sought to deport free Black people—basic beliefs that Black men and women disproportionately exhibited immoral behavior

---

10. Quoted in William Lloyd Garrison, *Thoughts on African Colonization* (Boston: Garrison & Knapp, 1832), 128.
11. Colonization was a movement to "return" people of African descent to colonies to be established in Africa. The nation of Liberia began its history as such a colony.
12. Garrison, *Thoughts on African Colonization*, 129.
13. Ibid., 128–29.
14. William Jay, *Miscellaneous Writings on Slavery* (Cleveland, OH: Jewett, Proctor & Worthington, 1853), 57.
15. Scott Christianson, *With Liberty for Some: 500 Years of Imprisonment in America* (Boston: Northeastern University Press, 1998), 145.

but that such criminality was a result of white hostility. In short, both movements blamed environmental barriers for Black degradation. Yet beyond that basic agreement, the two ideological camps diverged. Colonizationists believed that Black people could never be incorporated into the body politic of the new nation: Black people threatened to pollute the moral purity of white culture, and white hatred irreparably severed any hope of a biracial society. This lack of hope was due to whites' fear of Black people and resistance to "amalgamation." Henry Clay, a judge and a founder of the American Colonization Society, argued:

> Of all the descriptions of our population, and of either portion of the African race, the free people of colour are, by far, as a class, the most corrupt, depraved, and abandoned. There are many honourable exceptions among them, and I take pleasure in bearing testimony to some I know. It is not so much their fault as the consequence of their anomalous condition. . . . The laws, it is true, proclaim them free; but prejudices, more powerful than any laws, deny them the privileges of freemen. They occupy a middle station between the free white population and the slaves of the United States, and the tendency of their habits is to corrupt both. They crowd our large cities, where those who will work can best procure suitable employment, and where those who addict themselves to vice can best practice and conceal their crimes. If the vicious habits and propensities of this class were not known to every man of attentive observation, they would be demonstrated by the unerring test of the census.[16]

Clay argued that Black criminality was a result not of inherent depravity but rather of an "unfortunate situation."[17] But in his mind, that "unfortunate situation" was inevitable: middle class whites of honorable character refused to incorporate Black people into society. Other colonizationists similarly blamed the environment for the degraded character of free Black people. Thomas Marshall argued: "Neither the safety of the State nor the resources of any community would endure within its bosom such a nation of idle, profligate, and ignorant persons."[18] But Marshall also pointed out that "great as the degradation of the free black population is, no friend of Colonization has ever said

16. Henry Clay, "An Address Delivered to the Colonization Society of Kentucky, at Frankfurt, December 17, 1829, by the Hon, Henry Clay, at the Request of the Board of Managers," *African Repository and Colonial Journal* 6, no. 1 (March 1830): 12.
17. Ibid., 17–18.
18. Thomas Marshall, "The Speech of Thomas Marshall, in the House of Delegates of Virginia, on the Abolition of Slavery, Delivered Friday, January 20, 1832. Richmond," *African Repository and Colonial Journal* 9, no. 11 (January 1834): 322.

that their vices or crimes were of such a nature as to be incapable of reform."[19]

The colonizationists reflected the thinking of post-Revolutionary elites who rejected slavery but recoiled at the thought of racial equality, because for them, Black skin inevitably represented inner pollution. As early as 1817, a prominent politician of Maryland, General Robert Goodloe Harper, supported the plan to colonize free Black people because "such a class must evidently be a burden and nuisance to the community; and every scheme which affords a prospect of removing so great an evil, must deserve to be most favourably considered."[20]

> In reflecting on the utility of a plan for colonizing the free people of colour, with whom our country abounds, it is natural that we should be first struck by its tendency to confer a benefit on ourselves, by ridding us of a population for the most part idle and useless, and too often vicious and mischievous. These persons are condemned to a state of hopeless inferiority and degradation, by their colour; which is an indelible mark of their origin and former condition, and establishes an impassible barrier between them and the whites. This barrier is closed for ever, by our habits and our feelings, which perhaps it would be more correct to call our prejudices, or a mixture of both, make us recoil with horror from the idea of an intimate union with the free blacks, and preclude the possibility of such a state of equality between them and us, as alone could make us one people. Whatever justice humanity and kindness we may feel towards them as our inferiors; nor can they help viewing themselves in the same light, however hard and unjust they may be inclined to consider such a state of things.[21]

Northern resistance to an ideal of racial equality, like that exhibited by Harper, was widespread in the 1830s. But by that time, references to Black inferiority were much more nuanced. Leading proponents of colonization shied away from "inglorious" questions of natural Black inferiority and emphasized depressed conditions that led to crime. Ebenezer Baldwin, in his book *Observations on the Physical, Intellectual, and Moral Qualities of Our Colored Population*, stated that "degradation is not proof of incapacity."[22] However, Baldwin was convinced that colonization was the only solution in the conflicts resulting from the "cor-

19. Ibid., 325.
20. Robert Goodloe Harper, *A Letter from General Harper of Maryland, to Elias Caldwell, Secretary of the American Society for Colonizing Free People of Colour, in the United States, with their own consent* (Baltimore, 1818), 9.
21. Ibid., 6.
22. Baldwin, *Observations*, 14.

rupted characters" of the manumitted slaves: "It was perceived that, without education and without incentives to ambition, with a boundary line drawn by prejudice, but as impassable as if it had been established by justice, between the whites and the blacks, mere liberty, without change of habitation, was fruitful in crime, but rarely productive of happiness."[23] Thus, removal to another country was the only recourse.

Similarly, in his rebuttal of anti-colonizationist arguments, Rev. Calvin Colton argued that Black people could rise to a respectable rank in a society in which they had opportunities. But the hindrances embedded in US society resulted in the problem that "a stifling, strangling incubus seems to rest upon all their faculties. Rarely is there to be found a man of wealth among them; few possessed of comfort; the great mass are poor and wretched; and depravity, vice, and crime find a home among them."[24] Colton believed that black inferiority in intellect and moral force was solely due a "long-depressed and inferior *condition*."[25] At the same time, he argued, whites possessed a moral superiority that Black people could not achieve in the United States.

The argument that Black people were and must remain morally inferior in a country that barred their advancement found advocates among members of the Boston Prison Discipline Society, a benevolent organization led by prominent clergy and lay persons who were opposed to slavery. The society, founded by Louis Dwight in 1826, explicitly endorsed colonization if the character of the Negro population "could not be raised."[26] The first annual meeting passed a motion presented by two clergymen, the Reverend William Jenks and the Reverend Francis Wayland, which recognized the "degraded character of the coloured population" as the first "cause of the increase and frequency of crime."[27] These facts, the reformers stated, "are gathered from the Penitentiaries, to show how great a proportion of the convicts are coloured, even in those States, where the coloured population is small, show most strikingly, the connexion between ignorance and vice."[28] The writers pointed to disproportionate Black incarceration in six Northern states as proof of Black criminality. Blacks comprised one

23. Ibid., 41.
24. Calvin Colton, *Colonization and Abolition Contrasted* (Philadelphia: H. Hooker, 1839), 5.
25. Ibid.
26. Prison Discipline Society, *First Annual Report of the Board of Managers of the Prison Discipline Society, Boston, June 2, 1826*, 4th ed. (Boston: T. R. Marvin, 1827), 38.
27. Ibid., 4, 35.
28. Ibid., 35.

seventy-fourth of the Massachusetts population but one-sixth of the state inmates; they made up one thirty-fourth of the Connecticut population but one-third of the state convicts; there were less than one thousand Blacks in Vermont, but twenty-four were imprisoned in the state penitentiary.[29]

Jenks and Wayland were accurate in their assessment of the disproportionate incarceration of Black men and women. In 1820 in the state of New York, for example, Black people made up 2.9 percent of the general population.[30] Yet they were incarcerated at much higher rates. State assembly records show that in the same year, there were 468 white men and women and 112 Black men and women imprisoned in the New York State Prison in New York City, and 206 white and 12 Black inmates in Auburn Prison in Cayuga County.[31] In short, although Black residents constituted less than 3 percent of the state population, they made up 18 percent of state prisoners when the populations of the two state prisons were combined.

Observers Gustave de Beaumont and Alexis de Tocqueville, who traveled throughout the United States and assessed penitentiaries to gain insight into how the French government might replicate them, determined that approximately 25 percent of inmates in all of the prisons they investigated were Black. Consequently, the French visitors insisted that free Black people were more criminally oriented than free whites:

> In general, it has been observed, that in those states in which there exists one negro to thirty whites, the prisons contain one negro to four white persons. The states which have many negroes must therefore produce more crimes. This reason alone would be sufficient to explain the large number of crimes in Maryland: it is, however, not applicable to all the states of the south; but only to those in which manumission is permitted: because we should deceive ourselves greatly were we to believe that the crimes of the negroes are avoided by giving them liberty; experience proves, on the contrary, that in the south the number of criminals increases with that of manumitted persons; thus, for the very reason that slavery seems to draw nearer to its ruin, the number of freed persons will increase for a long time in the south, and with it the number of criminals.[32]

29. Ibid., 35–36.
30. United States Bureau of the Census, *Negro Population in the United States, 1790–1915* (New York: Arno, 1968), 51.
31. New York State Assembly, 44th Session, "Number of Prisoners in New-York State Prison, December 31st, 1820," *Journal of the Assembly of the State of New York*, 1821.

These French observers, then, were amongst those who argued that free Black people exhibited moral pollution, more so than slaves. The Reverend Colton, an advocate of colonization, proclaimed: "As to the comparative state of morals among them, it is ascertained to be fearfully below that of slaves and of whites."[33] In fact, many of the Black inmates in Northern penitentiaries were manumitted slaves[34]—thus their statements suggested that Black people needed authority figures to maintain self-control.

Advocates of the Boston Prison Discipline Society clearly believed that Black people in society polluted and corrupted whites—and that this was true within a prison setting as well. They argued that states should educate Black people in order to "raise their character to a level with that of the whites."[35] States should strictly rank inmates: "The obvious principles of classification, requires that males and females, old and young, condemned and uncondemned, blacks and whites, debtors and criminals, should be separated." Such distinction, the reformers dictated, was consistent with the purposes of justice and the principles of religion.[36]

Religious and Philosophical Approaches to Discipline in Northern Penitentiaries

The Christian ideals espoused by the Boston Prison Discipline Society did not aim at total conversion of prisoners. In this their views differed from another penal theory—the Quaker paradigm of spiritual conversion—which formed the basis of the Pennsylvania system of solitary confinement.[37] The Quaker reformers in Philadelphia believed that criminals, like all human beings, were individuals who embodied an inner light that rendered them capable of profound spiritual transformation. They devised a system of lengthy solitary confinement to

32. Gustave de Beaumont and Alexis de Tocqueville, *On the Penitentiary System in the United States and Its Application in France* (Philadelphia: Carey, Lea & Blanchard, 1833), 61–62.
33. Colton, *Colonization and Abolition Contrasted*, 5.
34. Adam Jay Hirsch, *The Rise of the Penitentiary: Prisons and Punishment in Early America* (New Haven, CT: Yale University Press, 1992), 73–74. In addition to freed slaves, Irish and German immigrants comprised a significant portion of penitentiary inmates.
35. Prison Discipline Society, *First Annual Report*, 37.
36. Ibid., 17–18.
37. For the purposes of this book, I will focus on the "Auburn" system implemented in New York, as this model was widely replicated in Northern and Southern states, while the Philadelphia model was not broadly adopted. A thorough investigation of the Pennsylvania system is beyond the scope of this book. However, as noted in the statistics compiled by the Prison Discipline Society, the racial demographics of Pennsylvania prisons were similar to those of other states.

foster individual contemplation and redemption while avoiding collective corruption and contamination. In Eastern State Penitentiary, built in 1829, prisoners were kept completely separate from one another. Newly arrived convicts donned a hood to walk to their cells so that other prisoners could not recognize them. Prisoners had their own yards, solitary tasks (such as shoemaking), and profound silence in which to examine themselves, recognize their guilt, and seek God's forgiveness.[38] As in other states, Black prisoners disproportionately made up the ranks of inmates incarcerated in Pennsylvania.

The Boston Prison Discipline Society and New York officials rejected solitary confinement when several inmates went mad or committed suicide during the first year of operating Auburn Penitentiary, New York's second state prison.[39] However, they believed that imprisonment could effectively foster industrious habits. The Boston Prison Discipline Society declared:

> It cannot be asserted that this or any other system of punishment, will change the heart of convicts, and produce sincere repentance;—but it will protect society, during the periods to which they are doomed: it will deprive offenders of the power of transmitting new vices to their fellow criminals, and will at least afford them an opportunity for reflection, by inculcating habits of order, industry, and temperance.[40]

Many inmates—impoverished whites and Blacks—were imprisoned for crimes related to theft.[41] Reformers identified penitentiaries as a way to morally indoctrinate ostensibly lazy whites—who were disproportionately immigrants[42]—and the subjugated Black race in the middle-class ethoses of restraint, discipline, and hard labor. Idleness was seen as both symptom and cause of deviant behavior: Those unwilling to work were prone to commit all types of offenses. Idleness also gave them time to corrupt and instruct fellow miscreants in a life of crime.[43] Thus, reformers advocated a system of hard labor to acculturate white

---

38. Muriel Schmid, "The Eye of God: Religious Beliefs and Punishment in Early Nineteenth-Century Prison Reform," *Theology Today* 59, no. 4 (January 2003): 551–53.
39. Beaumont and Tocqueville, *On the Penitentiary System*, 5.
40. Prison Discipline Society, *First Annual Report*, 84.
41. Michael Stephen Hindus, *Prison and Plantation: Crime, Justice, and Authority in Massachusetts and South Carolina, 1767–1878* (Chapel Hill: University of North Carolina Press, 1980), 63.
42. For example, a "Table of Prisoners Received into the New-York State Prison in the year 1827" shows that there were 153 Americans and 42 foreigners, 23 of whom were from Ireland, incarcerated in the New York City prison. See also David J. Rothman, *The Discovery of the Asylum: Social Order and Disorder in the New Republic* (Boston: Little, Brown, 1971), 240.
43. Rothman, *Discovery of the Asylum*, 103.

and Black inmates to the discipline necessary for financial independence and stability.

One spokesperson for the Boston Prison Discipline Society, Francis Gray, declared:

> The object of prison discipline is to induce [the convict] not merely to form good resolutions . . . but to support himself by honest industry. The only effectual mode of leading him to do this, is to train him . . . to accustom him to work steadily and diligently from 8 to 10 hours a day, with no other respite. . . . The discipline best adapted to such men, is that which inures them to constant and vigorous toil.[44]

Historian David J. Rothman thus summarizes this approach:

> The prison would train the most notable victims of social disorder to discipline, teaching them to resist corruption. And success in this particular task should inspire a general reformation of manners and habits. The institution would become a laboratory for social improvement. By demonstrating how regularity and discipline transformed the more corrupt persons, it would reawaken the public to these virtues. The penitentiary would promote a new respect for order and authority.[45]

A religious ethos informed the effort of Louis Dwight of the Boston Prison Discipline Society to reform the moral character of convicts. A former Andover Seminary student and tireless agent of the American Bible Society, Dwight had initially hoped to become a minister, but a lung injury prevented him from pursuing ordination. He found his calling in prison reform. Dwight believed that the need for prison reform derived from the natural and moral laws of God.[46] He considered convicts to be "creatures of the same glorious Creator with ourselves. . . . They have souls like our own, in their nature mysterious, in their existence immortal. . . . And they are objects of regard to the Son of God, the Lord Jesus Christ. . . . They are capable of love; but generally, when committed to Prison, they are filled with malice. . . . Their case is not hopeless."[47]

Dwight's Prison Discipline Society was composed of Sabbatarians and temperance advocates. They were part of a broad religious revival

44. Ibid.
45. Ibid., 107.
46. William Jenks, *A Memoir of the Rev. Louis Dwight, Late Secretary of the Boston Prison Discipline Society* (Boston: T. R. Marvin, 1856), 5; W. David Lewis, *From Newgate to Dannemora: The Rise of the Penitentiary in New York, 1796-1848* (Ithaca, NY: Cornell University Press, 1965), 96.
47. W. D. Lewis, *From Newgate to Dannemora*, 108.

that held crusades against drunkenness, Sabbath-breaking, and idleness. Sabbatarians strictly observed Saturday or Sunday as a period of respite from recreational activities. Along with temperance advocates, they sought an agenda of moral reform that emphasized fundamental transformation of human passion and inclinations, a shift that necessitated transformation of social institutions as well.

Tocqueville and Beaumont observed the role of religion in the prison reform movement during their travels:

> In America, the progress of the reform of prisons has been of a character essentially religious. Men, prompted by religious feelings, have conceived and accomplished every thing which has been undertaken; they were not left alone; but their zeal gave the impulse to all, and thus excited in all minds the ardour which animated theirs. So also is religion to this day in all the new prisons, one of the fundamental elements of discipline and reformation: it is her influence alone which produces complete regeneration; and even with regard to reformations less thorough, we have seen that it contributes much to obtain them.[48]

Religious impulses spurred a New York prison advocate, Thomas Eddy, to work for the moral reformation of convicts.[49] Yet by 1816, when Auburn Prison was established in upstate Cayuga County, belief that prisoners were inherently morally polluted had once again surfaced. Even Eddy admitted that his experiment had failed. There were escapes and riots, and Eddy himself expressed frustration that the prison had failed to reform many convicts. New York officials implemented a prison discipline model known as the "Auburn system," which enforced through corporal punishment silent, factory-style, collective work during the daytime and separate celling at night.[50] By 1821, elected and inspecting officials advocated the "Auburn system" as that

---

48. Tocqueville and Beaumont, *On the Penitentiary System*, 93.
49. He was considered the "John Howard" of the American penitentiary movement—a title bestowed in honor of an English prison reformer who had achieved celebrated successes in making English prisons uniformly sanitary and ventilated, with sufficient wholesome food for inmates. Eddy claimed the mantle of Howard in America by becoming the initial warden of New York State Prison in New York City in 1797. Following Howard's recommendations, Eddy built the prison near a river, on an airy spot. He drafted a comprehensive new penal code in New York that abolished the death penalty in all cases except treason against the State, murder, aiding or abetting murder, or stealing from a church; it also eliminated whipping as punishment for a crime and forbid corporal punishments, such as flogging, branding, and torture of convicts. Eddy sought to develop prison industries in an attempt to teach prisoners a trade. He further established a schedule for religious worship and encouraged local ministers to preach to the prisoners. He also started a night school, with classes restricted to well-behaved inmates, and devised a system of incentives to improve inmate conduct and productivity, with the stipulation that inmates who maintained a record of good behavior could receive a share of profits upon discharge. He applied his methods to Black and white convicts alike.

"which would be productive of economy to the state, and essential benefit to the morale of the prisoners."[51] Prison would be used for the purposes of economic development, then, as was enslavement of Black people in the South. Although prison officials did not articulate the expansion of penal systems as relating to slavery—indeed, Northern officials expressed disgust at the maintenance of racial bondage—Auburn Prison would mirror the system of forced servitude in many ways.

The Boston Prison Discipline Society propagated the "Auburn system," which they believed was "eminently a system of moral discipline, adapted to republican institution. It is compatible with humanity, justice and economy, and resembles in no degree, the bastilles and dungeons of despotic governments, or the gloomy cells of superstition, where men are frequently immured for their very virtues."[52] Yet there were vigorous debates about the moral vision of the "Auburn system," even as many citizen reformers, elected officials, and penal managers embraced its model of collective labor in silence and separate celling at night. Competing philosophies disagreed not with the Auburn system's *methods* (silence, work, and profits)—indeed, New York officials and Boston reformers displayed remarkable uniformity on these matters—but about whether and to what extent inmates—Black and white alike—had the capacity to be morally reformed. This debate mirrored Northern abolitionist and Southern proslavery arguments about the moral capacities of slaves. The conflict on state punishment played out between officials who advocated for chaplain services, fostered educational programs, instituted collective (silent) eating in dining halls, and limited application of the lash, and supervisors who rejected religious and educational instruction, restricted food, implemented solitary eating in cells, and applied the whip unsparingly.

Thus, two philosophical camps arose through the development of the "Auburn system." One school of thought insisted that education and religious instruction might lead to a better man.[53] Governor DeWitt Clinton of New York stated that any failure in the moral reformation of convicts was solely the fault of prison administration: "As the only

50. Orlando Lewis, *The Development of American Prisons and Prison Customs, 1776–1845, with Special Reference to Early Institutions in the State of New York* (Montclair, NJ: Patterson Smith, 1967), 86–87.
51. J. C. Spencer, New York State Assembly, *Journal of the Assembly*, 44th Session (1821), 904. Spencer was a member of the select committee appointed to visit the state prison at Auburn.
52. Prison Discipline Society, *First Annual Report*, 84.
53. At this time, female convicts were considered unredeemable. They, too, were incarcerated in state penal institutions. See W. D. Lewis, *From Newgate to Dannemora*, 158–75.

legitimate object of punishment is to prevent crime, by reforming the offender, by incapacitating him from perpetrating future mischief, or by deterring others . . . and as none of these consequences have resulted, the failure must be imputed to the system, its defective arrangement, or improper administration."[54] But moral reform, in Clinton's view, was possible: "In order to reform an offender, he must be placed beyond the influence of bad advice and example; his mind and passions must be disciplined by intellectual, moral, and religious instruction, and he must be subjected to privations, to labor and to solitude."[55]

Indeed, this was in line with the dominant ethos of the times, in which all malfeasance was attributed to environmental factors, and consequently, morally polluted people could be improved and reclaimed by middle class society. Northerners maintained this argument about Black people enslaved in the South and free Black people—some of who became imprisoned—in the North. Inspectors of the Auburn Prison contended that, in fact, some moral reform *was* taking place. In 1819, they reported: "The prisoners have been, in general, healthy, and with few exceptions have behaved themselves in a manner becoming their situations, and it is with pleasure the inspectors have it in their power to remark that an alteration in the mind and manners of some is apparent."[56]

There was, however, a competing school of thought. It reflected a penological approach that emphasized "rigid discipline"—that is, rational and instrumental approaches to punishment. According to this theory of deterrence, inflicting pain upon an offender was justifiable because it discouraged crime.[57] This world view found a corresponding ideology in proslavery ideology, which argued that Black slaves must be kept under strict authority because they would not obey social norms of their own volition. Reformers in this school sought to reduce the prisoner to an automaton and derive maximum benefits from his labor in the penitentiary shops. They doubted that adult criminals, Black and white alike, could ever be reformed, but rather insisted that the prison be established as a place of punishment and terror to potential offenders.[58]

---

54. DeWitt Clinton, "State of the State address," in *Journal of the Assembly*, New York State Assembly, 41st Session (1819), 16.
55. Ibid.
56. Prison Inspection Committee, "Report of the Inspectors of the State Prison in the Village of Auburn," in *Journal of the Assembly*, New York State Assembly, 41st Session (1819), 324–25.
57. W. D. Lewis, *From Newgate to Dannemora*, 6.

This approach, which found its fullest expression in the philosophy of warden Elam Lynds, rejected the approach of the Boston and New York reformers. Yet reformers, despite their advocacy for the educational and moral improvement of prisoners, fervently supported Lynds, who served as the first principle keeper and second warden at Auburn and later at Sing Sing prison.[59] Lynds believed that the purpose of prison was to break the spirit of the convict. He espoused racist ideas, arguing that nonwhite inmates were morally polluted, and indeed, closer to animals than humans.[60] He was thoroughly opposed to philanthropic ideals, which he identified as "impractical."[61] He furthermore did not believe in "*complete* reform, except with young delinquents." He stated in an interview with Beaumont and Tocqueville:

> Nothing, in my opinion, is rarer than to see a convict of mature age become a religious and virtuous man. I do not put great faith in the sanctity of those who leave the prison. I do not believe in the counsels of the chaplain, or the meditations of the prisoner, make a good Christian of him. But my opinion is, that a great number of old convicts do not commit new crimes, and that they even become useful citizens, having learned in prison a useful art, and contracted habits of constant labor. This is the only reform which I ever had expected to produce, and I believe it is the only one which society has a right to expect. . . . I would even say that the prisoner who conducts himself well, will probably return to his former habits, when set free. I have always observed that the worst subjects made excellent prisoners. They have generally more skill and intelligence than the others; they perceive much more quickly, and much more thoroughly, that the only way to render their situation less oppressive, is to avoid painful and repeated punishments, which would be the infallible consequence of insubordination; they therefore behave well, without being the better for it.[62]

Lynds insisted that curbing the spirit of the prisoner, and convincing him of his weakness, was the foundation for ruling prisoners. Furthermore, every head of a prison "must be thoroughly convinced, as I always have been, that a dishonest man is ever a coward. This convic-

58. Ibid., 82. Stephen Allen and Samuel M. Hopkins, two members of a legislative team that investigated prison conditions in 1820 and 1821, agreed upon three basic principles: convicts had not been treated with sufficient severity, too much faith had been placed in their reformability, and drastic changes would have to be made if the penitentiary idea were to succeed.
59. Thomas Eddy and Louis Dwight disapproved of the severity of whipping but otherwise admired Lynds unreservedly. See W. D. Lewis, *From Newgate to Dannemora*, 89.
60. Beaumont and Tocqueville, *On the Penitentiary System*, 162.
61. Ibid., 161.
62. Ibid., 164.

tion, which the prisoners will soon perceive, gives him an irresistible ascendancy, and will make a number of things easy, which, at first glance, may appear hazardous."[63]

Thus fear, intimidation, and flogging for the slightest offense against prison rules set the course for hard labor and lack of solidarity among prisoners.[64] The whip was indispensable for Lynds's approach to prison management: he referred to it as the most efficient method for discipline, as well as the most "humane." Similarly to Blacks under Southern enslavement, flogged inmates could be made to work in any way. Lynds supported silence not because it led to moral reformation—as was believed in Pennsylvania—but because it prevented plotting, escaping, and rioting. It served as a method of social control to the extent that a few prison guards could maintain authority over close to a thousand unchained men.[65] In reality, his method mirrored that of a white overseer supervising Black slaves, and the Northern prison took on the appearance of a slave plantation.

> The prison "overseers" were paid about the same amount as their Southern counterparts. Some resorted just as much to the whip, and they were expected to record their floggings in punishment logs like those that were kept down South. Keepers and clerks dutifully recorded data about each and every convict as he or she was acquired, substituting in their neat ledgers "sentence" columns for "price." Prison authorities increasingly began using slavekeepers' devices, such as iron masks and other restraints, that could be ordered through the agricultural journals.[66]

Moral Reform at Hard Labor

Lynds and his supporters' ideals of "moral discipline" referred to the work habits useful for an industrialized economy. Indeed, several theorists identify the penitentiary as a logical outgrowth of the industrial revolution; that is, the institution of the prison and the development of capitalism reinforced one another.[67] In his study of the penitentiary

63. Ibid., 165.
64. Lynds was not alone in his advocacy of corporal punishment. Often deputy prison guards believed that only a rigid system of discipline kept convicts in subjection.
65. The system of silence, hard labor, and flogging, instituted in 1822 at Auburn, was adopted in 1825 when Lynds took one hundred convicts from the upstate prison to build a new facility in Westchester County. Originally known as Mount Pleasant, Lynds and his keepers ruled Sing Sing as rigidly as they had Auburn.
66. Christianson, *With Liberty for Some*, 126.
67. Dario Melossi and Massimo Pavarini, *The Prison and the Factory: Origins of the Penitentiary System* (London: Macmillan, 1981); Georg Rusche and Otto Kirchheimer, *Punishment and Social Structure* (New York: Columbia University Press, 1939).

during the industrial revolution in England, Michael Ignatieff queries why it came to be considered just, reasonable, and humane to immure prisoners in solitary cells, clothe them in uniforms, regiment their day to the rhythm of the clock, and "improve" their minds with doses of Scripture and hard labor.[68] Indeed, the social function of punishment in the eighteenth and nineteenth centuries was to prevent "low and indigent persons" from finding means of support outside of the wage discipline of the factory system.[69] Bourgeois reformers insisted that anyone who honestly applied himself to his work could earn a daily living. Poverty was interpreted as a sign of divine malediction, for which reformers had a cure.[70] By internalizing factory-oriented habits—that is, routinization and repetition—the regimens of discipline would be internalized as moral habits.[71] Good moral habits, in turn, would lead to a middle-class bourgeois lifestyle that was more comfortable and more powerful than the existence experienced by the recalcitrant poor.

Forced labor in the English and American penitentiaries ostensibly trained idle people to develop industrious habits, but the goal of balancing the prison books—that is, ensuring that prisoner labor paid for the expenses of sustaining the institution—led to exploitation of inmate labor in Northeastern (and later Midwestern) states.[72] Prison labor operations mirrored forced labor under slavery. When they were not confined to their cells, convicts worked side by side in silence for ten hours a day, six days a week, manufacturing goods such as footwear, barrels, carpets, cotton ticking, carpenters' tools, and other items.[73]

---

68. Michael Ignatieff, *A Just Measure of Pain: The Penitentiary in the Industrial Revolution, 1750–1850* (New York: Penguin, 1978), 1.

69. Ibid., 26.

70. Melossi and Pavarini, *Prison and the Factory*, 28.

71. Michel Foucault, *Discipline and Punish: The Birth of the Prison*, trans. Alan Sheridan (New York: Random House, 1977). See also Ignatieff, *Just Measure of Pain*, 60–67. Ignatieff writes that in England, two schools of thought dominated the prison reform movement: In the religious camp, Quaker John Howard sought to morally reform the poor by turning their filth, laziness, and disease into cleanliness, honor, and health. In the materialist camp, reformers suggested that moral ideas were derived from external sensation; thus, they proposed, people could be socialized if officials took control over all sources of sensation. Both groups of reformers agreed that the English penitentiary should inculcate moral habits by depriving the mind from riotous living, sexual indulgence, and intemperance—in short, vice—and training the body to perform the rigorous, hard labor demanded by factory bosses. Finally, they proposed a third goal for the penitentiary: that it be financially self-sustaining as a result of the labor enforced within it. For further information on the English penal system, see Dario Melossi, "Prison and Labour in Europe and Italy during the Formation of the Capitalist Mode of Production," in Melossi and Pavarini, *Prison and the Factory*, 14.

72. By 1833, the Auburn system of collective hard labor in silence was replicated by Maine, New Hampshire, Vermont, Massachusetts, Connecticut, the District of Columbia, Virginia, Tennessee, Louisiana, Missouri, Illinois, Ohio, and Upper Canada (what is now the southern part of Ontario).

73. W. D. Lewis, *From Newgate to Dannemora*, 182. Other items manufactured in antebellum New York

> Both [prisons and chattel slavery] subordinated their subjects to the will of others. Like Southern slaves, prison inmates followed a daily routine specified by their superiors. Both institutions . . . frequently coerced their subjects to work, often for longer hours and for less compensation than free laborers. . . . The "overseer" resided in the penitentiary as well as the plantation, and he supervised the performance of "hard labor" by inmates as well as slaves. Inmates and slaves were both distinguished from the free community by a conspicuous insignia: the color and quality of their garb. And the most resonant symbol of the slave plantation—the clanking of chains—echoed just as loudly from within prison walls.[74]

Indeed, the establishment of prison shops in which inmates manufactured goods was central to the overarching goals of the New York penitentiary.[75] In order to ensure economic productivity while maintaining silence, "rigid discipline" increased. Reformers approved of the system of "moral" training in the industrial work enforced by corporal punishments such as whipping, even though such sanctions mirrored mistreatment of Black slaves in the South. Indeed, the Boston Prison Discipline Society was philosophically opposed to slavery but maintained its support of the "Auburn system" even as its leaders observed extensive flogging, deprivation of food, and subjection to solitary cells. Other forms of punishment included calculated humiliations to which each prisoner was subjected: Black-and-white striped uniforms, the gaze of tourists, and the lockstep, inline march in which prisoners stepped with downward gaze and one hand on the shoulder of the preceding inmate. In the eyes of prison officials and religious reformers, such methods led to moral habituation and industrious tendencies. These authority figures refused to acknowledge the ways in which Northern prisons had come to mirror Southern slavery, for

> prison was intended to improve on slavery by eliminating slacking and economic inefficiency. It offered a setting that in some ways resembled slavery, but minus certain distasteful features, such as sexual licentiousness, irreligiousness, idleness, and unjustified captivity. Prison silence would replace plantation singing. Masters would now erect walls to keep

penitentiaries included steam engines and boilers, combs, harnesses, furniture, and clothing. Sing Sing's principal industry was stonecutting.

74. Hirsch, *Rise of the Penitentiary*, 71–72.

75. Massimo Pavarini, "The Penitentiary Invention: The U.S. Experience of the First Half of the Nineteenth Century," in Melossi and Pavarini, *Prison and the Factory*, 131–35. There were six systems of prison labor instituted in New York during the Jacksonian era: public account (labor for the state); contract labor with private companies who brought supervisors and materials into the prison; piece-price, in which convict-made goods were sold on the public market; leasing, in which convicts were rented out to private agents; state use; and public use.

the captives in, the opponents out, and the do-gooders in check, leaving it to the great masses of the general public to only imagine what horrors lurked inside. Instead of being bred on plantations, these prisoners would be kept celibate and prevented from multiplying. Rather than being enslaved, not for any fault of one's own, but for being a member of the Negro race, convicts now would be committed pursuant to conviction of a specific crime. . . . Except in cases of particularly serious offenses, individuals would not be held for life, only for a set term of years. Persons would no longer be born into bondage; they would have to achieve it by their own illegal deeds. Individual masters would no longer own slaves, perhaps inherited with the livestock. Now, all citizens would relinquish such ownership to the state, and the state alone would serve as master and keeper. Such was the modus operandi of the new state prison.[76]

But forced labor upheld by whipping mirrored some of the worst practices that took place under slavery.

Corporal Punishment in Northern Penitentiaries

White convicts, along with imprisoned and enslaved Blacks, were subjected to horrific abuses and conditions. Inmates suffered inadequate medical care and diseases that flourished within the damp prison setting. They were routinely starved and fed moldy, bug-infested food. A state investigation was conducted after a prisoner attempted to eat food stolen from the prison kitchen too quickly and consequently died; the hearings that were conducted as a result revealed a setting in which prisoners were made to work long hours with inadequate sustenance.

> It appears that during the years 1837 and 1838, the complaints and expressions of the want of food by the convicts were more frequent and numerous than at any other period; that sometimes when the convicts failed to perform their usual tasks, and were reprimanded for such omissions, they would allege, with tears in their eyes, their inability, arising from the want of sufficient food to sustain them.[77]

The lack of food was further aggravated when prisoners were made to eat in their cells and keep their unwashed bowls in their cells

---

76. Christianson, *With Liberty for Some*, 104–5.
77. Documents of the New York State Assembly, 62nd Session, *Report of the Committee of State Prisons, in Relation to the Mount-Pleasant Prison*, vol. 6, no. 335 (1839), 5. Hereafter *Documents of the Assembly* will be referred to as *DA*.

overnight, resulting in rodent infestations and mouse droppings in foul-smelling food containers.[78]

In addition to diet-related abuses, prisoners endured horrific beatings, often for small infractions such as smiling and laughing. Many inmates were hospitalized and died as a result of whippings in which they were often stripped naked, bound with ropes, and fastened to a vice. Convicts reported that prisoners were whipped until "the blood ran down in streams" and old scabs on their backs became raw; prisoners were given one to two hundred lashes at one time.[79] Keepers admitted to flogging men until they needed to be hospitalized for offenses such as whispering.[80] It was not unusual for prison guards to apply salt and vinegar to the inmates' wounds after whipping them.[81] Guards were also known to knock down a prisoner and kick him mercilessly. Indeed, those associated with immorality were subjected to brutality.

Deprivation of food and severe beatings mirrored some of the worst abuses inflicted on slaves in the South. Furthermore, keepers (who functioned like overseers) were not the only officials in prison with the authority to corporally punish inmates. Contractors were also given the authority to beat prisoners they charged with slacking in their work.

> At one time . . . [a contractor] hauled [a prisoner] up to a vice and screwed his finger in, so that he could not pull them out, stripped him, and then gave him fifteen lashes; his fingers were changed in colour when they came out by being pinched too hard; this was not for bad conduct, but on account of heedlessness in his work; drew blood when he whipped, saw him cane several times; has seen a convict flogged twice for the same offence; agent himself flogged him a second time.[82]

In 1838, in response to the death of an inmate who drowned himself after being flogged, the *Hudson River Chronicle* opined: "that there are cases [at Sing Sing Prison], where cruelty, rather than punishment, is exercised, we have every reason to believe. . . . We believe that there is

78. Documents of the New York State Senate, *Testimony Taken by the Committee Appointed by the Senate, to Investigate the Affairs of the Auburn and Mount-Pleasant State Prisons*, vol. 2, no. 48 (1840), 5. Hereafter *Documents of the Senate* will be referred to as *DS*. The investigation revealed corruption in the upper levels of the prison administration, in which the keeper served as the food contractor and pocketed surplus funds that were supposed to be spent on the inmate's fare. Numerous testimonies from 1837–40 reveal the hunger pains of men incarcerated at Sing Sing. They were given codfish instead of meat, and mush without molasses; when meat was supplied, it was spoiled.
79. Testimony of William J. Dunn, *DA*, 62nd Session, vol. 6, no. 335 (1839), 26–27.
80. Testimony of Cortland Lawrence, ibid., 57.
81. Testimony of Giles G. Leach, ibid., 15–17.
82. Testimony of Bartown E. Powell, ibid., 29.

no propriety, certainly no mercy, exercised in flogging men with a cat-o'-nine tails upon their bare backs, until they are lacerated to jelly."[83]

The newspaper charged the keeper with "the scourging of convicts with hot irons, smashing their limbs in a vice, whipping with cats wound with wire, shooting convicts in their cells, inflicting from one to five hundred lashes with a six-tailed cat, and feeding, or rather, starving men upon a scarcity and insufficient allowance of unwholesome food."[84] It provided graphic details about the level of abuse of a white convict named Little:

> On a certain occasion, an officer of the Prison came into the hall in the darkness of nights, took a convict, named Little, from his cell, gagged him in the most inhuman manner, by jamming a large stick into his mouth, and lashing it behind his head—then stripping him naked, lashing him up by the hands, and whipping him with a cat-o'-nine tails, until life was nearly extinct—after promising him more as soon as he was able to bear it, thrust him into his cell, and locked him up. Little's offence was, that he had been singing or halloing in his cell. The first opportunity that offered, Little, to escape the other promised whipping, jumped into the basin, and drowned himself. He was taken out and buried without the Coroner being called.[85]

These abuses against white inmates were similar to those enacted against Black slaves. For Black prisoners in the penitentiary—many of whom were freed slaves—the floggings and restrictions imitated the institution of chattel slavery maintained in Southern states. A keeper named Burr severely punished a Black convict by flogging him three hundred times with the cat-o'-nine tails. "His back and breech and legs were very much lacerated; the convict was unable to labor in consequence of this whipping; was shut up in his room for several days, and kept on low diet; [the witness] says he appeared soon after to be deranged; says he thinks the agent and his deputy were both present at the whipping of this convict."[86]

An assistant keeper testified to beating a Black convict that he saw laughing. The assistant keeper ordered him to take off his shirt, and when the convict refused and raised his fist, the official inflicted thirty blows with the cat-o'-nine whip and subsequently called in another keeper to inflict another thirty stripes.[87]

83. Editorial, *Hudson River Chronicle*, vol. 1, issue 32, May 29, 1838, 4.
84. "Prison Investigation," *Hudson River Chronicle*, vol. 2, issue 22, March 19, 1839, 3.
85. "Prison Investigation," *Hudson River Chronicle*, vol. 1, issue 50, October 2, 1838, 2.
86. Testimony of John S. Mattocks, *DA*, vol. 6, no. 335 (1839), 26.

Another keeper testified that he whipped a Black inmate for disobeying orders: the keeper inflicted fifty blows with a whip and another fifty blows with a cat wound with wire.[88] Yet another guard noted that he used the cat on a "tough hided negro" named Howell and justified it by telling the investigating committee that "the cat was made for the occasion."[89]

Public reports on the abuses garnered responses from prison officials.[90] In this way, the prison differed from chattel slavery, for there was a level of public accountability that was not present where Black people were the private property of whites. Investigative committees found that in addition to starving inmates, the "Auburn system" approved excessive flogging and beating, such as the infliction of eighty to two hundred strokes with a cat-o'-nine tails for small offenses or omissions of duty, for smiling or speaking to another convict, or for looking off from one's work.[91] Prison officials often sent convicts to the hospital or to their death.[92] Elected officials expressed outrage that deputy keepers at both prisons, in inflicting chastisement upon convicts, had been left wholly to their own unchecked and irresponsible discretion, frequently flogging with extreme severity, without counting the stripes or blows or troubling themselves with making a report.[93] Officials furthermore criticized keepers for not limiting abuses.[94]

Investigative committees found that the keepers who followed Lynds's philosophical approach—to break the spirit of prisoners rather than morally reform them—contrasted starkly with the state's goal of reforming morally polluted convicts:

[We have found that] sufficient attention is not given to the operation upon the minds and feelings of the convicts; that it is not properly appre-

---

87. Testimony of Charles Wright, ibid., 34.
88. Testimony of Henry Pinckney, ibid., 44.
89. Testimony of Giles G. Leach, ibid., 64.
90. Report of the Committee on State Prisons, in relation to the Mount-Pleasant prison, ibid., 1–9. In 1839, a legislative committee investigated complaints of inmate abuse, lack of food, and unfettered warden power. Sixty-five witnesses corroborated that inspectors of the prison failed to inquire into the conduct of the agent or the assistant keepers about the feeding, treating, or punishing of convicts. Responses to infractions often were not officially recorded, and because such wide latitude was given to the keepers, often flogging was not reported to the warden.
91. Testimony of Joakin Urmy, DA, vol. 6, no. 335 (1839), 31.
92. There was great public unrest regarding the administration of Robert Wiltse when reports of two mentally ill men incarcerated at Sing Sing, known as Van Winkle and Judson, died as a result of maltreatment. There was also outcry in Cayuga County about Elam Lynds, who had returned as warden to Auburn Prison in 1838. Two inmates died after his return as a result of abuse during his administration.
93. DS, vol. 2, no. 48 (1840), 5.
94. Ibid., 9.

ciated that convicts, like the rest of mankind, are most effectually governed through the means of their mental faculties; that they are capable of reflection and judgment; actuated and impelled by the passions; influenced by hopes and fears; moved by stripes to anger and revenge; and entertaining even there, if permitted, pride and ambition. True they are sent there to receive the punishment adjudged by the law for their crimes, and are continually reminded of it by their abject condition, and their entire subjection to the will of their keepers. . . . [But] they should be led to believe that their sufferings are not aggravated, but rather alleviated by their officers; they should attribute their degradation to the strong arm of the law, and not be made to feel that their deepest suffering is the effect of petty tyranny. Their submission to discipline would not be impaired, but rather improved by these means; the effect upon their minds would be salutary; and the hopes of reformation would be promoted.[95]

These elected officials believed convicts to be "the worst, the most depraved, desperate, and in general the most ignorant of men" and that "in the bosoms of such the vilest passions reign with ungovernable sway." However, they expressed belief that the arbitrary and brutal punishments inflicted upon inmates at Sing Sing as well as Auburn prisons in the late 1830s were wholly unjustified and that prisons could bring about moral reformation.[96] They did not acknowledge the resemblance of the penitentiary to slavery.

In fact, historian Scott Christianson argues, the existence of the penitentiary may have soothed the anxieties of proponents of abolition, in that the penitentiary—even if the majority of inmates were white Americans and foreigners—continued a form of racial control in the aftermath of emancipation. Northern reformers, in fact, admitted a goal of social control, if not of racial control: they acknowledged that prisons were distinguished from enslavement precisely because penitentiaries indoctrinated prisoners in the moral virtues of factory work habits, temperance, and self-imposed discipline. Advocates and officials argued that an authoritative, controlled environment was needed to supervise those who deviated from middle-class Protestant virtues. These authority figures differed from their Southern counterparts because they believed Black people could achieve discipline and virtue, but they agreed with them that Blacks required a disciplinary, industry-oriented environment. In this way, Northern reformers and officials, like Southern slaveowners, perceived Black people as degraded,

95. *DA*, vol. 6, no. 335 (1839), 4–5.
96. *DS*, vol. 2, no. 48 (1840), 85.

criminal beings who, as a result of vice, were disproportionately incarcerated.

Southern Penal Institutions

Innate Black immorality was a dominant theme in nineteenth-century Southern racial discourse. From the 1830s to the 1860s, such discourse took two tracks: in one view, Black people were subhuman and needed to be restrained like animals; in the other, Black people were like children who acted out of control without the guidance of parental slaveowners.[97] In the postbellum period, references to innate Black criminality suggested continuity between antebellum and postwar versions of racism.[98]

As the South emerged from the Civil War, these ideological constructs buttressed the building of state penal systems. Indeed, as the South struggled to recover from widespread devastation, elites raised fears of Black immorality and mobility, for the pollution associated with Black people threatened the purity of white culture. White southerners espoused the necessity of establishing new laws and state penal systems. Criminal laws and state punishment, initially oriented toward punishing violent white men, shifted to controlling free Black people.

Discourses on Black Degradation in the Antebellum South

Southern ideological and theological constructs of Black criminality arose in response to the abolitionist fervor of the 1830s. In 1832, Professor Thomas R. Dew of William and Mary College crafted a proslavery argument in response to debates in the Virginia legislature on the merits of colonization. Slavery, in his view, contributed to the civilization of mankind; indeed, Black people were ferocious animals whose bestiality could only be moderated by slavery:

> There is nothing but slavery which can destroy those habits of indolence and sloth, and eradicate the character of improvidence and carelessness which mark the independent savage. He may truly be compared to the wild beast of the forest—he must be broke and tamed before he becomes fit for labor and for the task of rearing and providing for a family. There is nothing but slavery which can effect this—the means may appear exceedingly harsh and cruel—and, as among wild beasts many may die in the

97. Frederickson, *Black Image*, 56.
98. Ibid., 58.

process of taming and subjugating, so among savages many may not be able to stand the hardships of servitude.[99]

Dew's analysis spurred a trajectory of thought that identified the savage Black body as more beast than human. The following year, a writer named Richard Colfax argued that the distinct features of Black people, "woolly hair, thick lips, black skins, flat noses," are "characteristics of another species, differing vastly and very essentially from white men."[100] Black people were intermediate creatures between white men and apes, Colfax argued, with smaller brains than whites. Thus, they could not be intelligent beings competent enough to participate in the privileges of citizenship. Were slavery to be abolished, "we would eternally have our prisons filled and our public charities consumed because of the inability of the negroes to obtain respectable employments."[101] Slavery should be considered a virtuous institution, as it kept Black people from crime.

Alongside of the image of Blacks as beasts, another thread of public discourse asserted Black criminality by raising doubts about the capacity for self-elevation. The condition of the free Black person in the North contradicted any hope for "amalgamation of the races," argued William Drayton:

It cannot, however, be boasted, that his intellectual character has been materially elevated, or his moral nature greatly improved. The free blacks are, in the mass, the most ignorant, voluptuous, idle, vicious, impoverished, and degraded population of this country. They are seldom seen pursuing regular trades, and avoid all continuous labour with characteristic solicitude. They have sunk lower than the Southern slaves, and constitute but a melancholy proof of the advantages of abolition.[102]

Drayton castigated the Northern abolitionists for failing to acknowledge that their advocacy would lead to "the utter annihilation of all sense of virtue," that emancipation from slavery would "plunge the

---

99. Thomas R. Dew, *Review of the Debate of the Virginia Legislature of 1831 and 1832* (Richmond, VA: T. W. White, 1983), 30.
100. Richard H. Colfax, *Evidence Against the Views of the Abolitionists, Consisting of Physical and Moral Proofs of the Natural Inferiority of Negroes* (New York: James T. M. Bleakley, 1833), 21.
101. Ibid., 30.
102. William Drayton, *The South Vindicated from the Treason and Fanaticism of the Northern Abolitionists* (Philadelphia: H. Manly, 1836), 230.

race into a pit of fathomless and irretrievable degradation and perdition."

> The most fearful consequence to be anticipated from emancipation, is the violence and insurrections of the manumitted slaves. That this violence would be inevitable, cannot, we think, be doubted. Many causes would combine to render the vast population, thus suddenly freed from wonted restraint, fierce, unquiet, and insurrectionary. Idleness itself would prompt them to a war upon the whites, if for the mere enjoyment of excitement. The want that succeeds idleness would urge still more fiercely to hostilities. The vices that would flow in upon them, drunkenness, sensuality, and impatience of restraint, would also act as spurs to goad them on to deeds of violence and blood. Their conscious degradation could not fail to add to their discontent.[103]

The cruelty and crime that would ensue would be unequaled in all the earth, Drayton promised. A torrent of blood would sweep all southerners, regardless of age, and white women would be violently subjected to the "savage and brutal passions of their demoniac captors." For once emancipated, the Black slaves would be "without land, without money, without experience, or intelligence, but more than all, without habits of self restraint. Thus situated, he must sink to the lowest wretchedness." The only possible outcome of emancipation, according to Drayton, was the spread of "idleness, poverty, drunkenness, vice, suffering, and discontent."[104]

Drayton, espousing a viewpoint commonly held in the North as well as the South, determined that in addition to embodying violent propensities, Black people were inherently lazy. "Indolent from constitution, the moment he is allowed the privilege of abstaining from toil, no persuasion, no inducement, not even the stern voice of necessity, can bring him back to it."[105] Idleness fostered criminality, in that it led to poverty, theft, and violence. Abolition of slavery, then, would create a perpetual conflict between the "original white population and a black emigration, ignorant, savage, vicious, and idle."[106] It would lead all created beings to "sink into a depth of crime and infamy" and bring down "the curse of God and man."[107]

Religious justifications for slavery abounded. Some advocates of

103. Ibid., 243–44.
104. Ibid., 247–49.
105. Ibid., 240.
106. Ibid.
107. Ibid., 235–36.

slavery advanced a "positive good" argument: slavery made the Black person moral, whereas freedom fostered vice. In 1846, the Southern writer Matthew Estes argued that whereas free Northern Black people had descended into a state of viciousness and criminality, Southern slaves were very religious. "I think it probable that it could be made to appear, that the few free Negroes in the free States, are guilty of more crimes than our whole [Southern] black population," Estes wrote.[108] He quoted an 1843 article in the *Southern Literary Messenger*, which argued that the free Blacks of the non-slaveholding states "are vicious to an enormous extent," and that "the vices of the free blacks have increased in proportion to the time which has elapsed since their emancipation."[109] Despite the arguments of abolitionists, Estes argued, free Blacks in the North "are vicious, degraded and consequently pay but little attention to Christianity, or even to the rules of ordinary morals."[110]

Estes was an explicitly religious apologist. He was among many southerners who used theological concepts to defend racial bondage. He and his fellow religious proslavery advocates drew from more than a century of English exegesis, in which the concept of Blackness was loaded with theological meaning—of baseness, evil, danger, and repulsion, as opposed to the purity, virginity, virtue, and godliness conveyed by whiteness.[111]

His contemporary Samuel Cartwright argued in his 1843 *Essays* that Blacks were indeed human—the Bible determined that all men had the same origin—but that they had a distinctly servile nature. Indeed, Cartwright believed that the Bible confirmed the discoveries of naturalists like Voltaire, who argued that "Negroes" possessed a different constitution than did whites.[112] "All observation proves," Cartwright

108. Matthew Estes, *A Defence of Negro Slavery, as It Exists in the United States* (Montgomery: Press of the *Alabama Journal*, 1846), 107–8.

109. Ibid., 108.

110. Ibid., 109. Interestingly enough, in Estes's view, it was the entire Northern region that appeared to have a lax religious condition. Whites, "wretches" of both sexes, and members of the highest and lowest classes were unfriendly to religious improvement. Slaves, however, were provided for by their masters and contented with their position.

111. Jordan, *White over Black*, 41–42. Interpretations of Blackness from English explorers such as George Best reinforced Southern concepts of racial difference. Best equated Blackness with sexuality, the devil, and the judgment of a God who had originally created man not only "Angelike" but "white." Furthermore, Best focused upon self-discipline, linking "disobedience" and "carnal copulation" to something "black and loathsome." While this book does not focus on Blackness and sexuality, per se, there is a plethora of writing that emphasizes this theological strain in Southern proslavery arguments.

112. Samuel Cartwright, *Essays, being inductions drawn from the Baconian philosophy proving the truth of the Bible and the justice and benevolence of the decree dooming Canaan to be servant of servants* (Vidalia [LA], 1843), 5–6.

wrote, "that these people's pleasures are not so much those of reflection, as those of sense." History and science prove, Cartwright believed, that due to his physiology and anatomical structure, the Black person was the slave of his appetites and sensual propensities.

> He is, from necessity, more under the influence of his instincts, appetites, and *animality*, than other races of men, and less under the influence of his reflective faculties. There is not so much a deficiency of intellect as a want to balance between his animality and intellectuality. The former predominating rules the intellect and chains the mind to slavery—slavery to himself, slavery to his appetites, and a radical savage in his habits, whenever he is left to himself. His mind being thus *depressed* by the excessive development of the nerves of organic life, nothing but arbitrary power, prescribing and enforcing *temperance* in all things, can restrain the excesses of his animal nature and restore reason to her throne.[113]

Because of the heightened wantonness and excessive sexuality resulting from animality, Cartwright argued, the hand of the slaveowner must be maintained to ensure divinely ordained order:

> Certain it is, that nothing but compulsion has ever made him lead a life of industry, temperance and order; nothing but compulsion has ever converted him into a civilized being. When the compulsive hand of arbitrary power is withdrawn, he invariably relapses into barbarism; proving that when he has his personal liberty, he is not a free agent to choose the good and avoid the evil—whereas, under that government which God ordained for him, the excesses of his animality are kept in restraint and his free agency is restored.[114]

When ruled by the temperate slaveowner, Black people were mild, good natured, obedient, timid, and domestic. However, Cartwright argued, they could not be forced to overwork, or they were transformed into "stubborn demons" who felt no fear or pain.[115] This was true in a state of freedom as well as slavery; however, in freedom, Black people would work with less regularity. Indeed, slaveowners provided the force necessary if Black laborers were to be coerced to work.[116]

Cartwright was among those apologists who believed that the Black slave was akin to a child rather than a beast. His apologetics for slavery

---

113. Ibid., 11–12. Cartwright detailed the differences in the nerves of the spinal marrow and the abdominal viscera and argued that Blacks' brains were 10 percent less in volume and in weight.
114. Ibid., 12.
115. Ibid., 15.
116. Ibid., 34.

derived from the biblical exegesis of Genesis 9, in which Noah plants a vineyard. "And he drank the wine, and was drunken; and he was uncovered in his tent. And Ham, the father of Canaan, saw the nakedness of his father, and told his two brethren without."[117] In the story, Ham's two older brothers, Shem and Japheth, cover their father, a process that alerts Noah to the actions of Ham. "And [Noah] said, 'Cursed be Canaan: a servant of servants he shall be unto his brethren.'"[118] In the exegesis of Southern apologists, Noah cursed Ham for his degraded behavior and character. Ham was the "servant of servants" whose name meant "black."[119] Thus his descendants were to be slaves to Shem and Japheth—white and red men.[120]

The scriptural defense of slavery—and in particular, Noah's curse—became the most elaborate and systematic statement of proslavery theorists.[121] By comporting himself as a dishonorable son, Ham had embodied the very traits that distinguished the nature of the slave population: disorderly, offensive, criminal.[122] The minister Josiah Priest published an extensive treatise on the biblical justification of Black enslavement that became one of the most widely sold books in the South.[123] Priest proclaimed:

> the word [Ham] not only signified *black* in its literal sense, but pointed out the very disposition of his mind. The word, doubtless, has more meanings that we are *now* acquainted with, *two* of which, however, besides the first, we find are *heat* or *violence* of temper, exceedingly prone to acts of ferocity and cruelty, involving murder, war, butcheries, and even *cannibalism*, including beastly lusts, lasciviousness in its *worst* feature, going beyond the force of these passions, as possessed in common by the other races of men. Second, the word signifies deceit, dishonesty, treachery, low mindedness, and malice.[124]

Priest's justification of slavery focused primarily on an exegesis of Genesis 9. Although the biblical passage does not contain a reference

---

117. Genesis 9:20–22 NRSV.
118. Genesis 9:25.
119. Cartwright, *Essays*, 13, 16.
120. Stephen R. Haynes, *Noah's Curse: The Biblical Justification for American Slavery* (New York: Oxford University Press, 2002). See also Jordan, *White over Black*, 35–36. Church fathers such as Augustine, Luther, and Calvin cast Ham as inherently depraved.
121. Haynes, *Noah's Curse*, 8.
122. Ibid., 12.
123. Ibid., 69.
124. Josiah Priest, *Slavery, as it relates to the Negro, or African race: examined in the light of circumstances, history, and the Holy Scriptures: with an account of the origin of the black man's color, causes of his state of servitude and traces of his character as well as in ancient as in modern times: with strictures on abolitionism* (Albany, NY: C. Van Benthuysen, 1843), 33.

to Ham's color, Priest employed a unique hermeneutical approach to determine that Ham was Black and, therefore, vicious. Ham had "*always been a bad person, even from childhood*" Priest proclaimed.[125] Thus, God's curse was a divine judgment. Priest pointed to three points of evidence: (1) the fact that Blacks were created in a lower order of intellectuality; (2) the fact that Noah had proclaimed the curse, and thus he appointed Black people to the position they would hold; and (3) the "pervading fact of their degraded condition," which pointed to God's judicial decree.[126]

Priest and his contemporaries also read a sexual subtext into Genesis 9, thus reinforcing images of the Black male rapist. Pagan religious idols represented lewdness and "the wild passions of lascivious desires,"[127] which could only be controlled by authorities. Passages in Leviticus proved that Negroes outraged all order and decency in human society in that they did not distinguish between family members and animals in their sexual advances.[128] Priest described the Sodomites who attempted to rape Lot's visitors as members of the race of Ham.[129]

Priest furthermore noted biblical emphases on the colors white and Black. "White is the sign of life and being. . . . Black, in all ages, has been the *sign* of every hateful thing. If a man is uncommonly wicked, he is said to be a *black* hearted wretch, as a traitor, a liar, a thief, a murderer, &c."[130]

Priest thus concluded that Black people were decidedly immoral when compared to whites:

> The distinction of color, between white and black, is not more striking than is the difference between the *moral* feelings and *mental* endowments of the two races. They indulge almost universally in disgusting debauchery and sensuality, displaying everywhere a gross indifference to the mental pains and pleasures of others. Insensibility to order and metaphysical harmony, with an *entire* want of what is comprehended under the idea of elevated sentiment, manly virtue and moral feeling, is characteristic of the race.[131]

125. Ibid., 79.
126. Ibid., 83.
127. Ibid., 148.
128. Ibid.
129. Ibid.
130. Ibid., 138.
131. Ibid., 201–2.

Other religiously based proslavery writers agreed that the fixed character of the posterity of Ham rendered Black slaves as eminently suited for a state of servitude. The Reverend Leander Ker, in an 1840 Pennsylvania lecture, "Slavery Consistent with Christianity," proposed:

> This crime of Ham was the first transgression recorded after the flood, and probably the first committed. . . . Noah now was to the world what Adam was, when created—the official head—the *viceregent* of Heaven—and, therefore, the first deliberate and willful offence, as in the case of Adam, according to the moral government of God, must be punished with the utmost rigor of law.[132]

That Ham had dishonored his father meant that Ham refused to honor all governors—natural, civil, ecclesiastical, and divine. This exegetical analysis was particularly salient in the antebellum South, where dictates of honor formed a pervasive system of values.[133] In the minds of southerners, racial slavery dishonored all members of one class—Black people—and bestowed honor on another—whites. In short, slavery generated honor. Inseparable from dimensions of class and race, honor also formed a part of Southern culture that rested upon loyalty, particularly regard for the familial patriarch.[134]

Many Southern slaveholders regarded themselves as heads of household in the tradition of Noah, men who demanded filial respect from family members and slaves alike.[135] They also emphasized the "social death" that resulted from the status of slavery. Slaves were dishonored and dishonorable beings[136]—a stigma that was conferred on all Black

---

132. Leander Ker, *Slavery Consistent with Christianity* (Baltimore: Sherwood, 1840), 6.
133. See Edward L. Ayers, *Vengeance and Justice: Crime and Punishment in the 19th-Century American South* (New York: Oxford University Press, 1984); Haynes, *Noah's Curse*, 78–85.
134. Ayers, *Vengeance and Justice*, 13, 27. Ayers notes that the values of honor—the preoccupation with reputation, appearance, ostentation, worldly hierarchy, sport, and amusement—were checked by a Southern evangelicalism that demanded, like Northern notions of dignity, self-control and restraint.
135. Although Genesis 9 describes a scene in which Noah is inebriated, Southern readings of dishonor emphasized not Noah's inebriation but the fact that Ham, by looking upon his father's nakedness, dishonors him. Haynes argues that for readers formed by Southern honor, the point of the biblical story was not whether Noah had acted dishonorably but why Ham had discovered his shame and revealed it to others. He quotes Bertram Wyatt-Brown, who suggests that the greatest dread imagined by adherents of honor was "the fear of public humiliation," especially when it involved "bodily appearance [that] was an outward sign of inner merit." Haynes, *Noah's Curse*, 78–79. Haynes also analyzes the Southern antebellum culture of honor, which recognized a system of values in which a man possessed exactly as much worth as others conferred upon him. Honor and public opinion were considered synonymous. He quotes Kenneth Greenberg, who describes a momentous form of dishonor in the Old South in the shaming of an opponent through unmasking him "to identify an image as falsely projected and to show contempt for it." He analyzes: "When the man of honor is told that he smells, he does not draw a bath—he draws his pistol. The man of honor does not care if he stinks, but he does care that someone has accused him of stinking." Ibid., 80.

people by virtue of the fact that in the United States, only Blacks were enslaved. The similar status of convicts—dishonorable and dishonored beings—rendered an ideological continuity between antebellum slavery and postbellum convict leasing.[137]

State Punishment of Black People in the Antebellum South

The dishonored status of Black people, and the theological assurance that racial hierarchy was divinely ordained, reinforced the operation of antebellum Southern penal systems. Only whites were imprisoned in Southern penitentiaries, because white convicts were seen as committing a criminal *act*. They could be rehabilitated in the "Auburn system" that was replicated in Southern penitentiaries. Black convicts in the antebellum era were punished outside of prison walls. Identified as innately immoral, they were subjected to corporal punishments with no pretense of moral reform. Although most whites were convicted of a violent crime (assault) and most Black people were convicted of a property crime (theft), enslaved and free Black people were subjected to an entirely different penal code and mode of trial than were whites.[138] Enslaved and free Black people were accorded few procedural rights in courts, could be convicted without regard to legal charges, and were punished with substantial severity.[139]

> In criminal cases, as in all trials, blacks were not permitted to give sworn testimony, nor could they initiate prosecutions except through a guardian. All crimes for which whites could be arraigned were criminal when committed by blacks, but blacks were liable to be prosecuted for a great many additional offenses. If a black man wounded a white man, he could be executed; the third conviction for striking a white man was also capital. . . . Some crimes were considered more serious when committed by blacks. In 1843, for example, assault with intent to rape a white woman was made capital.[140]

---

136. Orlando Patterson, *Slavery and Social Death: A Comparative Study* (Cambridge, MA: Harvard University Press, 1982), 7–13. He writes: "The slave could have no honor because he had no power and no independent social existence, hence no public worth. He had no name of his own to defend. He could only defend his master's worth and his master's name. That the dishonor was a generalized condition must be emphasized, since the free and honorable person, ever alive to slights and insults, occasionally experiences and responds to specific acts of dishonor. The slave usually stood outside the game of honor." Ibid., 10–11.
137. Thorsten Sellin, *Slavery and the Penal System* (New York: Elsevier, 1976).
138. Hindus, *Prison and Plantation*, 139.
139. Ibid., 130.
140. Ibid., 131.

Furthermore, the testimonies of Black people were considered of lesser value than those of whites. Black people did testify—both in trials of other Blacks and on their own behalf against whites—but they were unable to successfully contradict any statement of a white witness or prosecutor, because whites assumed a Black proclivity for lying.[141] They were also convicted at much higher rates than whites: for example, South Carolina slaves were sentenced at approximately double the ratio for whites.[142]

State punishment of Black people in the antebellum era emphasized whipping and hanging. In some cases in South Carolina, slaves were sentenced to the local jail or the state workhouse.[143] Poor and immigrant white men, who made up the majority of white defendants, were sentenced to the penitentiary. Authorities made every effort to avoid biracial incarceration in state facilities. After 1818, only Louisiana consistently admitted slaves to its prison as an alternative to hanging.[144]

In the late 1850s, to avoid the problem of degraded honor posed by biracial imprisonment, states began to lease Black convicts to private entrepreneurs. Black prisoners worked outside of prison walls on canals, roads, bridges, railroads, and cotton factories. In general, during the antebellum period, while imprisoned white men were being "reformed" in state penitentiaries, convicted Black people who were formerly free suffered punishments that focused on inflicting pain on the body—as had slaves—rather than on redeeming moral character.

Punishment in the Postbellum South

Whites constructed Black people as irredeemably degenerate, and thus justified harsh criminal laws and emerging institutions of punishment in the aftermath of the Civil War. Southern officials disproportionately targeted Black people for criminal prosecution immediately after Southern surrender. In the fall of 1865, Governor Benjamin G. Humphrey of Mississippi declared that the freedom of Black people had limits: Black people occupied a place in the lower order of things, and

141. Ibid., 133.
142. Ibid., 144.
143. Ibid., 146–50.
144. Ayers, *Vengeance and Justice*, 61. He notes that in 1823, Virginia lawmakers decided to embark upon an experiment: they would sell into slavery free Blacks convicted of "serious" crimes. The law stayed in operation for four years but was abandoned after it proved to be "more in conflict with public feeling and sentiment, than it is common for the acts of our Legislature to be." Nevertheless, forty-four free Blacks were sold into slavery before Virginians decided that the law was "incompatible with every principle of morality and justice, and directly repugnant to the just, human, and liberal policy of Virginia." Ibid., 62.

that place was the cotton field. "Such was the rule of the plantation," said Humphrey, and the "law of God."[145]

In the antebellum period, when whites perceived Black character as inherently immoral, the institution of chattel slavery had represented authoritative control over the Black body. In the aftermath of the Civil War, the new reality of unrestrained Black mobility led to heightened fears of widespread criminality. Emancipation ended slavery, but it did not end the assumptions underlying slavery.[146] Southern whites continued to view Black people as inherently immoral and criminal; emancipation raised alarm about Black criminality to new heights. Chief among white anxieties was theft; yet another was sexual malfeasance.

Many in the postbellum era interpreted stealing by Black people as a biological flaw. "You can't find a white streak in 'em, if you turn 'em wrong side outwards and back again," one planter observed. "All the men are thieves, and all the women are prostitutes. It's their natur' to be that way, and they'll never be no other way."[147] In addition to theft and prostitution, whites in the postbellum period also expressed apprehension at the idea of "amalgamation"—particularly sex between white women and Black men.

Indeed, Southern racial ideology from the antebellum to the postbellum periods shifted from constructing Black men and women as alien pollutants in the community to defining them as enemies.[148] Upon emancipation, ideologies about Black criminality spurred the development of penal laws and practices that became "worse than slavery."[149]

Criminal laws known as Black Codes—aimed at curtailing Black mobility, exploiting Black labor, and maintaining white supremacy—were enacted in every Southern state between 1866 and 1867. Although the Thirteenth Amendment abolished forced labor for free persons, it permitted involuntary servitude solely as a punishment for a crime.[150] A key aspect of the Black Codes was a series of laws against vagrancy, which ensured the continued availability of cheap or free Black labor. The crime of "vagrancy" was defined in such a broad and ambiguous way that the statutes perpetuated de facto slavery.[151] Every former

---

145. David M. Oshinsky, *"Worse Than Slavery": Parchman Farm and the Ordeal of Jim Crow Justice* (New York: Free Press, 1996), 20.
146. Ibid., 17.
147. Ibid., 32.
148. Alex Lichtenstein, *Twice the Work of Free Labor: The Political Economy of Convict Labor in the New South* (New York: Verso, 1996), 21.
149. Oshinsky, *"Worse Than Slavery,"* 35.
150. Lichtenstein, *Twice the Work,* 2.
151. Ayers, *Vengeance and Justice,* 151.

Confederate state passed a vagrancy law. Mississippi's Black Code stated an explicit moral function. Its "Act to Amend the Vagrant Laws of the State" defined "vagrant" as runaways; drunkards; pilferers; lewd, wanton, or lascivious persons, in speech or behavior; those who neglect their employment, misspend their earnings, and fail to support their families; and "all other idle and disorderly persons." The penalty for this kind of vagrancy was a fine not exceeding $100 and not more than ten days in jail.[152]

The new legislation also mandated that each "Negro" must have a written labor contract or a license from local officials authorizing him or her to do irregular work. If any Black worker under contract left "without good cause," civil officers should, and any person might, arrest him and carry him back. The reward was five dollars plus ten cents per mile traveled and was to be held out of the culprit's wages.[153] Thus, the threat of arrest for vagrancy allowed planters and sheriffs to coerce Black workers into making and keeping their contracts for their labor. Virtually any freed slave who was not under contract to (and thus, the protection of) a white man could be arrested for vagrancy.[154]

The Florida Convention followed the state of Mississippi by enacting by special ordinance an interim vagrancy law, which ordered that anyone "leading an idle, profligate or immoral course of life" should be punished by fine, imprisonment, or "by being sold for a term not exceeding twelve months."[155] Similarly, legislators in South Carolina, Georgia, Alabama, Louisiana, and Texas copied Mississippi's Black Code, sometimes word for word.[156] On February 10, 1866, the Freedman's Bureau in Savannah, Georgia, issued the command:

To all idle and dissolute Freedmen:

You are hereby kindly exhorted to go to work at once and make contracts for the year. . . . We do not wish to resort to extreme measures, but we warn you that unless you procure some useful employment within three days for this date, you will promptly be arrested and proceeded against as vagrants: the chain gang will be your inevitable fate.[157]

---

152. Ibid., 68.
153. Ibid.
154. Douglas A. Blackmon, *Slavery by Another Name: The Re-Enslavement of Black People in America from the Civil War to World War II* (New York: Doubleday, 2008), 53–54.
155. Theodore Brantner Wilson, *The Black Codes of the South* (Tuscaloosa: University of Alabama Press, 1965), 66.
156. Oshinsky, *"Worse Than Slavery,"* 21.
157. Wilson, *Black Codes*, 84.

Although the federal government outlawed Black Codes in 1867, new state statutes restricting Black mobility and opportunity quickly replaced them.[158] Unlike the Black Codes, these new laws were not explicitly race-specific, yet it was widely perceived that they would rarely, if ever, be applied to whites. Mississippi's infamous "pig law" of 1876 defined the theft of any property valued at over ten dollars or of any swine as grand larceny.[159] In the 1880s, Alabama, North Carolina, and Florida enacted laws making it a criminal act for a Black man to change employers without permission, effectively removing former slaves' option of contracting out their labor freely.[160]

Black Codes forced freed slaves onto plantations and railroads and into mines. They formalized exploitation of Black labor in an era when labor was ostensibly free. But these laws served another function as well: remodeling the image of the recalcitrant Black slave into that of the thieving Black convict.

The act of rounding up freed slaves fed into an overarching system of threat, exploitation, and containing people who were associated with moral pollution. Similar to the role of the master of the antebellum slave era, local sheriffs in the postbellum era took on a powerful role in which they had complete authority over the lives of convicts.[161] This new dimension of power led to an extensive system of exploitation in which payment for crimes was enforced at the end of every criminal proceeding, with the accumulated fees lumped into the penalties ordered by the judge. The vast majority of persons found guilty and given fines were unable to pay. The companies that acquired the prisoners under lease paid these additional fees and required convicts to "repay" them through additional work, which added extraordinary lengths to their sentences. An organized market for prisoners began to evolve, with labor agents pursuing able-bodied Black men for arrest and sheriffs receiving the proceeds of a prisoner's lease.[162]

Many men rounded up and charged with crimes bargained for labor contracts closer to home, often on the same plantations where they had worked as slaves. Thus, they returned to conditions of uncompensated hard labor, in shackles, under the lash, physically compelled to work as an antidote to the immorality of "idleness." Indeed, the very

158. Blackmon, *Slavery by Another Name*, 53–54.
159. William Cohen, *At Freedom's Edge: Black Mobility and the Southern White Quest for Racial Control, 1861–1915* (Baton Rouge: Louisiana State University Press, 1991), 225–26.
160. Ibid., 54.
161. Blackmon, *Slavery by Another Name*, 64–66.
162. Ibid., 61–67.

punishments endemic to slavery were incorporated into the postbellum penal system.

As in the antebellum penal system and institution of chattel slavery, the postbellum penal system did not pretend to inculcate moral reform in people who were considered socially polluting and incapable of rehabilitation.

> The well-worn notion that blacks would only work under the threat of compulsion bolstered the forced labor central to the postwar southern penal system, a system socially legitimized by the supposed need to respond to the threat of so-called "negro criminality." Both its labor regime and its penological rationale virtually dismissed the possibility of "reforming" or rehabilitating the black lawbreaker. Reformation only entered the discourse of convict labor when the abysmal conditions found in southern convict camps were defended on the grounds that they represented an improvement over the health and welfare of the "average negro laborer," or when the hard labor required by convicts coincided with the "unskilled" heavy labor held suitable for blacks.[163]

The premise upon which Southern postbellum penal systems were established reinforced the notion that criminals possessed bodies but not souls. They were meant to work, not to improve. This construction of the criminal Black body allowed the "servant of servants" to continue as a menial drudge. In the postbellum period this exploited body provided the industrial labor to build a "New South."

The vast majority of prisoners were leased to private industrialists to labor on railroads, as well as in the coal, steel, and cast iron mines. By the end of Reconstruction in 1877, every formerly Confederate state except Virginia had adopted the practice of leasing Black prisoners into commercial hands. By the end of the 1880s, at least ten thousand Black men were slaving in forced labor mines, fields, and work camps in the formerly Confederate states.[164] Company guards were empowered to chain prisoners, shoot those attempting to flee, torture any who wouldn't submit, and whip the disobedient—naked or clothed—almost without limit.[165] There was little outcry, as the white public relied upon convict leasing to contain the threat of moral pollution posed by Black freemen.

---

163. Lichtenstein, *Twice the Work*, 21.
164. Blackmon, *Slavery by Another Name*, 90.
165. Lichtenstein, *Twice the Work*, 1–151; Blackmon, *Slavery by Another Name*, 56. Over eight decades, there were rarely penalties to industrialists who were leasing former slaves for their mistreatment or deaths.

Brutally severe conditions led to high rates of mortality. Convicts were routinely starved and beaten by farmers, government officials, corporations, and small-town businessmen intent on achieving the most lucrative balance between the productivity of captive labor and the cost of sustaining them. The consequences for Black prisoners were grim. For example, in the first two years that Alabama leased its prisoners, nearly 20 percent of them died. In the following year, the rate of mortality rose to 35 percent, and in the fourth year, nearly 45 percent were killed.[166] There were similar mortality rates in other Southern states. Florida's chief prison doctor argued that numerous "debasing habits," led by "lust" and "passion," resulted in high rates of death among Black prisoners.[167]

Conditions within mines were brutal as well. Prisoners digging in coal mines would dig about ten feet under the coal face and then blast the coal loose, pick out worthless pieces, load a car, and then push the car to the main shaft. This work entailed digging coal lying down or on one's knees, often in water, in a dark tunnel six to eight feet wide, illuminated only by the convict's head lamp, which frequently dripped oil in his eyes and overcame him with fumes.[168] Convicts were killed or badly hurt by the coal cars, by explosions, by pick wounds, and most frequently, "mashed by slate," "injured by slate," or "killed by slate fall."[169] Prisoners died in such drastic numbers, Texas officials contended, because the "average Black convict" was a "moral degenerate who entered prison with the 'seeds of disease' already in his system. The convict appeared normal until he was 'put to hard labor'—at which time the seeds flowered and he died."[170]

For eight decades, the white public turned a blind eye to the terrible conditions of convict leasing.

> On many railroads, convicts were moved from job to job in a rolling iron cage, which also provided their lodging at the site. . . . The prisoners slept side by side, shackled together, on narrow wooden slabs. They relieved themselves in a single bucket and bathed in the same filthy tub of water. With no screens on the cages, insects swarmed everywhere. It was like a small piece of hell, an observer noted—the stench, the chains, the sickness, and the heat. "They lie on their beds, their faces almost touching the

166. Blackmon, *Slavery by Another Name*, 57.
167. Oshinsky, *"Worse Than Slavery,"* 84.
168. Lichtenstein, *Twice the Work*, 134.
169. Ibid., 135.
170. Oshinsky, *Worse than Slavery*, 84.

bed above them. . . . On hot days . . . the sun streams down . . . and makes an oven of the place, and the human beings in it roast."[171]

The human beings who were subjected to postbellum criminal legislation, arbitrary arrest, and brutal convict leasing conditions were considered fundamentally immoral and thus held responsible for their own demise.

Conclusion

Nineteenth-century Southern penal systems and Northern penitentiaries exhibited numerous similarities and, at times, espoused similar ideologies. Both institutions of punishment emphasized the need to restrain immoral Black people who were viewed as prone to criminality in the aftermath of slavery.[172] Both systems relied on religious interpretations of Black immorality to buttress their advocacy for restraining Black people. Northern penitentiaries and Southern convict leasing each sought to exploit labor under a system of violent subjugation that relied upon the lash; in this way, prisons employed the disciplinary methods of chattel slavery. Both penitentiaries and convict leasing engaged in the production of goods while taking full advantage of a captive work force; this practice, too, mirrored forced racial bondage.[173] And both sought to produce earnings: Southern plantations were explicitly run for profit, and Northern prisons also sought not only to pay for the expenses associated with incarceration but also to produce a profit; this drive for revenue paralleled the motivations of slave owners. Finally, in disproportionately imprisoning Black people, both systems maintained racial hierarchies established during the preceding era of chattel slavery.

However, there were also substantial differences in the development of Northern penitentiaries and Southern penal systems. While each region most fully established state punishment in the aftermath of legal slavery—in the 1820s in the North and in the 1860s and 1870s in the South—Northern prison reformers assumed the duty of morally reforming individual prisoners. At the very least, officials and reformers sought to inculcate moral habits of work and reintegrate former prisoners—including Black people—into society upon release. While

---

171. Oshinsky, *"Worse Than Slavery,"* 59.
172. Hirsch, *Rise of the Penitentiary*, 73–74.
173. Ibid., 93.

there were divergent approaches to rehabilitating prisoners, prison officials and reformers alike agreed that inmates should learn work habits that would acculturate them to an industrial society. That Black people were disproportionately incarcerated in the North fostered ideas that they were disproportionately criminal—but white reformers and officials primarily pointed to environmental conditions that had fostered depravity. For the most part, they did not uphold ideas of innate Black criminality, and they hoped that Black people would adopt middle-class moral habits and work as free laborers. Reformers and officials toured penal facilities to ensure that prisoners were treated correctly and that there were programs that inspired moral reform.

These reformers did not acknowledge that penitentiaries resembled the institution of slavery even as these reformers critiqued slavery. They did not acknowledge the depth of sentiments about the fear of large numbers of free Black people, a perceived inability to accommodate large numbers of newly liberated slaves in a free society, and fear of crime. They refused to acknowledge the desire for a cheap and docile labor force for the state. In their eyes, prisons were meant to reform and ready participants for a democratic, industrial society, and thus elected officials held prison keepers accountable for horrific corporal abuses.

However, in the South, Black people were constructed as innately immoral, as descendants of the cursed Ham, a race of people who were designed by God to serve the white race. After emancipation, fears of predatory free Blacks and the loss of slave labor propelled officials to develop convict leasing systems that brutalized Black prisoners, with no pretense of moral reform. Southern elites readily acknowledged that they sought to exploit the labor of Black convicts in order to maintain an agricultural economy and develop new industries. Elite interpretations of the morality of convict leasing, and later of chain gangs and prison farms, buttressed the racial control embedded in the penal system.

Additional differences between North and South were heightened during the emergence of the Progressive era in the late nineteenth century. In the North, prison reformers advocated for individualized sentencing and new systems of supervision outside of the penitentiary: probation and parole.[174] Advocates identified the penitentiary system,

---

174. David J. Rothman, *Conscience and Convenience: The Asylum and Its Alternatives in Progressive America* (Boston: Little, Brown, 1980).

as it had been established, as brutal and contradictory to efforts at moral reform. Inspired by the Social Gospel, they sought to rehabilitate offenders through methods of social work and community supervision.

By contrast, during the same period, southerners implemented county and state chain gangs—a governmental response to the fury of free white laborers who identified convict laborers as competition. It was during this period that discourses of Blacks as brutes reemerged in public discourse.[175] Chain gangs proved just as brutal as private convict leasing. Ensuing public outcry led Southern states to establish massive prison farms in which convicts, dressed in black-and-white stripes, grew crops under the threat of the lash. To outside eyes, new Southern prisons resembled the antebellum plantations, with cattle, mules, vegetable crops, and cotton.[176] In the present day, prison farms still mark the landscape, now joined by state-of-the-art facilities in every region of the country.

175. Ayers, *Vengeance and Justice*, 238–52.
176. Oshinsky, *"Worse Than Slavery,"* 137.

3

Institutionalizing Pollution Boundaries: Policing, Imprisonment, and Reentry

Introduction

Policing systems function to corral and control bodies associated with moral pollution. In the contemporary period, disproportionate surveillance occurs in racially and class-segregated communities, with sophisticated technologies bolstered by the War on Drugs. Indeed, present-day policing practices, incarceration in jails and prisons, and post-reentry barriers operate as the primary social instruments for containing bodies associated with moral pollution. Today, there are 2.3 million people in US prisons—nearly half of whom are Black—and little recognition of the devastation wrought by drug task forces and sophisticated policing systems, mandatory minimum sentences and other harsh crime laws, the expansion of carceral institutions across rural America, or the legal and social "collateral consequences" of a felony conviction.

Images of Blackness, Images of Crime

The overrepresentation of people of African descent in carceral institutions has been magnified and reinforced by media stories on crime. Scholarly studies on visual representations in mass media consistently find that Blacks are associated with moral pollution: aggressive behavior and violent crime. Daytime talk shows, prime time television dramas, and nightly news shows depict negative images of Black character and bodies, thereby perpetuating a conceptual link between Blackness and criminality.[1]

Indeed, popular media disproportionately contains images of Blacks as shiftless, disorderly, and arrested (even if not convicted). These images carry powerful subliminal ideas. Political scientist Tali Mendelberg finds that visual images are the most effective way to communicate implicit messages:

> Images play an important and distinctive role in the way people perceive their world. . . . Indeed, visual images have proven to be powerful cues for evoking racial stereotypes. Stereotypical or threatening images can communicate derogatory racial meaning in a more subtle way than an equivalent verbal statement.[2]

In the same way in which theological discourses on Black criminality suffused nineteenth-century popular culture, in the contemporary period, visual representations perpetuate the image of Black criminality. Popular periodicals, television shows, and films play an influential role in depicting and shaping perceptions of Black people as morally polluted. Although popular media depicts Black professionals as successful and influential leaders in law firms, medical offices, and police stations, television also depicts images of Black immorality.[3]

The visual image of the criminal in popular media was not symbolically associated with Black bodies until the 1960s. Prior to that, the representation of the criminal in magazines and television shows was generally that of a white man who was capable of rehabilitation. In his survey of popular periodicals and films, communications theorist John Sloop describes the shift between the representation of the prisoner in the 1950s and the prisoner in the 1960s. In the 1950s, when 70 percent of the prison population was white, the dominant image of the pris-

---

1. Robert M. Entman and Andrew Rojecki, *The Black Image in the White Mind: Media and Race in America* (Chicago: University of Chicago Press, 2010), 57; John M. Sloop, *The Cultural Prison: Discourse, Prisoners, and Punishment* (Tuscaloosa: University of Alabama Press, 1996).
2. Tali Mendelberg, *The Race Card: Campaign Strategy, Implicit Messages, and the Norm of Equality* (Princeton, NJ: Princeton University Press, 2001), 9.
3. Katheryn Russell-Brown, *The Color of Crime*, 2nd ed. (New York: New York University Press, 2008), 1.

oner was of a person who shared a morality with the broader culture. His general failure to behave was understandable; it was the result of an uncomfortable, unfortunate living condition.

In this era, the rehabilitative model for the treatment of prisoners dominated penal philosophy, and officials responded to riots with an orientation toward fixing problems rather than imposing segregation or harsher punishments.[4] Sloop argues that "because prisoners shared the larger culture's sense of morality, their actions were configured as mistakes in judgment rather than proof of an evil nature."[5] In short, prisoners in popular media were portrayed as whites who, if treated decently, would respond in kind. This understanding of the prisoner as amenable to change was echoed in the reigning penal philosophy of the day. African Americans, who were constructed as shiftless and violent, were not widely represented in popular images of prisoners in 1950s mainstream periodicals.[6]

However, in the 1960s, popular media representations of prisoners began to change. Films and periodicals characterized prisoners as either redeemable or hopelessly irrational and immoral. During this period of intense civil rights struggle, redeemable prisoners were depicted as highly educated and more culturally diverse than those portrayed in the 1950s. At the same time, a second image emerged: that of a violent and brutal prisoner who was naturally polluted, and consequently could be changed through rehabilitation programs.[7] Popular media began to reflect Afrocentric movements, but Sloop finds that mainstream periodicals and films continued to emphasize the contrasting cultural images of the moral white prisoner and the immoral "other" who possessed dark skin.[8]

In the early 1970s, there emerged three depictions of prisoners. In addition to the white redeemable inmate and the recalcitrant, violent Black inmate, the images emerged of political prisoners George Jackson and Huey Newton, who defined the dominant political and cultural norms as oppressive and unjust. Thus, in this era, there was increased focus on what Christian Parenti calls "social dynamite" in addition to

4. Sloop, *Cultural Prison*, 33.
5. Ibid. Sloop also notes that during this time, it was common practice for pharmaceutical corporations and research institutions to utilize inmate populations as the subjects of experiments focusing on the safety and effectiveness of new medications, vaccinations, and treatments; see ibid., 34.
6. Ibid., 57.
7. Ibid., 64. Importantly, this is also a period when prisoners won several civil rights cases under the Warren Court. See also Marie Gottschalk, *The Prison and the Gallows: The Politics of Mass Incarceration in America* (New York: Cambridge University Press, 2006), 165–96.
8. Sloop, *Cultural Prison*, 78, 85.

"social junk"—both of which symbolized moral pollution. Media attention to the "social dynamite" image, one aspect of racial pollution imagery, reinforced the image of the Black revolutionary who posed a threat to the white social order:

> The incorrigible African American male is constructed as personally responsible for his actions, and, further, generally unable to rejoin the social order. . . . He is a free agent who chooses to violate the norms of moral behavior. Moreover, even though he chooses a life of immorality, he is paralyzed by his irrationality and incapable of rehabilitation; society's only answer is to punish him and keep him separate from the populace at large.[9]

The change in the image of the violent Black prisoner, from the 1960s to the early 1970s, highlighted the prisoner's free will and responsibility. The inherently violent Black prisoner was not the victim of a racist, unjust society but was rather a rational human being who had access to social institutions and opportunities and nevertheless chose an immoral course of life. He could only be punished, because rehabilitation programs could not reform him.[10]

In short, in the same way that prisoners in popular media came to be represented as Black, Black people in the popular media came to be symbolically represented as criminal. The image of the morally polluted Black man was in part evoked after the 1965 Watts rebellion and the more than one hundred riots during the summer of 1967. James W. Button's study of Black violence in the late 1960s and early 1970s shows that images of Blacks rioting spurred authority figures to address systemic barriers such as poverty, lack of educational and employment opportunities, and dilapidated housing.[11] Yet the representations of burning cities, Black Power activists, and street crime associated with young Black male drug dealers also generated revulsion from members of mainstream society.[12] A 1972 cover story in *Newsweek* stated:

---

9. Ibid., 116–17.
10. Ibid., 117–18. The present-day emphasis on incapacitation derives from prevailing ideas that Blacks are incapable of moral reform. A 1997 study in Kentucky found that adults who hold negative stereotypes of Blacks are likely to oppose furloughs for Black prisoners, in part because they regard African American prisoners as incorrigible and beyond rehabilitation. See Jon Hurwitz and Mark Peffley, "Public Perceptions of Race and Crime: The Role of Racial Stereotypes," *American Journal of Political Science* 41, no. 2 (April 1997): 386.
11. James W. Button, *Black Violence: Political Impact of the 1960s Riots* (Princeton, NJ: Princeton University Press, 1978).
12. Melissa Hickman Barlow, "Race and the Problem of Crime in 'Time' and 'Newsweek' Cover Stories, 1946 to 1995," *Social Justice* 25, no. 2 (1998): 172.

Few citizens actually die of fear, but its chilling effects have become a grim part of daily life for millions in and around the nation's cities. While some statistics suggest that the crime itself may actually be leveling off, the fear of crime seems to be escalating into a fortress mentality that alters the way people see themselves and the way they live their lives. . . . But like the paranoid who has real enemies, most Americans have good reasons to be afraid. Crime remains most highly concentrated in the ghetto, but it has long since pushed out into middle class residential neighborhoods and the suburbs, often following on the heels of the drug problem to which it is so closely tied. No one is completely safe. . . . The white middle class increasingly sees crime in terms of black against white.[13]

Whites associated Blackness with moral pollution: that is, violent criminality and drug abuse. In the 1980s, this symbolic association expanded. Popular periodicals linked Blacks with street crime and described the wide array of strategies and technologies employed in the fight against crime. Each of the cover stories on crime in *Time* and *Newsweek* during this period emphasized the violence of Black males. "In violent crimes committed by a single person, the victims in a quarter of the cases claim that the attacker was black," a 1981 story proclaimed.[14] "One fact that can't be questioned is that a vastly disproportionate number of violent criminals are black—an observation that until recently tended to be discreetly ignored as racist."[15] These *Time* and *Newsweek* stories on the problem of crime contained extensive discussion of the failure of the criminal justice system to protect innocent victims from violent, morally polluted Black criminals.[16]

The salience of the image of the criminal Black man came to the forefront of the mainstream news after the 1992 verdict in which four police officers were acquitted of beating Rodney King. It was further heightened by the cover picture of *Time*'s 1993 cover story entitled "America the Violent," which depicted a distorted cartoon image of a Black male criminal, whose clenched fists were restrained by handcuffs. The article, which provided the details of President Clinton's Crime Bill, discussed the importance of crime as a political issue and described anecdotal and statistical evidence that crime was a growing problem in the United States, never explicitly mentioned race.[17] The implicit message from the cover photo, however, was that the height-

13. "Living with Crime, USA," *Newsweek*, December 18, 1972, 31, quoted in Barlow, "Race," 173.
14. "The Curse," *Time*, March 23, 1981, 20, quoted in Barlow, "Race," 174.
15. "The Epidemic of Violent Crime," *Newsweek*, March 23, 1981, 50, quoted in Barlow, "Race," 174.
16. Barlow, "Race," 174.
17. Ibid., 176.

ened sentences and increased funding were meant to restrain the threat posed by morally polluted Black men.

Indeed, *Time* magazine's 1994 cover story, titled "Lock 'Em Up and Throw Away the Key," emphasized the intensity of public concern over crime despite statistical declines in crime rates. Crime rates had risen 23 percent over ten years, the article declared. Even though much of that rate of increase took place in neighborhoods where violence was concentrated, "the fear of crime also cuts across class and racial lines."[18]

Criminologists Coramae Richey Mann and Marjorie Zatz conclude that popular media representations of skin tone have been associated with varying levels of violence. "Generally speaking, the darker the color, the greater the evil associated with it and the more dehumanizing the stereotypes."[19] In a famous example, they argue, *Time* magazine altered O. J. Simpson's skin color to make him appear darker than he really is, in order to attract readers and provoke a negative reaction to Simpson after he was arrested for murdering his white ex-wife.

Salient images of Black moral pollution pervade not only popular media but also local and national news broadcasts. Communications theorists Robert Entman and Andrew Rojecki find that the media network ABC mainly discusses Black people when they suffer or commit a crime, or otherwise fall victim and require attention from the government.[20] They also find that on a nightly basis, television news portrays urban America as out of control, chaotic and violent.

> By tying appearances of Blacks so frequently to narratives of crime and victimization, the news constructs African Americans as a distinct source of disruption. Because stories featuring Whites in these circumstances are so much fewer as a proportion of all stories with Whites, the news can easily imply a baseline or ideal social condition in which far fewer serious problems would plague the society if only everyone in the United States were native-born Whites.[21]

In this way, public perceptions exaggerate symbols of Black moral pollution, for racial representation on television does not accurately represent crime statistics. Local news highlights Black perpetrators,

---

18. "Lock 'Em Up and Throw Away the Key: Outrage Over Crime Has America Talking Tough," *Time*, February 7, 1994, 52, quoted in Barlow, "Race," 176.
19. Coramae Richey Mann, Marjorie S. Zatz, and Nancy Rodriguez, eds., *Images of Color, Images of Crime*, 3rd ed. (Los Angeles: Roxbury, 2006), 8.
20. Entman and Rojecki, *Black Image*, 67.
21. Ibid. The authors also observe that the portrayal of Latinos is similar to Blacks in some respects.

downplays Black victims, and emphasizes white victims.[22] The racial subtext of televised violence encourages whites to focus their social aversions on Black people.[23] Racialized moral boundaries are articulated by mass media and internalized by average white families whose daily interactions are primarily with other whites and who are told that they have reason to fear Black people.

News agencies exaggerate the differences between racial groups and thus play a part in iterating racialized moral boundaries. By focusing on a range of behavioral traits amongst Blacks but not whites, news networks suggest that Black people exhibit behavior such as criminal activity and thus are a threat to the moral order.

Nightly news stories about violent crime disproportionately depict Blacks and also overwhelmingly depict Black people as threatening.[24] A 1993–94 study of local news in Chicago showed that television images attributed a heightened degree of threat to Blacks by showing them as physically uncontrollable.[25] "Night after night the parade of Blacks in the literal clutches of police authority, far more than White defendants, sends a series of threatening images that insinuate fundamental differences between the races."[26] A 1997 study of adults in Kentucky found that stereotypes of Black people influence judgments against Black defendants who are accused of a violent crime. When whites are confronted with a crime that accords with the racial "picture in their head," then stereotypes affect judgments.[27] Whites who view African Americans as violent and lazy are far more likely to believe them to be guilty of assault, with innate proclivities towards criminality.[28] Black people are associated with crime and whites with morality, but these bifurcated associations do not allow for traits to be correlated with the other group. Consequently, Black people in the news tend to look different from and more dangerous than whites, even when they commit similar crimes.[29] In short, news networks play an important role in fostering symbols of the morally polluted Black person, and consequently, have heightened racialized moral boundaries.

The stoking of white fear increased significantly in television and newspaper coverage of the 1980s "crack epidemic," in which Black peo-

22. Ibid., 81.
23. Ibid., 82.
24. Hurwitz and Peffley, "Public Perceptions," 376.
25. Entman and Rojecki, *Black Image*, 81.
26. Ibid., 83.
27. Hurwitz and Peffley, "Public Perceptions," 384.
28. Ibid.
29. Entman and Rojecki, *Black Image*, 84.

ple were portrayed as street thugs and strung-out junkies. Although people high on drugs committed a very small number of violent crimes, there was wide concern about crack-related chaos.[30] Major newspapers carried headlines such as "U.S. Breaks Up Major Crack Ring in New York"[31] and "Addict Guilty in Crack Rampage Killing."[32] Prominent magazines featured stories about the crack-related "homicidal violence that has turned the streets of many American cities into virtual war zones."[33] A 1986 cover of *Time* magazine showed a ravaged face with the words "Drugs: The Enemy Within." The article stated:

> Like a drunk waking up from a 20-year binge with a massive hangover, America is bitter, remorseful, and full of resolution. Though the drug epidemic appears to have peaked, drug abuse remains unacceptably high, and one virulent form, crack addition, seems to be spreading.[34]

Coverage of crack cocaine in the 1980s primarily depicted dark-skinned bodies. Indeed, the menace of crack cocaine—which carries the same potency as powder cocaine—alarmed whites and inflamed an already salient stereotype of the shiftless, violent Black male. This stereotype carried over into 1990s news coverage and justified extraordinary drug laws, police actions, and court proceedings.

Political campaign ads have similarly heightened perceptions of the Black criminal and thus also heighten the perception of stark moral differences between whites and Blacks, thereby reiterating social boundaries. A number of candidates for national and gubernatorial office have used the threat of violent Black crime to illustrate their campaign promises: for example, Pete Wilson in California, Jim Edgar in Illinois, and George W. Bush in Texas ran ads showing blurry black-and-white images of fictional gun-toting rapists.[35] But the political campaign that most persuasively manipulated the image of the Black male criminal was that of presidential candidate George H. W. Bush in 1988.[36]

During his campaign, Bush highlighted the case of William (Willie) Horton, a young Black man who was convicted of murder and sentenced to life in a Massachusetts prison. Horton escaped while on fur-

---

30. Ted Gest, *Crime and Politics: Big Government's Erratic Campaign for Law and Order* (New York: Oxford University Press, 2001), 118.
31. Arnold H. Lubasch, "U.S. Breaks Up Major Crack Ring in New York," *New York Times*, July 31, 1987.
32. Ronald Sullivan, "Addict Guilty in Crack Rampage Killing," *New York Times*, February 28, 1989.
33. "Slaughter in the Streets," *Time*, December 5, 1988.
34. "Fed Up and Frightened: U.S. Mounts a Crusade Against Drugs," *Time*, September 15, 1986.
35. Mendelberg, *Race Card*, 5.
36. Ibid., 135–65; Donald R. Culverson, "The Welfare Queen and Willie Horton," in Mann, Zatz, and Rodriguez, *Images of Color*, 140–50.

lough and assaulted a white couple in their home; he tied up the man and raped the woman. Bush repeatedly blamed his opponent, Democratic candidate Michael Dukakis, for Horton's attack, because as governor, Dukakis had supported the furlough program. Bush never mentioned Horton's race, but his campaign repeatedly flashed menacing photos of Horton in visual ads. After the election, voters most readily recalled the names Dukakis, Bush, and Horton.[37]

By depicting in his campaign ads a Black man who had committed a violent crime, Bush exploited the racial fears of mainstream white Americans and furthered the perception that Blacks and whites embody moral differences.[38] His ads relied upon subconscious fears in an ostensible "post-racial" period.[39] His strategy attracted white voters who felt underlying resentment at integration policies such as school busing, affirmative action, and antipoverty programs.[40] These white voters feared that ongoing, daily contact with Black people would morally corrupt the neighborhood, school, and workplace. In blaming Dukakis for the violence of an African American man against innocent whites, Bush justified whites' apprehension of the threat of Black moral pollution.

The War on Black Bodies: Policing

The success of promoting violent Black stereotypes in campaign ads, popular television programs, films, periodicals, local networks, and national media outlets has led to federal administrative policies that, while ostensibly race-neutral, effectively discriminate against Blacks. Indeed, public policies are a means to encode and enforce racialized moral boundaries. President Reagan's War on Drugs targeted the "dark evil enemy within" the United States. In one television appearance, Reagan announced:

> [In a] major and sweeping effort . . . we will utilize the FBI, the DEA, the IRS, the ATF, Immigration and Naturalization Services, and the Coast Guard. We intend to do what is necessary to end the drug menace and to eliminate this dark evil enemy within.[41]

37. Mendelberg, *Race Card*, 3.
38. Mendelberg argues that Bush exploited fears through an implicit appeal to historically charged constructions of the Black male rapist.
39. Mendelberg, *Race Card*, 5; Entman and Rojecki, *Black Image*, 73.
40. Thomas Byrne Edsall and Mary D. Edsall, *Chain Reaction: The Impact of Race, Rights, and Taxes on American Politics* (New York: W. W. Norton, 1992).
41. Ronald Reagan, "Remarks Announcing Federal Initiatives Against Drug Trafficking and Organized

The War on Drugs—and the images associated with the War on Drugs—has fueled a contemporary penal system that today incarcerates 2.3 million persons. Constructing Black bodies as immoral has justified Stop and Frisk policing practices, arrests for low-level offenses, mandatory minimum drug legislation, unprecedented levels of federal funding for drug task forces and surveillance equipment, and a prison building boom.

The public in the 1960s saw pervasive images of slothful Black people. The images were exploited alongside alarmist rhetoric by President Reagan during the 1980s. At the same time, in the sixties, self-identified revolutionary groups formed to struggle for the well being of Black people and to resist police violence against Black people.

Revolutionary groups pointed to systemic racism and poverty as pervasive in the United States. Their criticisms, as well as their tactics, exposed the state violence that undergirded democratic institutions. Indeed, the marginalized status of revolutionary actors positioned them as socially polluting beings. As their rhetoric and resistance to state violence gained traction, they formed an explicit threat to mainstream white society. Indeed, Black resistance was treated as an internal war against the state. Riots across the United States, beginning with the Watts riots in 1965, alarmed public officials. During the riots, police encountered gunfire from snipers and concluded that a guerilla war–like siege was taking place. Police officials responded by adopting equipment and tactics employed in war. Los Angeles Police Chief Daryl Gates established five-officer Special Weapons and Tactics (SWAT) units, consisting of a team leader, sniper, observer, scout, and rear guard to address "high-risk" situations. Implementation of war tactics against marginalized people of color, in particular people of African descent, functioned to curb the threat of violence that these groups increasingly directed toward the state. In short, war tactics were employed to clamp down on people who were perceived as social pollutants.

The first employment of SWAT teams was against a Black political community group in Los Angeles. In 1966, a revolutionary political organization, the Black Panthers, armed themselves to resist police brutality. The Panthers articulated a right to armed self-defense against disproportionate police violence in impoverished Black communities. The organization engaged in a wide range of community-

Crime," October 14, 1982. https://www.reaganlibrary.archives.gov/archives/speeches/1982/101482c.htm. Accessed March 9, 2017.

based activities, including offering free breakfast programs for impoverished Black children. They promoted a "Black is Beautiful" approach for psychological upliftment. The dominant image of the Black Panthers in the media, however, was that of armed, violent Black men who were enemies of the state. Indeed, police officials engaged with the Panthers as morally polluting beings who threatened the dominant message of white supremacy as well as the authority of police officers.

The Panthers embodied the threat of racialized moral pollution on symbolic and material levels. Their physical appearance rejected the white beauty standard, in that they sported prominent Afros. Furthermore, their advocacy of armed self-defense and carrying guns posed a visible challenge to police officers. Finally, the Panthers' community breakfasts for impoverished Black children articulated a resistance to entrenched poverty that disproportionately marginalized generations of Black residents in the urban North and West. The Panthers resisted the isolation and demoralization that marked Black youth and adults who were deemed polluted.

Sustained attacks by police forces, as well as federal infiltrators, eventually brought the demise of the Panthers. Indeed, militarized policing functioned alongside covert operations by federal authorities and succeeded in collapsing the Black Power organization. In the process, two interlocking militarized policing practices were established and subsequently sustained. First, the use of military training and tactics against civilians became a central aspect in the later War on Drugs. Second, this War on Drugs was carried out not in the white-collar professional buildings or predominantly white college campuses where drug use was common but rather on the very same streets that were embraced and protected by the Black Panthers. In short, the War on Drugs followed on the heels of the war against revolutionary armed Black people. By associating Black people with sloth and violence, the War on Drugs gained support from policy makers, who funneled financial resources toward police units and prison building, both of which disproportionately impact communities of African descent.

The War on Drugs perpetuates racialized pollution boundaries on multiple levels. First declared by President Nixon in 1973, the War on Drugs initially funded drug treatment even as policy makers argued for a harsh crackdown on drug sellers and users.

The more significant stage of the War on Drugs began in 1982, in the second year of Ronald Reagan's presidency. The Reagan administration appealed to conservatives by adopting strategies similar to

Nixon's War on Drugs and by arguing that crime derives from human vice rather than socioeconomic conditions: "Choosing a career in crime is not the result of poverty or of an unhappy childhood or of a misunderstood adolescence; it is the result of a conscious, willful choice made by some who consider themselves above the law, who seek to exploit the hard work and, sometimes, the very lives of their fellow citizens."[42] Shortly after his election to the presidency, Reagan announced:

> We can begin by acknowledging some absolute truths. . . . Two of those truths are: men are basically good but prone to evil; some men are very prone to evil—and society has a right to be protected from them. . . . The war on crime will only be won when an attitude of mind and a change of heart takes place in America—when certain truths take hold again . . . truths like: right and wrong matters; individuals are responsible for their actions; retribution should be swift and sure for those who prey on the innocent.[43]

In October 1982, Reagan officially announced his administration's War on Drugs with the covert purpose of controlling predatory, morally polluting individuals. There were numerous ramifications as policing forces sought to garner newly available resources from the presidential administration. Local precincts shifted their attention away from drunk drivers and other offenses. More significantly for already impoverished communities, due to federal asset forfeiture legislation passed by Congress, both federal and local police agencies could "seize any 'drug-related' assets of suspected drug dealers and use any seized funds to augment law enforcement agency budgets even if the suspect is never charged with a crime."[44]

In short, not only did local police forces redirect their attention to perceived drug dealing and low-level "crimes," they financially profited from doing so. By 1994, local police precincts had garnered more than $1.4 billion in profits from searching and seizing private property, even though 80 percent of the people whose property was seized were never convicted of a crime.[45] Thus, those who were identified as morally polluting were, at the same time, made to serve a hidden eco-

---

42. Ronald Reagan, quoted in Katherine Beckett, *Making Crime Pay: Law and Order in Contemporary American Politics* (New York: Oxford University Press, 1997), 49.

43. Ibid.

44. Marc Mauer and Ryan King, "A 25 Year Quagmire: The War on Drugs and Its Impact on American Society," *The Sentencing Project* (Washington, DC: 2007), 5.

45. Eric Blumenson and Eva Nilsen, "Policing for Profit: The Drug War's Hidden Economic Agenda," *University of Chicago Law Review* 65, no. 1 (1998): 35–114. In 2005, Congress passed new standards of proof for property to be legitimately seized and sold for profit.

nomic agenda, as law scholars Eric Blumenson and Eva Nilsen have argued.[46]

Most significant for police authorities was the establishment of federally funded investigatory units at the state level, which were comprised of multiple arms, including SWAT teams and Drug Task Forces. SWAT teams continued to function as they did in the 1960s, with units trained to respond to snipers and situations associated with terrorism. After the first team was established in Los Angeles, SWAT teams proliferated across the country, first in big cities and later in medium and small cities.[47] Drug Task Forces were a new creation of the Reagan administration's War on Drugs. These teams consisted of regional investigators especially hired to identify narcotics operations, smuggling over borders, and drug labs. While ostensibly geared toward stopping drug trafficking, Drug Task Forces often targeted low-level drug users and dealers in low-income Black communities, even when studies showed that middle-class whites used drugs in equal, if not higher, numbers.

SWAT teams and Drug Task Forces served different purposes, then, in the practice of corralling socially polluting people and communities. SWAT teams dealt with the "social dynamite" end of the spectrum of social pollution. These units were geared toward potentially explosive situations involving armed resistance to state violence, drug manufacturing and smuggling, and hostage situations. Drug Task Forces, on the other hand, emphasized confronting and arresting low-level drug users and "cleaning up the streets"—in short, containing those identified as "social junk."

SWAT teams and Drug Task Forces, then, bolster the efforts of local police officers whose primary tasks are to ostensibly maintain social order.[48] These policing forces—militarized as well as "community-based"—serve a broader function of reinforcing a racialized social order that is already divided along race and class lines. As the War on Drugs escalated during the Reagan administration, the first Bush

46. Ibid.
47. Christian Parenti, *Lockdown America: Police and Prisons in the Age of Crisis* (New York: Verso, 1999), 112.
48. The employment of SWAT teams alongside federal initiatives to curb drugs and violence has sanctioned police brutality. In addition to SWAT teams, a federal program implemented a "Weed and Seed" strategy that functioned from 1991 until 2010. This "Weed and Seed" approach to policing employed a two-pronged strategy of "weeding" out violent offenders, drug traffickers, and other criminals by removing them from the targeted area and "seeding" the area with human services and neighborhood revitalization efforts. Community policing was intended to serve as the "bridge" between weeding and seeding. See Terence Dunworth et al., "National Evaluation of Weed and Seed: Manatee/Sarasota Case Study," National Institute of Justice, 1999, 1–3.

administration, and finally the Clinton administration, local police forces were bolstered by an increase in funds as well as by SWAT teams and Drug Task Forces.

The number of police officers in the United States doubled between 1980 and 1990, and in 1994 the Senate passed a bill, strongly supported by President Clinton, that proposed adding another 100,000 police officers. This is a continuation of a policy begun under the Reagan administration that has seen the federal government increase its allocation of resources for criminal justice without a pause. The War on Drugs, with a budget of $1 billion in 1981, received $13.4 billion in 1993.[49]

William Chambliss, in a 1994 ethnographic article on policing practices in Washington, DC, describes racialized approaches to "cleaning" up streets inhabited by people associated with social pollution.

It is 10:25 at night when an undercover agent purchases $50 of crack cocaine from a young black male. The agent calls us and tells us that the suspect has just entered a building and gone into an apartment. We go immediately to the apartment; the police enter without warning with their guns drawn. Small children begin to scream and cry. The adults in the apartment are thrown to the floor, the police are shouting, the three women in the apartment are swearing and shouting "You can't just barge in here like this ... where is your goddam warrant?" The suspect is caught and brought outside. The identification is made and the suspect is arrested. The suspect is sixteen years old.

While the suspect is being questioned one policeman says:

"I should kick your little black ass right here for dealing that shit. You are a worthless little scumbag, do you realize that?"

Another officer asks: "What is your mother's name, son? My mistake ... she is probably a whore and you are just a ghetto bastard. Am I right?"

The suspect is cooperative and soft spoken. He does not appear to be menacing or a threat. He offers no resistance. The suspect's demeanor seems to cause the police officers to become more abusive verbally. The suspect is handled very roughly. Handcuffs are cinched tightly and he is shoved against the patrol car. His head hits the door frame of the car as he is pushed into the back seat of the patrol car. One of the officers comments that it is nice to make "a clean arrest."

When asked whether it is legal to enter a home without a warrant, the arresting officer replies:

"This is Southeast [Washington] and the Supreme Court has little

49. William Chambliss, "Policing the Ghetto Underclass: The Politics of Law and Law Enforcement," *Social Problems* 41, no. 2 (1994), 184.

regard for little shit like busting in on someone who just committed a crime involving drugs. . . . Who will argue for the juvenile in this case? No one can and no one will."[50]

The hostility and violence directed toward impoverished Black youth—who are identified as "worthless scumbag[s]" and "ghetto bastard[s]" reveals a racialized approach to people associated with social pollution. Indeed, Chambliss's article describes significantly different approaches to white males driving in and residing in predominantly white neighborhoods in Washington, DC. Contrary to the ways in which Black youth were treated by street cops, a white, male drug dealer was told that he had a "pretty face" and that the officer would see him at the country club.[51] But toward Black youth, police were—and are—overtly and consistently hostile. Chambliss's 1994 ethnographic findings on a culture of hostility in police forces were later corroborated by several different high-profile scandals that illuminated excessive and brutal policing practices, including Tulia, Texas, in 1999.[52]

The Drug Task Force sting in Tulia, Texas, illuminates how undercover drug agents serve a racialized social function of corralling bodies associated with moral pollution. On the morning of August 12, 1999, the Texas newspaper *The Tulia Sentinel* ran a front-page headline: "Tulia's Streets Now Cleared of Garbage." The newspaper was referring to a July 23 drug sting operation, in which local police officers roused from bed and arrested forty-six Tulia residents, thirty-nine of whom were Black. The officers paraded the accused, some of whom wore nothing but underwear and handcuffs, in front of local television cameras.[53] Despite the fact that Tom Coleman, the undercover agent, lacked corroborating evidence, and despite the fact that the arrests had not revealed any cocaine, drug paraphernalia, weapons, money, or any other sign of drug dealing, the forty-six residents were arrested for selling powder cocaine. The six defendants who went to trial were handed down sentences ranging from twenty to more than three hundred years.[54]

The arrests and harsh sentences in Tulia are a microcosm of how

50. Ibid., 178.
51. Ibid., 181.
52. For a description of police brutality in New York City, see chapter 4. For an overview of police brutality in Ferguson, see chapter 5.
53. Andrew Gumbel, "American Travesty," *Independent/UK*, August 20, 2002.
54. Tom Coleman, the undercover agent, admitted that he did not wear a wire, have a partner to back up his testimony, collect finger evidence, or use surveillance video or still images to prove guilt. See Nate Blakeslee, *Tulia: Race, Cocaine, and Corruption in a Small Texas Town* (New York: Public Affairs, 2005); Alan Bean, *Taking Out the Trash in Tulia, Texas* (Desoto, TX: Advanced Concept Design, 2010).

police officers, as the first link in the penal chain, maintain racialized pollution boundaries to contain bodies associated with moral pollution. The defendants arrested in Tulia on July 23, 1999, lived in a neighborhood formally known as "Sunset Addition" but referred to by Black residents as the "Flats" and by white residents as "Niggertown."[55] Mattie White, a fifty-year-old mother of six, was never accused of selling drugs, but her daughter, two sons, one brother-in-law, two nephews, one son-in-law, one niece, and two cousins were arrested.[56] Her daughter Kizzie was sentenced to twenty-five years. Her son Kareem received sixty years; another son, Donnie, was sentenced to twelve. Kizzie's partner, a white man named William Cash Love and the father of their biracial daughter, was charged with selling a whole ounce of cocaine and making deliveries. He received the longest sentence of all: 341 years in state prison.[57]

The Whites' neighbors were similarly targeted. Joe Moore, a sixty-year-old hog farmer who lived in a one-room shack, was designated the "kingpin" and sentenced to ninety years. Freddie Brookins Jr., a twenty-six-year-old former high school star athlete, was handed twenty years.[58] In total, half of the adult Black male population was arrested and penalized in the Swisher County court system, based solely on Tom Coleman's testimony.[59]

The mass arrests and harsh sentences were meant to send a signal, the local District Attorney announced. Indeed, the drug sting *did* send a message to the white residents of Tulia who remained convinced that Black people were to blame for the anxiety they experienced. Nate Blakeslee, a reporter for the *Texas Observer*, observed that the drug sting was not about drugs but rather white residents' apprehension of moral decay.

For two decades, there had been repressed fears that Tulia was in decline. In the mid-1980s, the federal Conservation Reserve Program began reducing farming in Swisher County. This led to decreased revenue in the town's economy and increased reliance on federal farm subsidies.[60] By the 1990s, abandoned warehouses and storefronts dotted Tulia's main street.[61]

55. Jennifer Gonnerman, "How the Lingering Effects of a Massive Drug Bust Devastated One Family in a Small Texas Town," *The Village Voice*, July 31, 2001.
56. Ibid.
57. Northwestern Law Bluhm Legal Clinic, "Texas 'Officer of the Year' Chalked up 38 Wrongful Convictions," http://www.law.northwestern.edu/cwc/exonerations/txtuliasummary.html.
58. Leung, "Targeted in Tulia, Texas?"
59. Gumbel, "American Travesty."
60. In 1999, farm subsidies totaled $28.7 million for Swisher County. See Blakeslee, *Tulia*, 188.

White residents pointed to a perceived drug trade by Black Tulians as the reason for this decline.[62] Economic shifts and media messages—decreased employment opportunities, increased funding for the War on Drugs, national public fury over narcotics, and strategic political messages linking Black people to welfare and crime—fueled their anxiety. There had been reports of drug use by athletes at the local high school, and indeed, several local heroes had become hooked on crack cocaine.[63] The fear of drugs pervaded educational politics; prior to the July 23 drug bust, parents had attempted to require mandatory drug testing of all Tulia high school students.

But the Black residents in Tulia, their white allies, and outside observers identified the drug bust as a proxy for deeper anxieties. White residents expressed resentment at what they perceived as preferential treatment for minorities. Whites believed that Swisher County had a reputation as an easy place to get welfare, and consequently poor Black people sought to live in Tulia.[64] The Flats contained public housing units, and were associated with drinking and drug use.

> The basic tenets of the pioneer worldview—that survival is a product of hard work and nobody is entitled to anything beyond the fruits of his or her own labor—were widely held in Swisher County. Equally prevalent was the belief that blacks in Tulia did not adhere to the pioneer ethic, that they were in fact the great counterexample to the ethic: many of them did not work but did not starve, either; they paid no rent yet they had shelter; they seemed to assume that they were entitled to things that other people had to work for, though they did not pay their fair share of taxes.[65]

In addition to public assistance recipients, there were interracial families in the Flats,[66] a taboo that transgressed moral boundaries and conjured images of social decay. One defendant elucidated why white residents singled out William Cash Love, who received the longest sentence: 341 years for selling an ounce of cocaine. Tulia's white residents were trying to send a message to the town's white youth, Billy Wafer explained. Love hung out with the Black residents, had a relationship with a Black woman, and had fathered a biracial child. "When we saw

61. Ibid., 38.
62. Ibid., 183.
63. Ibid., 112–15.
64. Ibid., 187.
65. Ibid., 184.
66. Ibid., 92, 146, 156.

Cash we didn't see white. We saw black. They [whites] don't want 'em crossing over."[67]

The white families were also uneasy about a hip-hop culture that threatened to drain the "purity" of their youth. Another defendant, Donnie Smith, summarized the general sentiment: "If you're a white or Spanish guy hanging out with the blacks, you already in trouble."[68] In fact, all the whites arrested in the bust had ties to the Black community, although none of them were paraded before the cameras on the morning of July 23. Wafer succinctly summed up the threat of Black popular culture: "The young white kids are so intrigued by the slang, the talk, the way of life, how them young black kids walk the street all the time," he said. "That's what they're so fearful of, the influence on their kids, and that's the reason things are happening the way they are now."[69]

Tom Coleman, the undercover Drug Task Force agent, provided a perfect remedy to ameliorate their fears. He liberally used racial epithets to describe Black people in front of his superiors at the Tulia police station,[70] he was a card-carrying member of the Ku Klux Klan,[71] and although he himself was arrested while working undercover in Tulia, in 2000 the Texas Attorney General designated him "Officer of the Year."[72]

Coleman was hired through the Panhandle Narcotics Task Force, one of approximately one thousand drug task forces throughout the country that was funded by federal War on Drugs grants and operated with little oversight or accountability. Swisher County Sheriff Larry Stewart had not done a background check on Coleman—a fact that came back to haunt Tulia authorities when probing attorneys discovered negative character accounts and an arrest warrant served by a former employer. Furthermore, District Attorney Terry McEachern did little homework on Coleman and simply continued to prosecute the defendants, even when discrepancies in Coleman's reports and testimony became public.

Despite the ensuing problems with Coleman's undercover methods and courtroom statements, white residents in Tulia defended the drug bust. The *Tulia Sentinel* praised Sheriff Stewart and McEachern for

67. Quoted in Nate Blakeslee, "Color of Justice: An Undercover Drug Bust Opens Old Wounds in Tulia, Texas," *The Austin Chronicle*, July 28, 2000, 13.
68. Ibid.
69. Ibid.
70. Leung, "Targeted in Tulia, Texas?"
71. Northwestern Law Bluhm Legal Clinic, "Texas 'Officer of the Year.'"
72. Blakeslee, "Color of Justice," 2.

rounding up the "scumbags" in town.[73] Supporters of Sheriff Stewart, including clergy, publicly expressed their confidence in Stewart.[74] Local townspeople berated advocates of the accused.[75] Community members ostracized friends and family members who participated in a local activist group, "Friends of Tulia," which publicized the perspectives of the defendants. The activists were accused of dragging Tulia's name through the mud and disparaging the reputation of Sheriff Stewart.[76]

The white townsfolk, then, saw the drug bust as protecting something sacred in Tulia: a sense of identity defined against "them" and a respectable social order. As a result, they affirmed racially specific policing methods and the state system of punishment to mitigate their anxieties and forge their vision for a moral society. Yet Tulia is but one example. Indeed, while the travesty in Tulia appears to be a shocking miscarriage of justice, the use of militarized policing forces and state prisons maintain racialized pollution boundaries on a daily basis.

Crime Bills and the Proliferation of Prisons

As militarized policing forces became more routine, Congress passed unprecedented crime bills. Political elites sought to capitalize on whites' fears. In 1973, New York State legislators signed legislation that became known as the "Rockefeller Drug Laws," which stipulated a fifteen-year-to-life sentence for selling two ounces, or possessing four ounces, of a narcotic. The public associated narcotics with the image of a cocaine addict from the "inner city"—a euphemism for a dark, dangerous zone inhabited by animals.

Mandatory minimum sentences for drugs created one of the most dramatic changes in the US penal system.[77] After the passage of the Rockefeller Drug Laws, every state enacted mandatory minimum sentencing laws. In the 1980s, the federal government also enacted mandatory minimum drug laws. As a result, the prison population doubled between 1972 and 1984, and again between 1984 and 1994.[78]

73. Ibid, 1–2.
74. Blakeslee, Tulia, 183.
75. Ibid., 164.
76. Ibid.
77. Marc Mauer, Race to Incarcerate (New York: New Press, 1999), 142–61; Steven R. Donziger, ed., The Real War on Crime: Report of the National Criminal Justice Commission (New York: HarperPerennial, 1996), 24–27.
78. Devah Pager, Marked: Race, Crime, and Finding Work in an Era of Mass Incarceration (Chicago: University of Chicago Press, 2007), 11.

Although statistics revealed that Blacks and whites engaged in drug offenses—possession and sales—at comparable rates,[79] in every year from 1980 to 2007, Black people were arrested nationwide on drug charges at rates 2.8 to 5.5 times higher than white arrest rates.[80] In sum, elected officials responded to stoked fears about the threat of drugs and the threat of immoral Blacks—coalesced into the same fear—by enacting laws that were disproportionately applied to Black individuals residing in impoverished Black communities. Thus, Black bodies and Black spaces were simultaneously targeted.

The Sentencing Reform Act of 1984 abolished parole in the federal system and allowed the Sentencing Commission to radically alter the established sentencing guidelines in favor of much harsher and longer sentences. The federal courts were then required to follow the guidelines, such as mandatory minimums and to increase punishments for repeat offenders.[81] Judges were thus unable to take into account extenuating circumstances or to sentence defendants to prison terms that were proportionate to their sentences. Many of the seven hundred pages of the new sentencing guidelines were aimed at minor regulatory offenses rather than violent crimes.[82] A Truth in Sentencing provision mandated states seeking federal criminal justice funds to require violent offenders to serve 85 percent of their maximum sentence.[83] The result was a drastic increase in the prison population, primarily of impoverished Black people who played minor roles in the drug trade, at a time when there were increasingly few job opportunities for workers without college degrees.[84] Yet, the rationale for disproportionately

---

79. Jamie Fellner, *Targeting Blacks: Drug Law Enforcement in the United States* (New York: Human Rights Watch, 2008).
80. Jamie Fellner, *Decades of Disparity: Drug Arrests and Race in the United States* (New York: Human Rights Watch, 2009).
81. Joel Dyer, *The Perpetual Prisoner Machine: How America Profits from Crime* (Boulder, CO: Westview, 2000), 154. Similar laws that had existed one hundred years earlier had been deemed ineffective, overly costly, unjust, and fuel for dangerous conditions within prisons.
82. Ibid., 155.
83. Dyer, *Perpetual Prisoner Machine*, 168, 171. States seeking federal funding are required to adhere to Truth in Sentencing policies in order to receive grants. Seventy-five percent of people incarcerated under Truth in Sentencing are imprisoned for nonviolent crimes.
84. Other "get tough on crime" legislation has been enacted as well. "Three strikes" statutes mandate that an individual who has committed three crimes must be incarcerated under a life sentence for the third crime. First enacted in California in 1994, three strikes can be applied to nonviolent as well as violent offenses. Twenty-three states, as well as the federal government, have enacted a three strikes law that excessively penalizes repeat offenders. See Donziger, *Real War on Crime*, 19–22; Dyer, *Perpetual Prisoner Machine*, 157. The death penalty, like three strikes legislation and Truth in Sentencing statutes, gained widespread public support during the tough-on-crime culture of the last four decades. The Supreme Court abolished the death penalty in *Furman v. Georgia* in 1972 because of discrimination and arbitrariness in its infliction, only to uphold new death penalty statutes enacted on a state-by-state basis in 1976. Researchers have demonstrated racial

incarcerating Black people was attributed to shiftless decision making and violent demeanors—that is, to moral pollution.

The most drastic increase of the mass imprisonment of Black people arose in the wake of the threat of crack cocaine. Even while the War on Drugs was underway, mass imprisonment did not rapidly expand until the passage of the Anti-Drug Abuse Acts of 1986 and 1988, when crack cocaine was identified as a national menace. Congress imposed sentences that were one hundred times as long for crack cocaine as sentences for powder cocaine. Experts determined that the potency of crack and powder cocaine is the same; crack is powder cocaine cooked with baking soda and thus cheaper. Because it is less expensive, crack rather than powder is sold in small amounts on the streets in impoverished Black communities. The 1986 act required mandatory minimum sentences for trafficking crack cocaine—distribution of five grams of crack cocaine carried a minimum five-year federal prison sentence—while for powder cocaine, distribution of five *hundred* grams carried the same sentence. The Anti-Drug Abuse Act of 1988 mandated minimum sentences of five years for simple *possession* of five grams of crack cocaine or five hundred grams of powdered cocaine. The 100-to-1 sentencing ratio revealed that Congress sought to eliminate a moral threat: Black dealers selling drugs. Even under revisions signed by the Obama administration, in which the ratio was lowered to 14-to-1, the imbalance in sentencing indicates that the crack cocaine associated with Blacks is considered more dangerous than the powder cocaine associated with whites. The disproportionately harsh sentences embedded in mandatory minimums are maintained to prevent morally polluted Black people from targeting and corrupting white communities.

Additionally, the 1994 Crime Bill, the largest crime bill in history, provided federal funding for state and local law enforcement ($10.8 billion), crime prevention programs ($6.1 billion), federal law enforcement ($2.6 billion), and construction of new state prisons ($9.7 billion)—a total of $30 billion over a six-year period.[85] By the end of the

---

bias in capital punishment juries. Legal scholars have demonstrated that the death penalty is largely a means for achieving political popularity, particularly for district attorneys and governors seeking reelection. Despite ample evidence of racism, ineffectiveness at deterrence, and wrongful accusations, the death penalty is flourishing once again in the United States. See Stephen B. Bright, "Discrimination, Death, and Denial: The Tolerance of Racial Discrimination in Infliction of the Death Penalty," in *From Lynch Mobs to the Killing State: Race and the Death Penalty in America*, ed. Charles J. Ogletree Jr. and Austin Sarat (New York: New York University Press, 2006), 216; and Mona Lynch, "Stereotypes, Prejudice, and Life-and-Death Decision Making: Lessons from Laypersons in an Experimental Setting," in Ogletree and Sarat, *From Lynch Mobs*, 182–207.

1990s, one million Black adults were in prison, and Black men in their thirties were more likely to have been to prison than to have graduated from college with a four-year degree.[86] These staggering rates of incarceration of Black men have continued into the twenty-first century, thereby perpetuating the use of imprisonment to contain dark-skinned people associated with moral pollution.

In the effort to warehouse threatening Black bodies, funding for prison construction has driven an unprecedented boom in state-of-the-art prison facilities across the country. Economic restructuring in the 1980s led to widespread unemployment in rural communities, which sought prisons just as the federal government offered significant grants. "Between 1990 and 1999, 245 prisons were built in rural and small town communities—with a prison opening somewhere in rural America every fifteen days."[87] During the most rapid increase in the 1980s, the number of state prisons grew by as much as 12 percent in a single year.[88] Even with changing racial demographics in prisons in recent years—the number of whites sentenced for participating in the methamphetamine trade has risen—Black people are disproportionately imprisoned. Thirty-eight percent of all state and federal inmates are Black, although Black people make up just 12 percent of the U.S. prison population; 34 percent of prisoners are white.[89]

Furthermore, the disproportionate number of Black people in prison corresponds to shifts in penal philosophy: no longer is reform the ostensible goal of confinement. Since the early 1970s, as "social dynamite" and "social junk"—that is, armed racial justice activists and higher numbers of addicts—began to fill prisons, educational, vocational, and drug rehabilitative programming within prisons decreased. The shift in penal philosophy arose at a time in which racially undergirded prison riots became increasingly common and officials prioritized control over reform.[90] The shift from a rehabilitative to a punitive

85. United States Department of Justice, "Violent Crime Control and Law Enforcement Act of 1994," October 24, 1994, http://tinyurl.com/jas9j9p.

86. Western, *Punishment and Inequality in America* (New York: Russell Sage Foundation, 2006), xii; Michelle Alexander, *The New Jim Crow: Mass Incarceration in the Age of Colorblindness* (New York: New Press, 2010).

87. Tracy Huling, "Building a Prison Economy in Rural America," in *Invisible Punishment: The Collateral Consequences of Mass Imprisonment*, eds. Marc Mauer and Meda Chesney-Lind (New York: New Press, 2002), 198.

88. Marc Mauer, "The Changing Racial Dynamics of Women's Incarceration," The Sentencing Project, February 27 2013, PDF p. 3, http://tinyurl.com/hpbrxmh.

89. Erica Goode, "Incarceration Rates for Blacks Have Fallen Sharply, Report Shows," *The New York Times*, February 27, 2013.

90. Situations of intense conflict and riots were not new in prison history—indeed, major newspapers recorded a series of riots in US prisons in the 1920s and 1950s in particular. But in the 1970s, a

model began in 1973, when the first mandatory minimum drug laws were enacted.[91] An article by researcher Robert Martinson and colleagues garnered significant attention. Martinson and his colleagues asked "What works in prison reform?" and subsequently determined that "nothing works."[92] Prisoners were irredeemable. It is not a coincidence that Martinson's scholarly analysis thoroughly discredited the rehabilitative ideal in penal philosophy just as increasing numbers of African Americans and Latinos entered the prison system.[93] Martinson's theory supports the argument that Black people were and are constructed as incapable of moral reflection and action.

As funding for rehabilitative programs was withdrawn, support for scholarly endeavors first grew and then retracted. In 1995, Congress made prisoners ineligible for Pell Grants that paid for prison college programs—even though the amount paid for these programs was less than 1 percent of the total funding for Pell Grants.[94] The assumption

time when ideologies of revolutionary action were taking hold in Black communities, Black prisoners began to insist upon their civil rights as well as to coordinate resistance to guards' abuse. Two well-known riots in California and New York prisons forced the issue of prison violence onto the front page of national media. The 1971 riot at California's San Quentin led to the deaths of three officers and three inmates. Among the three prisoners killed was George Jackson, author of *Soledad Brother: The Prison Letters of George Jackson* (New York: Bantam, 1970). The 1971 uprising at Attica Prison in New York State resulted in an unprecedented number of deaths of prisoners as well as guards. Forty-three citizens died between September 9 and 13, 1971. Thirty-nine were killed and more than eighty others wounded by gunfire during the fifteen minutes it took the state police to retake the prison on September 13. See also New York State Special Commission on Attica, *Attica: The Official Report of the New York State Special Commission on Attica* (New York: Bantam, 1972), xi. The nine-member commission notes that with the exception of the massacres of Native Americans in the late nineteenth century, the state police assault that ended the four-day prison uprising was the bloodiest one-day encounter between Americans since the Civil War.

91. The change was not entirely driven by law-and-order forces: radical activists severely criticized the function of the prison and notions of rehabilitation. In 1971, the American Friends Service Committee, a Quaker organization, published a report on prisons entitled *Struggle for Justice*, which criticized the individualized treatment model as theoretically faulty and systematically discriminatory, and supported the prisoners' rights movement as well as broader struggles for social justice. See David Garland, *The Culture of Control: Crime and Social Order in Contemporary Society* (Chicago: University of Chicago Press, 2001), 57. Journalist Jessica Mitford's widely read book on rehabilitation criticized prison bureaucracy and rehabilitation programs from the perspective of prisoners; she also suggested that Blacks and Latinos were targeted by police officers because they fit a social type labeled as "dangerous." See Jessica Mitford, *Kind and Usual Punishment: The Prison Business* (New York: Alfred A. Knopf, 1973), 52–53.

92. The empirical evidence of treatment failure was summarized in 1974 by Robert Martinson in a widely read and endlessly summarized article in *The Public Interest* entitled "What Works in Prison Reform?" On the basis of an analysis of 231 evaluation studies dating from the period 1945 to 1967, Martinson offered the devastating conclusion that "with few and isolated exceptions, the rehabilitative efforts that have been reported so far have had no appreciable effect on recidivism." Before long, Martinson's findings were widely viewed as conclusive empirical evidence of the system's failure and became the basis for the claim that "nothing works." Within a few years, this claim was to become the new conventional wisdom. See Garland, *Culture of Control*, 58.

93. Francis A. Allen, *Decline of the Rehabilitative Ideal: Penal Policy and Social Purpose* (New Haven, CT: Yale University Press, 1981).

94. Wendy Erisman and Jeanne Bayer Contardo, *Learning to Reduce Recidivism: A 50-State Analysis of*

underlying this shift, which took place just as the number of Black people in prison rose, was that the prison functioned as a punitive place of containment. It did not attempt—for it could not implement—restoration of those prisoners associated with distributing mayhem and violence—that is, polluting the social environment.

At the same time that increasing numbers of Black defendants were sent to prison and rehabilitative programs were withdrawn, violence in prisons escalated. In the 1970s, as increased numbers of Black men were sentenced to state and federal prisons, conditions within institutions of confinement fostered spiraling levels of violence. The significant rise in prison sentencing led to overcrowding, which resulted in escalated levels of animosity between incarcerated persons as well as between inmates and staff. For example, in the California prison system, inmate fights and yard attacks intensified, resulting in deaths of both inmates and officers.[95] The swell in individual and group antagonism was evident not just in higher numbers of deaths within prisons but also in rising numbers of riots and the proliferation of supermax units and facilities throughout the country. Rather than investigating changing conditions, officials blamed the inherent nature of dark-skinned persons: they were violence prone and dangerous; therefore, the only solution was segregation and warehousing.

The riots, and consequent policy solutions, occurred as elected officials linked Black bodies to images of violence and prison officials rejected notions of rehabilitation. Incidents of riots, in turn, led to justification for a new type of supermax prison that today proliferates across the landscape of US prisons. Built as stand-alone facilities or units within maximum-security prisons, they are known as Administrative Control Units, Special (or Security) Handling Units (SHU), Control Handling Units (CHU), or colloquially as maxi-maxis.[96] The National Institute of Corrections (NIC) has defined supermax prisons as "freestanding facilities, or a distinct unit within a facility, that provides for the management and secure control of inmates who have been officially designated as exhibiting violent or seriously disruptive behavior while incarcerated."[97] Supermax facilities function as the ultimate

Postsecondary Correctional Education Policy (Washington, DC: Institute for Higher Education Policy: 2005), x.

95. Inmate assaults on guards rose from thirty-two statewide in 1969 to eighty-four in 1973. Kate King, Benjamin Steiner, and Stephanie Ritchie Breach, "Violence in the Supermax: A Self-Fulfilling Prophecy," *The Prison Journal* 88, no. 144 (March 2008): 146.

96. Jeffrey Ian Ross, "Supermax Prisons," *Society* 44, no. 3 (March 2007): 60.

97. Jesenia M. Pizarro and Raymund E. Narag, "Supermax Prisons: What We Know, What We Do Not Know, and Where We Are Going," *The Prison Journal* 88, no. 1 (March 2008): 23.

container for those who are associated with moral pollution: they to completely remove human beings from society for indefinite periods of time—sometimes decades.

The origin of the supermax has an identified history that coincides with the rise of numbers of Black inmates and a conservative ideology that rejects theories of rehabilitation. In October 1983, after the fatal stabbing of two correctional officers at the federal maximum-security prison in Marion, Illinois, prison administrators implemented a twenty-three-hour-a-day lockdown of all convicts. Over time, the institution shifted its policies to continue perpetual twenty-three-hour-a-day lockdown. Other states that experienced heightened violence within prisons followed by building their own supermax facilities. In 1994, the federal government opened a facility in Florence, Colorado, specifically designed to hold prisoners in total isolation twenty-three hours a day. There are now eighty thousand individuals who wake up in solitary confinement on a daily basis in state and federal prisons.[98] They have been identified as the "worst of the worst"—that is, persistent rule breakers, convicted leaders of criminal organizations such as the mafia and gangs, serial killers, and political criminals such as spies and terrorists. However, in some states, the criteria for subjecting an individual to total isolation are very loose or nonexistent.[99] Classifying an inmate as "very dangerous" or the "worst of the worst," then, is a subjective process. As Black and brown prisoners are identified as inherently irredeemable and disproportionately sentenced to solitary confinement, they are also disproportionately characterized as "the worst of the worst."

Black and Latino prisoners make up the majority of those housed in solitary confinement cells.[100] They are treated as "waste" in a management facility that specializes in warehousing bodies that are associated with social pollution.[101] While in the SHU, they have minimal contact with human beings. They are housed in twelve-by-seven-foot cells with artificial light, poured concrete beds, desks, and stools, and stainless

---

98. According to a 2015 BBC documentary, there are 80,000 people in solitary confinement in the US. See https://www.youtube.com/watch?v=cF2_UqD1JRM.

99. Ross, "Supermax Prisons," 61.

100. King, Steiner, and Breach, "Violence in the Supermax," 162. Mentally ill patients are also disproportionately incarcerated in the SHU. Some scholars estimate that half of all prisoners in twenty-three-hour lockdown exhibit symptoms of mental illness, which are exacerbated by the conditions of solitary confinement.

101. Pizarro and Narag, "Supermax Prisons," 36. I am indebted to Jonathan Simon (*Governing through Crime: How the War on Crime Transformed American Democracy and Created a Culture of Fear* [New York: Oxford University Press, 2007], 152–53) for the concept of prisoners as "waste."

steel sinks and toilets. They are constantly watched under sophisticated surveillance apparatuses and consequently do not experience personal privacy. They exercise in outdoor cages that are the same size as indoor cells, one hour a day, five days a week. Some prisons are completely automated; thus, there is scant communication with even guards. Communication takes place through a narrow window in the steel door of the cell or through an intercom system. Access to phone and mail is strictly supervised or restricted. Often, reading materials and television are limited or prohibited.[102] These measures suggest that persons in the SHU are associated with animals and physical functions rather than intellectual and spiritual capacity.

Human Rights Watch has determined that

> the conditions of confinement are unduly severe and disproportionate to legitimate security and inmate management objectives; impose pointless suffering and humiliation; and reflect a stunning disregard of the fact that all prisoners—even those deemed the "worst of the worst"—are members of the human community.[103]

Individuals imprisoned in solitary-confinement cells lack access to therapeutic programming. Indeed, there is no pretense on the part of officials that they believe the individuals locked down in isolation units possess minds and the capacity for reflection. In the quest to contain "the worst of the worst," prison officials revert to philosophies espoused by nineteenth-century officials who implemented the Auburn model of imprisonment and those with a financial stake in Southern convict leasing. Prisoners were, and are, bodies to be warehoused or exploited. They are not human beings capable of reason or social participation. The memoirs and reflections of people who have been sentenced to solitary confinement—writers and poets who survived solitary confinement and emerged to become outspoken activists against the function of the prison—exhibit how the supermax prison relies upon a narrow interpretation of individual and group immorality.

Isolation often leads to deranged behavior; this has been seen in solitary confinement units in maximum-security prisons. Indeed, extreme reactions to the prison environment are common today. The impact of isolation leads prisoners in "the box" to defiant use of their body prod-

102. Ross, "Supermax Prisons," 62.
103. Quoted in King, Steiner, and Breach, "Violence in the Supermax," 163.

ucts. Prisoners throw feces, urine, blood, and semen at staff; sometimes they smear feces around their cells and on themselves.[104] Thus, they are associated with polluted bodily fluids that have become symbolically associated with dark skin.

Yet, living in the "general population" can foster psychological imbalance as well. Even prisoners who seek to meditate, study, write, and transform themselves testify to the moral and intellectual corruption that prisons inflict upon those who are confined within them. The heightened sense of fear, constant threat of abuse, acts of rape, and overall violent atmosphere are contemporary replicas of nineteenth-century penitentiaries in which prison environments corrupt rather than reform the bodies and souls sentenced to them.[105] Furthermore, due to the disproportionate numbers of Black men and women who are imprisoned, the violence of prison excessively damages those individuals who are already associated with moral pollution and marginalized in mainstream society. The twenty-first century's attempts to warehouse those who threaten the social order has led to an institutionalized process of dehumanization that reflects nineteenth-century ideologies: Black people are morally polluted beings who threaten the purity of white society.

Profiting from the Prison Boom

If contemporary prisons—like their nineteenth-century predecessors—serve to keep immoral Black people from polluting white society, who profits from the extraordinary rise in mass imprisonment? In recent years, not only taxpayers but also private corporations have jumped onto the prison bandwagon. Public workers and private stakeholders have become deeply invested in controlling and containing the "polluted elements" of society in ways that echo nineteenth-century enslavement and incarceration. Political power is consolidated today by counting the bodies of prisoners—albeit nonvoting prisoners—in much the same way that slaves were counted as three-fifths of a person in order to bolster the political clout of Southern states in federal rep-

104. Lorna A. Rhodes, *Total Confinement: Madness and Reason in the Maximum Security Prison* (Berkeley: University of California Press, 2004), 43–44.
105. This fact was not lost on three historians who debunked the myth of rehabilitation in carceral settings in the 1970s. See Michel Foucault, *Discipline and Punish: The Birth of the Prison*, trans. Alan Sheridan (New York: Random House, 1977); David J. Rothman, *The Discovery of the Asylum: Social Order and Disorder in the New Republic* (Boston: Little, Brown, 1971); and Michael Ignatieff, *A Just Measure of Pain: The Penitentiary in the Industrial Revolution, 1750-1850* (New York: Penguin, 1978).

resentation.[106] The *New York Times* editorial writer Brent Staples wrote in 2004:

> The New York Republican Party uses its majority in the State Senate to maintain political power through fat years and lean. The Senate Republicans, in turn, rely on their large upstate delegation to keep that majority. Whether those legislators have consciously made the connection or not, it's hard to escape the fact that bulging prisons are good for their districts. The advantages extend beyond jobs and political gerrymandering. By counting unemployed inmates as residents, the prison counties lower their per capita incomes—and increase the portion they get of federal funds for the poor. This results in a transfer of federal cash from places that can't afford to lose it to places that don't deserve it.... Prisoner rights advocates have recently begun to argue that prison district politicians are more concerned about keeping the prisons full than about crime. The idea of counting inmates as voters in the counties that imprison them is particularly repulsive given that inmates are nearly always stripped of the right to vote. The practice recalls the early United States under slavery, when slaves were barred from voting but counted as three-fifths of a person for purposes of apportioning representation in Congress.[107]

In 2010, the New York legislature outlawed the practice of counting prisoners in the districts in which they are incarcerated; the legislatures of Maryland and Delaware outlawed the practice as well. But the practice is still legal and, indeed, conducted in forty-seven other states. In the 2010 census, more than two million people were counted as residents of the districts in which they were incarcerated rather than the districts from which they came.[108] This practice, known as "prison-based gerrymandering," results in conservative control of houses within state legislatures, thus making it difficult to pass progressive drug law reforms or to downsize prison populations.[109] It occurs in Texas and California, the two states with the largest prison populations,[110] and indeed perpetuates the punitive culture that has come to

106. This was known as the "Three-Fifths Compromise of 1878." Brent Staples, "Why Some Politicians Need Their Prisons to Stay Full," *New York Times*, December 27, 2004.
107. Ibid.
108. Peter Wagner, Aleks Kajstura, Elena Lavarreda, Christian de Ocejo, and Sheila Vennell O'Rourke, "Fixing Prison-Based Gerrymandering after the 2010 Census: A 50 State Guide," The Prison Policy Initiative, March 2010, http://tinyurl.com/gwgy2rp.
109. Peter Wagner and Eric T. Lotke, "Prisoners of the Census: Counting Prisoners Where They Go, Not Where They Come From," *Pace Law Review* 24, no. 2 (2004): 587–608.
110. Aleks Kajstura and Peter Wagner, "Importing Constituents: Prisoners and Political Clout in California," The Prison Policy Initiative, March 2010, http://tinyurl.com/gwgy2rp; Peter Wagner and Rose Heyer, "Importing Constituents: Prisoners and Political Clout in Texas," The Prison Policy Initiative, November 8, 2004, http://tinyurl.com/jyes8gy.

dominate the United States over the last four decades. Prison-based gerrymandering continues to rely on racialized interpretations of immoral bodies; in order to exploit the system, Black people must be seen as polluted elements that, in turn, must be locked away for long periods of time.

Relying on the bodies of incarcerated people to consolidate political power has an additional benefit: as state representatives have sought prisons for their districts, they are able to fulfill the promise of employment to largely white, rural communities.[111] Entire rural economies have come to rely on prisons. Small businesses, such as restaurants and hotels, benefit from local employment and money spent by travelers who are visiting their loved ones.[112] Small towns with prison facilities further receive subsidies from the state to improve water and sewage systems.[113] In sum, predominantly white, rural economies that have lost manufacturing and farming opportunities in a globalized economy now rely on imprisoning Black bodies to fill the void.

Prison guard unions have become particularly powerful in the political economy of punishment. In 2002, the California Correctional Peace Officers Association (CCPOA) donated more than $3 million to the reelection campaign of incumbent governor Gray Davis, who oversaw California's $5.6 billion prison system.[114] The CCPOA also played a significant role in passing harsh crime policies, such as "three strikes"; in influencing state and local races, such as local district attorney elections; and in bolstering the visibility and influence of victims' rights organizations.[115] Prison guard unions in other states have also been immensely influential. In 2007, the New York State Correctional Officers and Police Benevolent Association, which had donated at least $1.8 million to state politicians in previous years, opposed a commission to study and recommend prison closures. The president of the union, Lawrence Flanagan Jr., stated flatly, "We're not open to any closures at this point."[116] Indeed, although New York State prison populations had

111. Nicholas Confessore, "Spitzer Seeks Panel to Study Prison Closings," *New York Times*, February 5, 2007; Joseph T. Hallinan, *Going Up the River: Travels in a Prison Nation* (New York: Random House, 2003), xi.
112. Hallinan, *Going Up the River*, 1–20.
113. Huling, "Building a Prison Economy," 200.
114. Ben Carrasco, "Assessing the CCPOA's Political Influence and Its Impact on Efforts to Reform the California Corrections System," California Sentencing and Corrections Policy Series (Stanford Criminal Justice Center, Working Paper, January 2006), 4–7.
115. Ibid., 7–11; Dan Pens, "The California Prison Guards' Union: A Potent Political Interest Group," in *The Celling of America: An Inside Look at the U.S. Prison Industry*, ed. Daniel Burton-Rose, Dan Pens, and Paul Wright (Monroe, ME: Common Courage, 1998), 134–39.
116. Confessore, "Spitzer Seeks Panel."

decreased significantly, it was several years before the state legislature voted to close any prisons. Meanwhile, as politicians and rural residents have relied on prisons to maintain rural economies and a conservative status quo, Black people remain disproportionately incarcerated: in New York, Blacks make up 17.5 percent of the state population; they constitute 49.5 percent of a prison population of fifty-six thousand individuals.[117] While the prison population has decreased dramatically in recent years—largely due to changes in minimum-sentence drug laws—Blacks remain disproportionately incarcerated in relation to their population numbers. Black bodies have become fodder for what scholars term the "prison-industrial complex."

Corporate industries, in addition to rural communities, have come to depend on mass incarceration as well. Numerous sectors within the US economy have become reliant on prisons, so that the penal system is now "self-perpetuating."[118] These various tentacles consist of industries that supply prisons with services and products, industries that rely on cheap prison labor, and corporations that run private prisons. Activists identify this dynamic as a pattern that mirrors antebellum Northern penitentiaries and postbellum convict-leasing enterprises.[119] Angela Y. Davis writes:

> Just as newly freed black men and a significant number of black women constituted a virtually endless supply of raw material for the embryonic southern punishment industry and provided much-needed labor for the southern states as they attempted to recover from the devastating impact of the Civil War—so in the contemporary era do unemployed black men, along with increasing numbers of black women, constitute an unending supply of raw material for the prison industrial complex.[120]

Private corporations contract with prisons to provide health care and prisoner transportation.[121] They supply everything from food to barbed wire to $100,000 cells.[122] The eagerness of corporations to exploit the

117. Dan Bernstein with Hyejung Kim, "Under Custody Report: Profile of Incarcerated Offender Population Under Custody on January 1, 2012," State of New York Department of Corrections and Community Supervision, December 2012, PDF, p. 5, http://tinyurl.com/z7jkmr6.

118. Dyer, *Perpetual Prisoner Machine*. This argument echoes Michel Foucault's analysis in *Discipline and Punish*. Foucault argued that disciplines incorporated into every level of modern society anticipate and perpetuate the prison.

119. Paul Wright, "Slaves of the State," in Burton-Rose, Pens, and Wright, *Celling of America*, 102–6; Dyer, *Perpetual Prisoner Machine*, 15.

120. Angela Y. Davis, "From the Convict Lease System to the Super-Max Prison," in *States of Confinement: Policing, Detention, and Prisons*, ed. Joy James (New York: St. Martin's, 2000), 68.

121. Dyer, *Perpetual Prisoner Machine*, 14–16; Hallinan, *Going Up the River*, 159–62.

prison boom has been documented by state governments and activists alike.[123] Journalist Joel Dyer notes that

> the variety of corporations making money from prisons is truly dizzying, ranging from Dial soap to Famous Amos cookies, from AT&T to health care providers to companies that manufacture everything from prefab cells, leather restraints, cooking utensils, food, leg bracelets for home monitoring, security systems, razor wire, computer programs, knife-proof vests, laundry detergent, and so on.[124]

Corporate contracts with state governments have proven extremely lucrative. VitaPro Foods of Montreal, Canada, contracted at $34 million a year to supply Texas prisons with a soy-based meat substitute.[125] When MCI and, later, Verizon contracted with the state of New York to provide telecommunication services to prisoners and their families, the state received a 57.5 percent kickback from profits made off of the people who received collect calls from prisons. The loved ones paid $3 to connect and 16 cents per minute thereafter, resulting in more than $200 million in profits since 1996 in the form of commissions.[126] Nationally, the prison telephone market now generates more than $1 billion a year by charging exorbitant rates.[127] The financial gains reaped from mass imprisonment are made on the backs of often impoverished Black people.

Indeed, there are multiple motives at work in the quest to contain bodies that are seen as immoral and threatening. Mass incarceration also creates new markets for law enforcement technology. In his book *American Furies*, journalist Sasha Abramsky describes that at a prison-equipment trade show

> [salespeople] promise that their wares will deliver wonderful, transformative results. There's a table with a picture of a fully armoured guard, his eyes covered in thick goggles, pointing a gun straight at the observer. "Tactical and Survival Specialties, Inc.: Equipment Your Life Can Depend On," reads the sign. There's the Red-Man training gear, featuring a

122. Sasha Abramsky, *American Furies: Crime, Punishment, and Vengeance in the Age of Mass Imprisonment* (Boston: Beacon, 2007), ix–xiv.
123. Gottschalk, *Prison and the Gallows*, 29–30.
124. Dyer, *Perpetual Prisoner Machine*, 14.
125. Ibid.; Dan Pens, "VitaPro Fraud in Texas," in Burton-Rose, Pens, and Wright, *Celling of America*, 147–48.
126. Center for Constitutional Rights, "New York's Highest Court to Hear Challenges to Discriminatory Prison Telephone Charges," CCRJustice.org, October 23, 2007, http://tinyurl.com/z5ulkpw; see also Dyer, *Perpetual Prisoner Machine*, 14.
127. Dyer, *Perpetual Prisoner Machine*, 14.

dummy decked out from head to toe in red armor plates made of some indescribably strong plastic-looking material . . . [and] there are more mundane exhibits: the various forms of stun-gun weapons; the new, light-weight batons; the acoustic grenades that disorient inmates with bursts of unbearable noise; the various dispensers of tear gas, pepper spray, and mace.[128]

Journalist Joseph Hallinan also catalogued an annual trade show sponsored by the American Correctional Association. The exhibition hall was filled with corporations seeking to take advantage of a market estimated to be worth more than $37.8 billion a year.[129] "If there is a buck to be made off the prison boom, then those who will make it are here."[130] Companies such as Proctor & Gamble and Helene Curtis Industries, Inc., benefit from lucrative prison contracts, as have smaller corporations such as African-American Products Supply Company, which seeks to sell to African Americans, who spend $17.5 million a week in prison commissaries.[131] One of the biggest clients of corporations is the Federal Bureau of Prisons (BOP), which needs "services of cardiologists and radiologists, not to mention hobby craft instructors and parenting instructors. Bids are even solicited for coffee service and carbonated drinks."[132] The desire to exploit the contemporary penal system has expanded as corporations seek new clients, even at the cost of Black lives.

Corporations supplying goods and services—and thus profiting from the incarceration of Black people—are one facet of the prison-industrial complex. Prisons also provide cheap labor for corporations. Hallinan suggests that prisons across America are turning into for-profit factories, "cashing in on a tight labor market and public disenchantment with rehabilitation programs."[133] As of 1998, there were 1,310 industries in operation in the US prison system, accounting for total sales of $1.63 billion.[134] Hallinan notes that although inmates must be paid market wages, employers offer no retirement, vacation, or health benefits, nor do they pay for Social Security, workers' compensation,

128. Abramsky, *American Furies*, ix–xiv. For examples of correctional trade journal advertisements offering everything from food trays to stun guns, see Rhodes, *Total Confinement*, 42, 51, 86, 87, 89, 135, 168, 178.
129. Hallinan, *Going Up the River*, 156. He notes that corporate investment in the prison industry is bigger than either major league baseball or the porn industry.
130. Ibid., 157.
131. Ibid.
132. Ibid., 159.
133. Ibid., 143.
134. Dyer, *Perpetual Prisoner Machine*, 19.

or Medicare. Altogether, hiring people who are in prison can cut an employer's payroll costs by 35 percent.[135] It is thus extremely profitable for private corporations such as Microsoft, Boeing, Eddie Bauer, Planet Hollywood, AT&T, and Toys"R"Us to exploit prison labor.[136] Prison officials, in turn, keep a significant portion of workers' salaries, "to offset the expense of incarcerating them."[137] Furthermore, prison officials withdraw portions of prisoners' salaries for various public disbursement programs, such as victim restitution funds (this occurs even if the person is incarcerated for a victimless crime, such as a drug offense).[138] This practice harkens back to penal practices during convict leasing, when convicted Black "criminals"—who were often rounded up and charged with petty offenses—subsequently worked years to pay off fines charged by the state, thus serving as both fodder and labor for an expanding penal system.

In the contemporary era, unions serve as a complicating factor. Unions fight to preserve jobs in prisons as well as to keep prisons open and to increase severe crime policies. At the same time, unions are fighting the emergence of private prisons, which are yet another facet of the prison-industrial complex.[139] The private prison industry operates contracts to imprison nearly 5 percent of the US prison and jail population.[140] Private prisons are one of the fastest-growing segments of the prison-industrial complex.[141] Indeed, they are among the most recent political forces to profit from the public's antipathy to people who are deemed to be socially polluting. Two corporations dominate the private-prison market: Corrections Corporation of America (CCA), which controls about half of the private-prison industry, and Wackenhut Corrections Corporation, which operates about 25 percent. Private prison companies have become billion-dollar industries that mirror the convict leasing schemes of the nineteenth century.[142] The financial

135. Hallinan, *Going Up the River*, 143–44; Adrian Lomax, "Prison Jobs and Free Market Unemployment," in *Prison Nation: The Warehousing of America's Poor*, ed. Tara Herivel and Paul Wright (New York: Routledge, 2003), 133.
136. Dan Pens, "Microsoft 'Outcells' Competition," in Burton-Rose, Pens, and Wright, *Celling of America*, 119; Gordon Lafer, "The Politics of Prison Labor: A Union Perspective," in Herivel and Wright, *Prison Nation*, 121.
137. Pens, "Microsoft 'Outcells' Competition," 117.
138. Paul Wright, "Making Slave Labor Fly," in Herivel and Wright, *Prison Nation*, 115. In total, approximately 80 percent of prisoners' salaries are seized by the state.
139. Parenti, *Lockdown America*, 226.
140. Paul Wright, "The Private Prison Industry," in Herivel and Wright, *Prison Nation*, 137; Parenti, *Lockdown America*, 218. Parenti (*Lockdown America*, 226) notes that the union that set the model and still leads the fight against privatization is the CCPOA.
141. Dyer, *Perpetual Prisoner Machine*, 17.
142. Parenti, *Lockdown America*, 219.

success of private prisons is largely determined by occupancy: a facility must be at least 90 percent full to be profitable.[143]

Private prisons are notoriously abusive. There is extraordinary violence in private prisons, including disproportionate use of force and teargassing. A significant goal of private prisons is to hold down costs, resulting in decreased programming, high rates of staff turnover, and unreliable methods of addressing conflicts with prisoners.[144] Sixty percent of the cost of incarceration is labor, and because food and health care are fixed expenses, private prisons lower employee salaries.[145] There is a notorious lack of accountability for the conditions within private prisons; such abuse reflects a contemporary arrangement that originated during nineteenth-century convict leasing arrangements. Indeed, the contemporary prison must be understand as a current manifestation of enduring philosophies and practices that control Black bodies.

Invisible Sentences: Post-Incarceration Pollution Boundaries

The association of social pollution with dark bodies is sustained in multiple, disparate policies and practices that impact the reentry process. Upon reentry into the community, formerly incarcerated people encounter barriers to employment, housing, health care, voting, and funding for higher education. These barriers function as disparate, invisible pollution boundaries; indeed, administrative laws and social practices permanently lock people with felony convictions out of mainstream society. In this process, individuals with criminal convictions are permanently polluted: they must self-identify as former felons while they are simultaneously rendered invisible, unable to participate in mainstream society.

Indeed, the institutions that manage individuals who have been marked "felons" have expanded in an era of mass imprisonment. While 2.3 million people are in prison, nearly 5 million individuals are on probation and parole.[146] Consequently, barriers to reentry function as indefinite, perpetual prison sentences beyond prison walls. Reentry barriers extend the forms of racialized pollution boundaries that drive and sustain disproportionate policing and mass imprisonment. Indeed,

143. Dyer, *Perpetual Prisoner Machine*, 204.
144. Judith Greene, "Entrepreneurial Corrections: Incarceration as a Business Opportunity," in Mauer and Chesney-Lind, *Invisible Punishment*, 140.
145. Dyer, *Perpetual Prisoner Machine*, 213.
146. "One in 100: Behind Bars in America," Pew Charitable Trusts, February 28, 2008.

reentry barriers normalize pollution boundaries in mainstream society. Individuals marked "felon" are barred from many trade and professional workplaces, public housing complexes, college and university campuses, and from civic participation. Concurrently, they are more exposed to diseases such as HIV and AIDS, yet are less likely to receive adequate medication and care upon release from prison. In short, individuals with felony convictions are treated as permanently polluting entities in society and thus must be legally and socially controlled.

The function of civil law, then, is to maintain hurdles that prevent those who are deemed immoral from polluting mainstream society. The approximately 650,000 "permanently polluted" individuals reentering society from prison each year reflect the racial dynamics of the disproportionately policed and imprisoned population. Nearly 70 percent of the reentering population is Black and Latino, thus reifying the racialized pollution boundaries sustained by policing and imprisonment. Thus, those who are barred from many forms of employment, public housing, higher education institutions, and voting, are also disproportionately Black and brown. Whereas prior to incarceration they were largely quarantined in impoverished communities of color, subjected to violence, and living without access to living-wage employment, decent housing, or quality schools, after imprisonment they are *legally* barred from these institutions.

National recognition of the challenges facing individuals after prison arose in the early twenty-first century during the presidential administration of George W. Bush. "Prisoner reentry" became a popular theoretical framework for addressing individual behavioral patterns of incarcerated persons in an era of mass incarceration. Using the mantra "But They All Come Back," policy makers at state and federal levels acknowledged that 95 percent of incarcerated people would reenter the community at some point. Thus, Jeremy Travis and others concluded, officials must sentence offenders with the goal of successful reentry. Yet from the beginning, this theoretical approach contained philosophical flaws: as did reforms during the twentieth-century progressive era, this new approach to reentry focused solely on individuals and not on racialized patterns of arrest, plea bargains, and imprisonment. As members of the research group CLEAR (Community, Leadership, and Education after Reentry) wrote:

> Concerned with the failures of the criminal justice system, the focus of reentry on the individual was really about high recidivism rates, styled,

however, in the individualistic terms of *relapse,* a concept taken from addiction programs and appropriate to the emerging forms of what we are referring to as *population racism.* Not only was reentry imagined as a way to "assist" the individual prisoner in recognizing his or her vulnerability to repeat "antisocial behavior"—strengthening the individual prisoner's will to reform. But a close surveillance of the prisoner in reentry was argued to be warranted. . . . From the state, reentry's focus on the individual was not so much meant to evaluate the specific needs and capacities of individuals but rather to reconstitute the individual in reentry as one in need of therapeutic management and control.[147]

Establishing barriers to reentry, then, functioned to control formerly incarcerated people and, simultaneously, to argue that the hundreds of thousands of people with felony convictions deserved a "second chance." This approach to formerly incarcerated people achieved bipartisan support in Congress, when President Bush signed H.R. 1593, "The Second Chance Act of 2007." This bill provided funding for faith-based and secular organizations to "help America's prisoners find renewal and hope."[148] Bush went on to say:

The country was built on the belief that each human being has limitless potential and worth. Everybody matters. We believe that even those who have struggled with a dark past can find brighter days ahead. One way we act on that belief is by helping former prisoners who've paid for their crimes—we help them build new lives as productive members of our society. The work of redemption reflects our values. It also reflects our national interests. Each year, approximately 650,000 prisoners are released from jail. Unfortunately, an estimated two-thirds of them are rearrested within three years. The high recidivism rate places a huge financial burden on taxpayers, it deprives our labor force of productive workers, and it deprives families of their daughters and sons, and husbands and wives, and moms and dads.[149]

The political framework employed by Bush individualized the reentry process and deflected attention away from the systemic cycle of disproportionate policing and imprisonment of Black and brown bodies. While attempting to humanize people with felony convictions, Bush

---

147. Vivian Nixon, Patricia Ticineto Clough, David Staples, Yolanda Johnson Peterkin, Patricia Arlyne Zimmerman, Christina Voight, and Sean Pica, "Life Capacity beyond Reentry: A Critical Examination of Racism and Prisoner Reentry Reform," *Journal of Race and Ethnicity* 2, no. 1 (Autumn 2008): 29–30.
148. See "President Bush Signs H.R. 1593, the Second Chance Act of 2007," George W. Bush White House Archives, April 9, 2008, http://tinyurl.com/jsuw325.
149. Ibid.

simultaneously refrained from addressing racialized laws and practices employed in the War on Drugs. In so doing, he emphasized individual redemption and effectively kept in place the systems of punishment that maintain racialized pollution boundaries.

Simultaneously, state and local laws prohibit people with felonies from accessing employment, a key part of the reentry process. Many formerly incarcerated people are eager to find work in order to avoid reincarceration. However, the stigma of a felony conviction inhibits the vast majority from finding employment due to social suspicion and state legal barriers, lack of socialization in mainstream white communities that foster particular social skills in a service economy, and lack of training in technological fields as blue-collar jobs have moved overseas. These barriers to employment—social, legal, and technical—result in sustained demarcation between the impoverished communities of color that are associated with moral pollution and the middle-class and affluent communities that seek to maintain moral purity.

Scholars debate the reasons that formerly incarcerated persons have fewer job opportunities and lower wages than individuals without felony conviction: the patterns may indicate lack of skills and an involvement in the underground drug economy,[150] or the possession of a felony conviction may convey moral failings that automatically raise the suspicions and concerns of employers. While the conclusions of sociologists vary, the majority assert the same point: mass imprisonment has compounded the disadvantages of young Black men, as well as deepened the divisions between impoverished communities of color and middle-class white communities.

State legislation maintains pollution boundaries that are heightened by a felony conviction. Thirty-three states, as well as the District of Columbia, impose some kind of licensing restriction of formerly incarcerated persons.[151] A 2004/2009 study, *After Prison: Roadblocks to Reentry: A Report on State Legal Barriers Facing People with Criminal Records*, identified numerous restrictions enshrined in civil law. The study, conducted by the Legal Action Center,[152] determined that all fifty states impose barriers to reentry.[153] States may impose mandatory barriers, which

---

150. Sociologists such as Bruce Western (*Punishment and Inequality in America*, 109) refer to this as "selection effort."
151. Pager, *Marked*, 33.
152. The Legal Action Center is a New York City–based nonprofit advocacy and service organization. See www.lac.org.
153. Paul Samuels and Debbie Mukamal, *After Prison: Roadblocks to Reentry: A Report on State Legal Barriers Facing People with Criminal Records* (New York: Legal Action Center, 2004).

result in flat rejection of license seekers; however, the majority of licenses are labeled "discretionary" and thus the "nature of the crime" is taken into account. Devah Pager notes: "Some occupational licenses, for example, while not officially off-limits to ex-offenders, become so in practice because of a general requirement that license holders demonstrate 'good moral character.'"[154] For example, New York State Correction Law Article 23-A stipulates that formerly incarcerated persons demonstrate "good moral character" before being issued occupational licenses for more than one hundred trades—including electrical, plumbing, and barbering—that contain discretionary barriers. Because the vast majority of incarcerated people in New York State are Black, the practice of linking "good moral character" clauses in criminal law reiterates symbolic constructs of Black people as morally polluted.

Furthermore, if morality clauses frame the conceptual constructs of criminal laws, and if people with criminal convictions are deemed polluted, then *formerly incarcerated people are indelibly associated with moral pollution.* As has been argued in previous chapters, the historical constructs of Black immorality and the contemporary practices of disproportionate policing and imprisonment result in the perpetuation of linking pollution with racialized bodies. Post-incarceration licensing barriers represent one facet of maintaining racialized pollution boundaries, yet unlike in policing and imprisonment systems, licensing barriers function on a wholly invisible level. Rather than overt representations of state control, in the bodies of police officers or stone warehouses with barbed wire, pollution boundaries function in form letters denying formerly incarcerated applicants occupational licenses because they lack "good moral character" based on the "nature of the crime."

In 2004, after three decades of intensive prison building, states began to make progress in removing barriers to employment, housing, food stamps, and other opportunities.[155] However, in the same period, states have increasingly allowed employers greater access to criminal records through the internet. Today, employers may simply type a name and social security number into a database to access not only conviction records but in many cases arrest records as well (even if the arrest did not result in a conviction). The increased online access to arrest records and criminal records perpetuates the association between crime and moral pollution. Online technologies buttress racialized

154. Pager, *Marked*, 34.
155. Samuels and Mukamal, *After Prison*, 2.

social barriers between people with criminal convictions and those without by ensuring that employers (and thereby, future customers) never have to interact with formerly incarcerated persons in person. Thus, as physical social spaces have become increasingly segregated, online communications facilitate a further severing of social interaction. Morally polluted bodies are kept at a far distance, buttressed by state laws that allow online access to past criminal charges and convictions.

Thus the state operates reentry barriers at two levels: state licensing agencies legalize mandatory or discretionary barriers to people with felony convictions; these agencies furthermore regulate employer access to past criminal charges and convictions. Access to online criminal records impacts job opportunities for formerly incarcerated people: employers often have little stake in the reentry process.[156] Thus, while legal barriers impact formerly incarcerated individuals who seek to work in trade occupations, the flourishing of online access to criminal records results in *social* stigmatization and discrimination in hiring.

Indeed, the mark of a felony conviction results in multiple, overlapping consequences in the job market that render formerly incarcerated people permanently marginalized. Bruce Western assessed that formerly incarcerated men become "permanent labor market outsiders, finding only temporary or unreliable jobs that offer little economic stability."[157] However, he argues, this trend can be seen even *before* incarceration: Black men living in impoverished communities were less likely to have jobs, and if they did, they made lower wages than white men of similar educational attainment.[158]

Thus incarceration worsens the ability of formerly incarcerated people to find stable employment, for employers view a criminal conviction as an indication of untrustworthiness and danger.[159] Two studies of post-incarceration employment practices illuminate the degree to which race and possession of a felony conviction function to maintain racialized pollution boundaries. Pager conducted a 2007 study in which white and Black testers applied for jobs in the Milwaukee area. One team of testers possessed resumes that indicated time served in prison,

---

156. Pager, *Marked*, 26.
157. Western, *Punishment and Inequality*, 109. Much of Western's research exposes the perilous circumstances in which young men try to make ends meet prior to incarceration. He argues that pernicious poverty has already altered the life courses of young men in the inner city.
158. Ibid., 110.
159. Ibid.

while a second team of testers submitted otherwise identical resumes that did not. Pager found that

> White applicants *with* a criminal record are just as likely to receive call-backs (17%) as black applicants *without a criminal record* (14%). . . . Being black in America today is just about the same as having a felony conviction in terms of one's chances of finding a job.[160]

In short, a white man with a felony has the equivalent social status as a Black man without a felony: whites become polluted by their actions, whereas Black skin represents an inherently polluted character. Consequently, Black men must work twice as hard as equally qualified whites simply to overcome the stigma of their skin color.[161]

Pager's qualitative study further identifies how social barriers between white employers and Black applicants function to maintain patterns of stigmatization and pollution. She determines:

> In contrast to blacks with clean records, personal contact did little to improve the outcomes of black ex-offenders. Indeed, quite different from the situation with white applicants, where personal contact increased the likelihood of a callback for all testers and narrowed the gap between those with and without criminal records, for black applicants, personal contact actually widens the disparities. . . . Among those who had no contact with the employer, black testers with criminal records were roughly 40 percent less likely to be called back than those without criminal records. Among those who did have personal contact, by contrast, there was a more than 80 percent difference. Black ex-offenders are thus substantially worse off relative to nonoffenders when they have the opportunity to interact with employers. Far from the payoff we saw to white ex-offenders following conversations with employers, black ex-offenders fall ever further behind. . . . Even though these testers were bright, articulate, and personable, these traits appear insufficient to overcome the intense negative attributions that accompany the combination of blackness and criminal background.[162]

These social barriers are further exacerbated by the suburbanization of entry-level work, particularly in the service economy. Indeed, Western notes that physical remoteness and social discrimination reinforce one another.[163] Oftentimes, employment opportunities presented two

160. Pager, *Marked*, 91.
161. Ibid., 99.
162. Ibid., 106.
163. Western, *Punishment and Inequality*, 86.

stark difficulties: lack of public transportation and racial discrimination. "For suburban employers, being black and an ex-offender represents almost full grounds for exclusion."[164] Thus, the spatial separation functions to maintain pollution boundaries between middle-class white managers and formerly incarcerated Black job seekers.

Pager's Milwaukee study was further illuminated by a 2006 New York City study by Pager and Western that included male Latino testers, "Race at Work: Realities of Race and Criminal Record in the NYC Job Market."[165] Pager and Western sent matched teams of "testers" to apply for 1,470 real entry-level jobs throughout New York City over ten months in 2004.

The [white, Latino, and Black] testers were well-spoken young men, aged 22 to 26; most were college-educated, between 5 feet 10 inches and 6 feet in height, recruited in and around New York City. They were chosen on the basis of their similar verbal skills, interactional styles and physical attractiveness. Additionally, testers went through a common training program to ensure uniform style of self presentation in job interviews. Testers were assigned matched fictitious resumes representing comparable profiles with respect to educational attainment, quality of high school, work experience, and neighborhood of residence. Testers presented themselves as high school graduates with steady work experience in entry-level jobs. In some conditions, testers presented additional evidence of a felony conviction.[166]

Pager and Western found that white testers were highly preferred, followed by Latino testers. Black applicants were far less likely to receive a positive response from employers. Company representatives would assess suitability for a service based first on appearance rather than qualifications.[167]

In one case, for example, the three test partners reported experiences that, in the absence of direct comparisons, would have revealed no evidence of discrimination. In recording his experience applying for this retail sales position, Joe, one of our African American testers, reports: "[The employer] said the position was just filled and that she would be calling people in for an interview if the person doesn't work out." Josue, his Latino test

164. Pager, *Marked*, 112.
165. Pager and Western's "Race at Work" was released as part of the New York City Commission on Human Rights conference "Race at Work—Realities of Race and Criminal Record in the NYC Job Market," held on December 9, 2005 at the Schomburg Center for Research in Black Culture.
166. Pager and Western, "Race at Work," 1–2.
167. Ibid., 4.

partner, was told something very similar: "*She informed me that the position was already filled, but did not know if the hired employee would work out. She told me to leave my resume with her.*" By contrast, when Simon, their white tester, applied last, his experience was notably different: "*. . . I asked what the hiring process was—if they're taking applications now, interviewing, etc. She looked at my application. 'You can start immediately?' Yes. 'Can you start tomorrow?' Yes. '10 a.m.' She was very friendly and introduced me to another woman (white, 28) at the cash register who will be training me.*"[168]

As noted previously, white applicants, even those with criminal convictions, fare better than Black and Latino applicants. A qualitative example by Pager and Western describes a scenario in which a white tester whose resume indicated a felony conviction was hired over his Black and Latino counterparts, who indicated no criminal record:

> As just one example, the following case records this team's experience applying for a position at a local auto dealership. Joe, the black tester, applied first and was informed at the outset that the only available positions were for those with direct auto sales experience. When Josue, his Latino partner, applied, the lack of direct auto sales experience was less of a problem. Josue reports: "*He asked me if I had any customer service experience and I said not really. . . . He then told me that he wanted to get rid of a few bad apples who were not performing well. He asked me when I could start. . . .*" Josue was told to wait for a call back on Monday. Keith, their white ex-felon test partner, was first given a stern lecture regarding his criminal background. "*I have no problem with your conviction, it doesn't bother me. But if I find out money is missing or you're not clean or not showing up on time I have no problem ending the relationship.*" Despite the employer's concerns, and despite Keith having no more sales experience than his test partners, Keith was offered the job on the spot.[169]

In sum, these qualitative studies indicate not only that a criminal conviction marks a person as polluted but, furthermore, that dark skin represents a polluted character, whether or not a Black person has been convicted of a crime.

The association of dark skin with an immoral, polluted character similarly impacts formerly incarcerated individuals who seek public housing—*but only those who have been convicted of a drug crime.* The War on Drugs has elevated the image of a convicted drug dealer, as well as a person convicted of possessing drugs, as a morally polluting per-

168. Ibid., 4–5.
169. Pager and Western, "Race at Work," 7.

son who may not share physical premises with people who have not been convicted. However, the ban on occupying public housing does not apply to those convicted of violent crimes—only drug crimes.

Similar to employment and housing, persons with felony convictions are barred from voting in every state but Maine and Vermont. In 2006, Jeff Manza and Chris Uggen found that due to high rates of felony convictions under mass imprisonment, one in seven Black men is currently denied the right to vote, and in several states, one in four Black men are disenfranchised.[170] Manza and Uggen suggest that there are two subconscious rationales for barring persons with felonies from voting: maintaining the "purity of the ballot box" and keeping untrustworthy people who have violated the social contract from decision making.[171]

Manza and Uggen estimate that there were 5.3 million disenfranchised felons on Election Day 2004.

> This [number] represents 2.5 percent of the voting age population and 2.7 percent of the "voting eligible" population. With the 600,000 in county jails, almost 6 million Americans were prevented from voting in the 2004 election because of a criminal conviction. . . . In 14 states, more than 1 in 10 African Americans have lost the right to vote by virtue of a felony conviction, and 5 of these states disqualify over 20 percent of the African American voting age population. . . . The entire nation has an African American disenfranchisement rate of 5 percent or higher.[172]

Barriers to voting prevent people with felony convictions from polluting the body politic. Along with employment, housing, and higher education, restricting the franchise functions to keep morally polluted people from contaminating the social body.

Conclusion

Contemporary mass imprisonment relies on a war against Black people, who have been symbolically constructed as immoral beings that threaten to pollute the pure society of disciplined, hardworking white citizens. Police officers corral threatening bodies associated with "social dynamite" and indolent bodies associated with "social junk" by militarizing equipment and employing brutal methods. Wide-spread prison building has facilitated the wholesale transfer of Black people

170. Jeff Manza and Chris Uggen, *Locked Out: Felon Disenfranchisement and American Democracy* (New York: Oxford University Press, 2006), 10, 80.
171. Ibid., 12.
172. Ibid., 79–80.

from impoverished urban communities to sprawling compounds in rural areas, where union employees, political representatives, and corporations benefit. In many respects, the contemporary penal system mirrors nineteenth-century antebellum penitentiaries and postbellum convict leasing practices: public and private entities profit from incarcerating Black bodies. Post-incarceration reentry barriers permanently lock out people with felony convictions from participating in mainstream economic and political systems.

The historical and contemporary practices of controlling Black bodies are sustained in popular imagery, spatial segregation, and public policy. Mass incarceration is a system of racial control that bears down directly on people who are associated with immorality, sequestered in poor communities, and shipped to rural communities where their bodies are exploited, and released back into their communities only to be demonized as polluting "ex-cons" and "felons." As symbols of permanent pollution, formerly incarcerated persons have difficulty finding jobs and housing, and participating politically. As such, they are perpetually marginalized and ostracized from mainstream society.

PART II

Racial Justice
Movements

4

Policing Dark Bodies in Polluted Spaces: Stop and Frisk in New York City, 1993–2013

Introduction

Grassroots resistance to stereotyping Black people as morally polluted bodies arose in New York City from 1993 to 2013. A series of high-profile incidents of police brutality, as well as routine police practices, sparked organizing, campaigns, and court cases. Sustained outrage led to favorable court rulings and the passage of citywide legislation. This chapter argues that the anti-Stop-and-Frisk movement facilitated important organizing and consciousness building, but due to the movement's strategic reliance on court cases and legislation, it did not lead to a mass uprising that confronted the construction of Black people as morally polluted.

Resisting Police Brutality in New York City

Communities demonstrated in the wake of a brutal incident on August 9, 1997, in which police officers arrested and detained a thirty-year-old

Haitian immigrant, Abner Louima, following a fracas outside a Brooklyn nightclub.[1] At the 70th Precinct, the officers battered and sodomized Louima with a wooden stick. Soon thereafter he underwent emergency surgery to treat the injuries that the police officers had inflicted on his intestine and bladder.[2]

Communities also protested two years later, following an incident on February 4, 1999, when police officers from the New York Police Department (NYPD) Street Crime Unit fired forty-one bullets at Amadou Diallo, a street vendor from Guinea, West Africa.[3] Nineteen of the bullets struck his body, puncturing Diallo's spleen, kidney, liver, aorta, intestines, and spinal cord. The officers claimed that Diallo had reached for a weapon, at which point they opened fire. However, Diallo was unarmed; he had been reaching for his wallet. The four white officers were acquitted of all charges on February 25, 2000.[4]

Police shootings of these unarmed men, whose dark skin associated them with moral pollution, occurred alongside other police killings: of Anthony Rosario, Hilton Vega, Patrick Dorismond, and Anthony Baez. Indeed, police brutality has spurred marches and community organizations, as well as lawsuits against the city and legislative proposals at the city and state levels.[5] Multifaceted mobilization began when members of Mothers Against Police Brutality brought the use of police beatings and deadly force during Stop and Frisk practices to a coalition of organizations that began to coordinate a public response and hold the NYPD accountable.[6] Since 2010, this movement has grown and gar-

1. Andrea McArdle, introduction to *Zero Tolerance: Quality of Life and the New Police Brutality in New York City*, ed. Andrea McArdle and Tanya Erzen (New York: New York University Press, 2001), 2.
2. Ibid.: "At the May 1999 trial in federal court, Officer Justin Volpe pleaded guilty to violating Abner Louima's civil rights in connection with the assault, and was later sentenced to thirty years imprisonment; Charles Schwartz was convicted by a jury of holding Louima down during the station-house attack." Other officers involved in the attack were convicted of fabricating reports; three were acquitted of participating in the assault against Louima.
3. Ibid.
4. Ibid.: "The officers—Sean Carroll, Edward McMellon, Richard Murphy, and Kenneth Boss—were indicted on charges of intentional and reckless murder, and, after being granted a change of trial venue to Albany County, were acquitted of all charges on February 25, 2000."
5. See Clifford Krauss, "Clash over a Football Ends with a Death in Police Custody," *New York Times*, December 30, 1994, at B1 (discussing the death of Anthony Baez); Thomas J. Lueck, "Mayor May Face Inquiry in Dorismond Case," *New York Times*, November 22, 2000, at B2 (discussing death of Patrick Dorismond); Matthew Purdy, "Pathologist Says 2 Men Killed by Police Were Shot While Lying on the Floor," *New York Times*, August 3, 1995, at B5 (discussing the shooting of Anthony Rosario and Hilton Vega).
6. Ron Daniels, "The Crisis of Police Brutality and Misconduct in America: The Causes and the Cure," in *Police Brutality: An Anthology*, ed. Jill Nelson (New York: W. W. Norton, 2001), 240. Organizations that mobilized on the issue of police brutality included the National Congress for Puerto Rican Rights, the Committee Against Anti-Asian Violence, the Black Panther Collective, the December 12 Movement, Black Cops against Police Brutality, the Malcolm X Grassroots Movement, Jews for Racial and Economic Justice, the New York chapter of the National Lawyers Guild, Refuse and

nered greater support from the public, largely as a reaction to former mayor Michael Bloomberg's approval of extensive Stop and Frisk practices in economically depressed Black and Latino neighborhoods.[7]

This chapter investigates how critical activists in New York City employed multiple strategies over a twenty-year period as they resisted the excessive criminalization and policing of Black New Yorkers. As these critical activists analyzed and organized a grassroots movement and filed court cases, they sought to redefine racialized concepts of moral pollution and therefore shift racialized pollution boundaries that reflexively correlate bodies and spaces. While some of the activists in these organizations are active in the Movement for Black Lives, many activist initiatives took place before the killing of Michael Brown in Ferguson on August 9, 2014, when the Black Lives Matter call for action became a street movement. Therefore, I examine the anti-Stop-and-Frisk movement as a predecessor to the nationwide movement that arose after activists in Ferguson heightened public consciousness on unchecked police brutality. In this chapter, I examine two campaigns that challenged NYPD officers as they stopped, questioned, and frisked marginalized people. One campaign addressed legislation and practices on the city level. The other aimed to decriminalize marijuana in state law. Although the critical activists who engaged in the two campaigns employed similar strategies, each campaign addressed racialized pollution boundaries in different ways, due to the differing political affiliations of powerful elected officials at the city and state levels. I conclude with an analysis of how these two campaigns focused on controlling and containing Black people who were associated with moral pollution, but did not lead to a mass street uprising.

Racialized Bodies in Racialized Spaces

Stopping and frisking young Black and Latino men became common practice under the mayoral administration of Rudolph Giuliani (1994–2001) and further escalated under the mayoral administration of Michael Bloomberg (2002–13). During Bloomberg's reign, between Jan-

Resist, the NAACP Legal Defense and Education Fund, and the Asian American Legal Defense and Education Fund.

7. Al Baker, "Paterson Is Urged to Veto Bill That Parses Stop-and-Frisk Database," *New York Times*, July 3, 2010, at A14 (discussing Bloomberg's opposition to a state bill that would eliminate a database "of mostly young blacks and Hispanics" who have been stopped and frisked but were "not accused of any crime or violation").

uary 2004 and June 2012, the NYPD made 4.4 million stops. More than 80 percent of these stops were of Black and Hispanic New Yorkers.[8]

Black youth were stopped in numbers far disproportionate to their population: in 2011 alone, 52.9 percent of the nearly seven hundred thousand individuals stopped and frisked were Black.[9] The NYPD routinely argued "that the disproportionate number of stops of black people [was] justified because blacks are disproportionately involved in violent crimes."[10] Incredibly, in 2011 "the number of stops of young black men . . . actually exceeded the total number of young black men in the city (168,126 compared to 158,406)."[11]

The 2013 *Floyd v. City of New York* class action court case found:

Fifty-two percent of all stops were followed by a protective frisk for weapons. A weapon was found after 1.5% of these frisks. In other words, in 98.5% of the 2.3 million frisks, no weapon was found. Eight percent of all stops led to a search into the stopped person's clothing, ostensibly based on the officer feeling an object during the frisk that he suspected to be a weapon, or immediately perceived to be contraband other than a weapon. In 9% of these searches, the felt object was in fact a weapon. 91% of the time, it was not. In 14% of these searches, the felt object was in fact contraband. 86% of the time it was not. Six percent of all stops resulted in an arrest, and 6% resulted in a summons. The remaining 88% of the 4.4 million stops resulted in no further law enforcement action. In 52% of the 4.4 million stops, the person stopped was black, in 31% the person was Hispanic, and in 10% the person was white. In 2010, New York City's resident

8. *Floyd v. City of New York*, 959 F. Supp. 2d (S.D.N.Y.2013), at 1. On page 19, *Floyd* states: "The Supreme Court has held that under the Fourth Amendment, it is constitutionally reasonable for the police to 'stop and briefly detain a person for investigative purposes if the officer has a reasonable suspicion supported by articulable facts that criminal activity "may be afoot," even if the officer lacks probable cause.' This form of investigative detention is known as a *Terry* stop."
9. New York Civil Liberties Union (NYCLU), "Stop-and-Frisk 2011," May 9, 2012, PDF, p. 5, http://tinyurl.com/j39q7tq (noting that in New York City, 33.7 percent of individuals frisked were Latino, and 24.5 percent of the state prison population was Latino); Dan Bernstein with Hyejung Kim, "Under Custody Report: Profile of Incarcerated Offender Population Under Custody on January 1, 2012," State of New York Department of Corrections and Community Supervision, December 2012, PDF, p. 5, http://tinyurl.com/z7jkmr6. Anti-Stop-and-Frisk activists in New York City struggle against the racial profiling of Blacks and Latinos. Where able, I will distinguish between the two populations. However, congruent with the approach of activists, I will highlight that Stop and Frisk policy is enacted against young men whose physical appearance renders them outside of the white dominant culture. Critical activists also assert that NYPD officers profile transgender people, immigrants, and Muslims and Arabs. See Center for Constitutional Rights, "Stop and Frisk: The Human Impact," July 2012, PDF, 11–12, 14, http://tinyurl.com/zw3l4va.
10. NYCLU, "Stop-and-Frisk 2011," 5. In 2011, 52.9 percent of stops were of Blacks and 33.7 percent of stops were of Latinos; conversely, whites accounted for only 9.3 percent of the stops (ibid.); see also Center for Constitutional Rights, "Stop and Frisk," 27n2. The number of stops represents an increase of over 600 percent since Mayor Michael Bloomberg came into office (Center for Constitutional Rights, "Stop and Frisk," 4).
11. NYCLU, "Stop-and-Frisk 2011," 7.

population was roughly 23% black, 29% Hispanic, and 33% white. In 23% of the stops of blacks, and 24% of the stops of Hispanics, the officer recorded using force. The number for whites was 17%. Weapons were seized in 1.0% of the stops of blacks, 1.1% of the stops of Hispanics, and 1.4% of the stops of whites. Contraband other than weapons was seized in 1.8% of the stops of blacks, 1.7% of the stops of Hispanics, and 2.3% of the stops of whites. Between 2004 and 2009, the percentage of stops where the officer failed to state a specific suspected crime rose from 1% to 36%.[12]

Because nearly 90 percent of stops are not related to a suspected violent crime, "the race of those involved in violent crime generally cannot explain the disproportionate number of black New Yorkers stopped every year."[13] Indeed, this chapter argues that it is not participation in violence, but rather, the perception that Black bodies symbolize the *threat* of moral disorder, that explains disproportionate stops.

In order to legally stop a person, a police officer must have reasonable suspicion that the person has committed, is committing, or is about to commit an unlawful act. To frisk a person, however, the officer must have reason to believe the person stopped has a weapon that poses a threat to the officer's safety—a higher and more specific standard.[14] Police reports on Stop and Frisk—known as UF-250 forms—show that between 2005 and 2008, 85 percent of Stop and Frisks were Blacks and Latinos and only 8 percent of Stop and Frisks were whites.[15] In a similar pattern, police were also more likely to use force against Blacks and Latino New Yorkers.[16]

It is against the law in every jurisdiction in the country for police departments to institute quotas on actions such as Stop and Frisk.[17] However, NYPD officers are required to meet "productivity measures," with performance indicated by the number of UF-250 forms they fill out after conducting a Stop and Frisk.[18] These productivity measures function as what one officer called a "highly developed" system that mandates numerical quotas for arrests, summonses, and Stop and Frisk encounters.[19] Police officers document stopping people for vague rea-

12. *Floyd*, at 6–7.
13. NYCLU, "Stop-and-Frisk 2011," 5.
14. *Terry v. Ohio*, 392 U.S. 392 U.S. 1, 88 S. Ct. 1868, 20 L. Ed. 2d 889 (1968), 1, 24.
15. Center for Constitutional Rights, "Racial Disparity in NYPD Stops-and-Frisks: The Center for Constitutional Rights Preliminary Report on UF-250 Data from 2005 through June 2008," January 15, 2009, PDF, p. 4, http://tinyurl.com/jnthspa.
16. Ibid., 27.
17. Benjamin Weiser, "Officer's Lawsuit over Quotas Is Reinstated," *New York Times*, November 28, 2012, at A25 (reporting on a retaliation lawsuit filed by a New York City police officer who publicized "the existence of an illegal arrest-quota system").
18. Ibid.

sons listed on the UF-250 form, such as "Suspicious Bulge/Object," "Furtive Movements," and "Wearing Clothes/Disguises Commonly Used in the Commission of Crime."[20] In 2011, as in previous years, the most common reason given for stops was "furtive movements."[21] Such imprecise language can justify what is in reality the practice of racially profiling Blacks and Latino persons whose bodies represent moral pollution.

The 2013 court case *Floyd v. City of New York* illuminates the multiple dimensions in which dark bodies are targeted by police officers not because of conduct but rather because of appearance. Court testimony shows that police officers stopped—or refrained from stopping—people because of their race. Federal Judge Shira Scheindlin found that New York City police officials "adopted a policy of indirect racial profiling by targeting racially defined groups for stops based on local crime suspect data."[22]

This has resulted in the disproportionate and discriminatory stopping of blacks and Hispanics in violation of the Equal Protection Clause. Both statistical and anecdotal evidence showed that minorities are indeed treated differently than whites. For example, once a stop is made, blacks and Hispanics are more likely to be subjected to the use of force than whites, despite the fact that whites are more likely to be found with weapons or contraband. I also conclude that the City's highest officials have turned a blind eye to the evidence that officers are conducting stops in a racially discriminatory manner. In their zeal to defend a policy that they believe to be effective, they have willfully ignored overwhelming proof that the policy of targeting "the right people" is racially discriminatory and therefore violates the United States Constitution. One NYPD official has even suggested that it is permissible to stop racially defined groups just to instill fear in them that they are subject to being stopped at any time for any reason—in the hope that this fear will deter them from carrying guns in the streets. The goal of deterring crime is laudable, but this method of doing so is unconstitutional.[23]

19. Ibid. "The officer, Craig Matthews, a veteran of the 42nd Precinct in the Bronx, had claimed in the lawsuit that he was subjected to a 'campaign of retaliation and harassment' after he complained about a 'highly developed' system that mandated numerical quotas for arrests, summonses and stop-and-frisk encounters."
20. Delores Jones-Brown, Jaspreet Gill, and Jennifer Trone, "Stop, Question and Frisk Policing Practices in New York City: A Primer," John Jay College of Criminal Justice, March 2010, PDF, p. 9, http://tinyurl.com/zszbxtf. The UF-250 form that New York police use also lists several other possible reasons for the stop that officers can check off, including "Fits Description," "Sights and Sounds of Criminal Activity," and "Area Has High Incidence of Reported Offense of Type under Investigation" (high-crime area).
21. NYCLU, "Stop-and-Frisk 2011," 4.
22. *Floyd*, at 13.

Black people were more likely to be arrested (instead of summoned) after a stop for the same suspected crime.[24] Black people were 14 percent more likely, and Hispanics 9 percent more likely, to be subjected to the use of force.[25] Furthermore, Black people were stopped more than whites but were less likely to receive a sanction, indicating that Blacks were stopped for less suspecting reasons than were whites.[26]

Superiors often encouraged rank-and-file officers to racially profile Black and brown youth, regardless of conduct. Scheindlin noted that police officers checked "furtive movements" to justify stopping Black and brown youth between the ages of sixteen and twenty-one. In 2009, officers indicated "furtive movements" as a basis for the stop nearly 60 percent of the time.[27] Yet, Judge Scheindlin also determined that "furtive movements"—even as the label indicated vagueness and extraordinary discretion—were not, in fact, the reason that youth were stopped. Scheindlin highlighted testimony by police chief Joseph Esposito to support her claim that racial profiling operated as a policy—albeit unwritten—in daily practices. *Floyd v. City of New York* describes that "Chief Esposito, the highest ranking uniformed member of the NYPD throughout the class period and the chair at Compstat meetings,[28] was especially frank about the NYPD's policy of targeting racially defined groups for stops, provided that reasonable suspicion is also present":

> Q. Quality stops are stops that are in the right place at the right time, correct? A. Yes. Q. And targeting . . . the right people, correct? A. Among other things. Q. And the right people would be young black and Hispanic youths 14 to 20, correct? A. At times. [pause] You failed to mention reasonable suspicion. Chief Esposito conceded that not all stops are based on a spe-

23. *Floyd*, at 13.
24. *Floyd*, at 56.
25. *Floyd*, at 56.
26. *Floyd*, at 56.
27. *Floyd*, at 35.
28. According to *Floyd*, "Compstat" was introduced in 1994. It is the NYPD's statistics-based performance management system, which focuses on tracking crimes in certain locations. "The system collects and analyzes statistical and other data about local crime and enforcement activities, conducts weekly meetings during which senior officials question local commanders about the data, and holds commanders accountable for addressing crime conditions and improving the quantitative measures of their performance." During the *Floyd v. City of New York* trial, police chiefs testified that the number of UF-250s that a unit submitted were taken into account in the process of evaluating the unit's performance. Deputy Chief Marino stated: "They can do things like they can put up computer maps and show robberies up in this area. And then they will show a lot of activity in this area." See *Floyd*, at 64–66. The introduction of Compstat put significant pressure on numerical "productivity" and was related to the Quota Law of 2010, in which the NYPD established a written policy for prohibiting retaliation against police officers for failing to meet quotas for stops, arrests, or other enforcement activities.

cific suspect description from a crime complaint. In fact, officers check "Fits Description" on only 13% of UF-250s. Nevertheless, Esposito testified, the NYPD uses criminal suspect data to target certain individuals for stops even when there is no suspect description: Q: Do you believe the disparity in stop, question and frisk among black and Latino men is evidence of racial profiling? A: No. I don't believe that. . . . Because the stops are based on complaints that we get from the public. . . . THE COURT: But there are many street stops that have nothing to do with complaints, right? THE WITNESS: Correct. THE COURT: It's observed conduct. . . . It's not based on a complaint of a victim. THE WITNESS: It's based on the totality of, okay, who is committing the—who is getting shot in a certain area? . . . *Well who is doing those shootings? Well, it's young men of color in their late teens, early 20s.*[29]

For Chief Esposito, then, people matching the general demographics (race, age, and location) of the local population are "the right people"—that is, suspicious due to appearance and geographical position, rather than because of individual conduct. *Floyd v. City of New York* contains additional evidence from recordings made by Officer Pedro Serrano that corroborates Chief Esposito's testimony.[30]

Deputy Inspector Christopher McCormack explained to Officer Serrano that stopping "the right people, [at] the right time, [in] the right location" meant not stopping "a 48-year-old lady [who] was walking through St. Mary's Park when it was closed." He continued as follows:

INSPECTOR: This is about stopping the right people, the right place, the right location.

SERRANO: Okay.

INSPECTOR: Again, take Mott Haven where we had the most problems. And the most problems we had, they was robberies and grand larcenies.

SERRANO: And who are those people robbing?

INSPECTOR: The problem was, what, male blacks. And I told you at roll call, and I have no problem telling you this, *male blacks 14 to 20, 21.* I said this at roll call.

Deputy Inspector McCormack testified that his statements in the recording were based on suspect descriptions from victims. But *he also acknowl-*

29. *Floyd,* at 83–84. See also Jennifer Gonnerman, "Officer Serrano's Hidden Camera: The Stop-and-Frisk Trials of Pedro Serrano: NYPD Rat, NYPD Hero," *New York Magazine,* May 19, 2013.
30. Officer Pedro Serrano secretly recorded meetings with superior officers.

edged that the descriptions of the suspects consisted only of the information stated here: males, black, between 14 and 21.

Earlier in the recording, when challenged by Officer Serrano, Deputy Inspector McCormack clarified that he does not believe "every black and Hispanic" is subject to being stopped based on the crime suspect data. Deputy Inspector McCormack, like Chief Esposito, recognized that reasonable suspicion is required for every stop. But both believe that, within the pool of people displaying reasonably suspicious behavior, those who fit the general race, gender, and age profile of the criminal suspects in the area should be particularly targeted for stops.[31]

The testimonies of these high-ranking police officials demonstrate that racialized bodies are to be stopped, checked, frisked, and intimidated. Indeed, these bodies are constructed as shiftless, dangerous, and violent, and are thus held in check by hostile police officers who are simultaneously encouraged and protected by superiors.

Furthermore, the racialized bodies of young men who are stopped and frisked are correlated with public spaces deemed dangerous, violent, and consequently held in check. Indeed, police officers checked "Area Has Incidence of Reported Offense of Type under Investigation" (that is, a "High Crime Area") on 55 percent of UF-250 forms.[32] Expert witnesses, including Dr. Jeffrey Fagan, found that within any area, regardless of its racial composition, Black and brown people were more likely to be stopped than whites, controlling for racial composition, crime rate, patrol strength, and socioeconomic conditions.[33] In fact, most stops take place in impoverished neighborhoods such as East New York, Brownsville, or Mott Haven. Judge Scheindlin found that

(1) The NYPD carries out more stops where there are more black and Hispanic residents, even when other relevant variables are held constant. The racial composition of a precinct or census tract predicts the stop rate above and beyond the crime rate. (2) Blacks and Hispanics are more likely than whites to be stopped within precincts and census tracts, even after controlling for other relevant variables. This is so even in areas with low crime rates, racially heterogenous populations, or predominately white populations.[34]

---

31. *Floyd*, at 84–85. Italics mine.
32. *Floyd*, at 45–46. The City argued that more crime takes place in identified areas. However, expert witness Dr. Jeffrey Fagan asserted that checking off "High Crime Area" is a reflexive action and it is likely inaccurate that 55 percent of crimes took place in neighborhoods designated as "High Crime Areas."
33. *Floyd*, at 59, 62–63.
34. *Floyd*, at 9.

Judge Scheindlin's analysis indicates that racialized spaces operate reflexively with racialized bodies, in that racialized spaces are directly associated with mayhem and depravity. Philosopher Charles W. Mills similarly argues:

> The norming of space is partially done in terms of *racing* the space, the depiction of space as dominated by individuals (whether persons or subpersons) of a certain race. At the same time, the norming of the individual is partially achieved by *spacing* it, that is, representing it as imprinted with the characteristics of a certain kind of space. So this is a mutually supporting characterization that, for subpersons, becomes a circular indictment: "You are what you are in part because you originate from a certain kind of space, and that space has those properties in part because it is inhabited by creatures like yourself."[35]

Indeed, in these morally polluted spaces—demarcated by neighborhood names and police precinct numbers—inhabitants are to be continually watched and physically held in check. The "right people" are to be stopped in "the right location." Mills elaborates on the concept of racialized spaces that are demarcated to contain fearsome morally polluting bodies:

> The battle against this savagery is in a sense permanent as long as the savages continue to exist, contaminating (and being contaminated by) the non-Europeanized space around them. So it is not merely that space is normatively characterized on the macrolevel *before* conquest and colonial settlement, but that even *afterward*, on the local level, there are divisions, the European city and the Native Quarter, Whitetown and Niggertown/Darktown, suburb and inner city. David Theo Goldberg comments, "Power in the polis, and this is especially true of racialized power, reflects and refines the spatial relations of its inhabitants."[36]

Thus the justification for disproportionate stops in "High Crime Areas" is that the Black and brown people inhabiting such spaces must be intimidated, subjugated, and made to "know their place" so that they do not escape the boundaries that have been established. The police, then, function as boundary holders between polluted and pure spaces. Stopping and frisking people of color *because they are Black in ostensibly dangerous Black spaces, as well as safe white spaces,* sends a message that

---

35. Charles W. Mills, *The Racial Contract* (Ithaca, NY: Cornell University Press, 1997), 41–42.
36. Ibid., 47–48.

the police hold authority over Black bodies, in morally polluted Black neighborhoods and in "pure" white spaces.

Yet conservative politicians argue that only spaces—not racialized bodies—are targeted. Accusations of police racism are unwarranted in that police who engage in Stop and Frisk practices do not target *people* with a particular skin color but *neighborhoods* with the highest crime rates. Mike Long, Chairman of the New York State Conservative Party, stated:

> If you're having more gun violence, and you're having more robberies, and you're having more problems in a particular area, regardless, that's where you apply your police attention. And sadly, the black and Latino constituents are the largest victims of crime in our city. . . . I don't doubt that there are some police officers that go over the top, and we can't be blind to that, but I get so annoyed, whether they be black or Latino activists, that are constantly saying things and screaming the race card, when the fact is that the police officers are really protecting their communities.[37]

Indeed, between 1993 and 2013, NYPD officers referred to demarcated neighborhoods as "hot spots" and developed a policing strategy specific to those places. Officer Pedro Serrano recounted how officials flooded "crime hot spots" with cops and ordered them to give out summonses and perform Stop and Frisks, ostensibly to prevent more serious crimes.[38]

A sophisticated crime tracking system known as "Compstat" has been employed since the 1990s to track and stop smaller crimes in order to stop bigger crimes and to pinpoint "hotspots" where crimes are clustered.[39] Compstat meetings to hold high-ranking officials accountable take place regularly. Journalist Jennifer Gonnerman in a *New York Magazine* article described:

> Once a commander returned to the station house [from a Compstat meeting], of course, he passed down that pressure to everyone else: to the lieutenants, the sergeants, down to the officers. For every crime hot spot, the precinct commander had to show that he was on top of the situation, that his cops were taking action. He had no way of counting exactly how many crimes he'd prevented—how do you count robberies and shootings before

37. Interview with Mike Long, Chairman, New York State Conservative Party, March 2013.
38. Gonnerman, "Officer Serrano's Hidden Camera."
39. Jonathan Dienst, Rich McHugh, and Evan Stulberger, "An Inside Look at the System That Cut Crime in New York by 75 Percent," NBC News, April 16, 2016, http://tinyurl.com/hkcfo7o.

they happen?—but he could offer up the next best thing: high numbers of 250s and summonses.[40]

Stop and Frisk, then, was a strategy integral to maximizing Compstat information. Should Black and brown young people choose to venture out of demarcated bounds, police officers strive to humiliate and subjugate them within a broader culture of hostility. In 2010, Officer Adrian Schoolcraft, an eight-year veteran of the NYPD, published recordings from secretly taped meetings and informal interactions that occurred between June 1, 2008, and October 31, 2009, in the 81st Precinct in Bedford-Stuyvesant, a historically Black neighborhood in Brooklyn. The recordings display supervisors' extraordinary contempt and hostility toward Black and Latino people in impoverished neighborhoods. For example, at a roll call on November 8, 2008, Lieutenant Jean Delafuente stated:

> All right, I went out there [to Howard and Chauncey] yesterday and . . . we've got the old man out there with the grey hairs. A loud mouth. He thinks since he's 55 years old he's not going to get locked up. Well, guess what? I don't tolerate shit out there. He went in and two of his pals went in. All right? So we've got to keep the corner clear. . . . Because if you get too big of a crowd there, you know, . . . they're going to think that they own the block. We own the block. They don't own the block, all right? They might live there but we own the block. All right? We own the streets here. You tell them what to do.[41]

Similarly, Lieutenant Delafuente reminded the officers at a roll call on November 1, 2008, that they are "not working in Midtown Manhattan where people are walking around smiling and happy. You're working in Bed-Stuy where everyone's probably got a warrant."[42]

As further evidence of a culture of hostility in the 81st Precinct, Sergeant Raymond Stukes said the following at a roll call on March 13, 2009:

> If you see guys walking down the street, move 'em along. Two or three guys you can move, you can't move 15, all right? If you want to be a[n] asshole or whatever you want to call it, make a move. If they won't move, call me over and lock them up [for disorderly conduct]. No big deal. We could leave them there all night. . . . The less people on the street, the easier our

40. Gonnerman, "Officer Serrano's Hidden Camera."
41. *Floyd*, at 72–73.
42. *Floyd*, at 73.

job will be. . . . *If you stop them[,] 250, how hard is a 250. I'm not saying make it up but you can always articulate robbery, burglary, whatever the case may be. That's paperwork. . . . It's still a number. It keeps the hounds off, I've been saying that for months.*

Similarly, Sergeant Stukes stated at a roll call on November 23, 2008: "If they're on a corner, make them move. They don't want to move, you lock them up. Done deal. *You can always articulate later.*"

In a speech at roll call on Halloween in 2008, Deputy Inspector Mauriello stated:

Tonight is zero tolerance. It's New Years Eve all over again. Everybody goes. I don't care. . . . They're throwing dice? They all go, promote gambling. I don't care. Let the DA discuss what they're going to do tomorrow. . . . They got [bandanas] on and they're running like nuts down the block, chasing people? Grab them. Fuck it. You're preventing a robbery. . . . You know that and I know that.[43]

Deputy Inspector Steven Mauriello connected manner of dress and place with justification for stops—regardless of the person's actual conduct. At a roll call on November 8, 2008, he stated:

I'm tired of bandanas on their waist and I'm tired of these beads. Red and black beads mean Bloods. Their bandanas—if they're walking down the street and they've got a bandana sticking out their ass, coming out there—they've got to be stopped. A 250 at least. At least.[44]

Routinely, then, high-level police administrators advocated stopping and frisking, with a subtext of violent subjugation. These sergeants demonstrated utter disregard for the dignity and constitutional rights of Black and brown New Yorkers; indeed, they encouraged officers to fill quotas "to keep the hounds off." At a December 8, 2008, roll call, Sergeant Raymond Stukes instructed:

This job is so easy. Just keep the hounds off. A parker, a 250, you could book somebody walking down the street. You know what? I stopped and asked—so what? I did a 250. What's the big deal? Let him go. He doesn't want to give you no information, who cares? It's still a 250.[45]

43. *Floyd*, at 73–74.
44. *Floyd*, at 75.
45. *Floyd*, at 75. See also Graham Raymond, "The NYPD Tapes: Inside Bed-Stuy's 81st Precinct," *The Village Voice*, May 4, 2010: "[The secret recordings] reveal that precinct bosses threaten street cops if

The contempt displayed by police supervisors permeated every level of the NYPD. Sergeants associated dark skin with moral corruption, as they regarded all Black and brown bodies—regardless of conduct—with violent crime and mayhem. A culture of hostility buttressed the violations enacted by rank-and-file officers who stopped and frisked community members, filled quotas, and perpetuated racialized pollution boundaries between white, Black, and brown New Yorkers.

Officials' Responses

Former New York City mayor Michael Bloomberg justified Stop and Frisk practice as a violence-prevention procedure that took illegal weapons off the streets.[46] During his administration, Stop and Frisk procedures rose 600 percent,[47] even though in the first half of 2011 only 1.9 percent of all frisks resulted in a weapon found.[48] In 2011, when police officers stopped 700,000 individuals, 780 guns were recovered.[49] The ineffectiveness of increasing Stop and Frisk practices is obvious when compared to 2003 when 160,851 stops were conducted and 604 guns were found.[50] Bloomberg responded to criticism of the extraordinary increase in Stop and Frisks under his administration by supporting state-level legislation that would decriminalize possession of twenty-five grams or less of marijuana in public view.[51] At the same time, he defended Stop and Frisk policies even as the city's police force significantly reduced the number of stops it conducted in 2012.[52]

The NYPD responded to critiques by justifying "the high percentage of stops of black and Latino New Yorkers. Officials contended that those high percentages merely reflect[ed] the concentration of stop-

they don't make their quotas of arrests and stop-and-frisks, but also tell them not to take certain robbery reports in order to manipulate crime statistics."

46. Kate Taylor, "Stop-and-Frisk Policy 'Saves Lives,' Mayor Tells Black Congregation," *New York Times*, June 11, 2012, at A14.
47. Ibid.
48. NYCLU, "Stop-and-Frisk 2011," 8.
49. Ibid, 13.
50. Ibid.
51. Center for Constitutional Rights, "Stop and Frisk," 7: "In June 2012, first Governor Andrew Cuomo and then Mayor Michael Bloomberg and Commissioner Kelly added their support to those calling for the decriminalization of small amounts of marijuana in public view in order to reduce the number of such arrests." "Decriminalization" refers to charging people with a violation, which carries a fine, rather than a criminal misdemeanor; "under decriminalization . . . the acquisition, use, and possession of drugs can be punished by a citation much like traffic violations are." Carl L. Hart, "Holder's Proposal Is Insufficient: Congress Needs to Decriminalize Drugs," *Huffington Post*, August 16, 2013, http://tinyurl.com/jqzaay3. In New York State, it is already a violation to possess twenty-five grams of marijuana without putting it into public view.
52. John Eterno and Eli Silverman, "Mike Bloomberg's Fact-Free Defence of Stop-and-Frisk," *The Guardian*, September 11, 2013, http://tinyurl.com/jymmaa3.

and-frisk activity in high-crime precincts" in which the majority of residents are Black and Latino.[53] However, the 2011 data revealed that disproportionate numbers of "blacks and Latinos [were] stopped in precincts that have substantial percentages of white residents."[54]

Thus, actions alone do not account for the high number of stops of Black and Latino New Yorkers. While officials may justify the criminalization of certain individuals, their desire to maintain a racialized moral order is a more convincing explanation for Stop and Frisk policing practices.

Bloomberg, who continued a quality-of-life campaign initiated under Rudolph Giuliani's mayoral administration, rejected the charge that his administration was engaging in a form of social control by focusing on fear of crime.[55] He argued that leniency toward even minor offenses—such as turnstile jumping in the subways—reduced the city's overall quality of life and promoted a culture encouraging of more serious crime.[56]

The argument that a decrease in violent crime and an increase in police officers on the street would support an intensified quality-of-life campaign justified the ongoing program of force and harassment against low-income Blacks and Latinos in New York City. As Tanya Erzen wrote:

> For everyone deemed capable of creating disorder, from panhandlers to neighborhood teenagers to the homeless, the Quality of Life initiative represents a concerted assault upon the right to exist in the city and to move in public spaces. The campaign's premise is two-pronged. First, the same people who jump a turnstile or wash a windshield may very well be felons and robbers, rapists and burglars. Second, a broken window, a trash-strewn street, or a homeless person asleep on a bench symbolize [sic] disorder. This disorder initiates a snowball effect whereby drug dealers, vandals, and other urban predators begin to engulf a neighborhood.[57]

These ideas follow the well-known "broken windows theory," of which criminologists George Kelling and James Q. Wilson were the first pro-

---

53. Ibid.
54. Ibid.: "For instance, the population of the 17th Precinct, which covers the East Side of Manhattan, has the lowest percentage of black and Latino residents in the city at 7.8%, yet 71.4% of those stopped in the precinct were black or Latino. Similarly, the 6th precinct, covering Greenwich Village, is 8% black and Latino, yet 76.6% of stops in that precinct were of blacks and Latinos."
55. Tanya Erzen, "Turnstile Jumpers and Broken Windows: Policing Disorder in New York City," in McArdle and Erzen, *Zero Tolerance*, 19.
56. Ibid.
57. Ibid.

ponents.[58] Kelling and Wilson proposed that police officers target individual vagrants and "drunks" to avoid destruction of an entire community: "This wish to 'decriminalize' disreputable behavior that 'harms no one'—and thus remove the ultimate sanction the police can employ to maintain neighborhood order—is, we think, a mistake."[59] Together they published a 1982 article in *The Atlantic* that argued for causal links between visual disorder and serious crime.[60] Successive Giuliani administrations in the 1990s applied the broken windows theory to people who washed windshields, slept on park benches, or panhandled, thereby casting them as threats to the social order.[61]

Giuliani's policies gained support, particularly from middle-class city residents who avoided certain areas or expressed annoyance at the "squeegee men" who offered to wash the windshields of cars stopped at red lights in hopes of being paid for the service.[62] Mike Long, the New York Conservative Party Chairman, argued that the first priority of city government should be "safety"—which he equated with controlling undesirable people in public spaces.[63]

While Long represents far-right politicians who argue that the primary, if not sole, function of government is to protect "the people" at all cost, even sociologists who deplore mass imprisonment have supported broken windows policing strategies and Stop and Frisk patterns of policing.[64] Michael Jacobson, former commissioner of New York City Probation and Corrections, has argued that increased surveillance, frisks, and arrests ultimately reduce state incarceration.[65] If the goal of public policy is to "downsize prisons," he encouraged Stop and Frisk policing.[66] In a 2013 policy paper coauthored with James Austin, Jacobson wrote:

> This report concludes that a change in New York City's policing strategy created [a drop in imprisonment]. Beginning in the 1990s, the New York Police Department shifted toward making more arrests for misdemeanors

58. Ibid.
59. George L. Kelling and James Q. Wilson, "Broken Windows: The Police and Neighborhood Safety," *The Atlantic*, March 1982, http://tinyurl.com/jfx2egl.
60. Ibid.
61. Erzen, "Turnstile Jumpers," 20.
62. Ibid.
63. Interview with Mike Long, Chairman, New York State Conservative Party, March 2013.
64. Inimai Chettiar, foreword to *How New York City Reduced Mass Incarceration: A Model for Change?*, by James Austin and Michael Jacobson, Brennan Center for Justice, January 2013, PDF, p. 3–4, http://tinyurl.com/hgb425w (discussing how the "broken windows" and Stop and Frisk policies led to reduced rates of incarceration in New York).
65. Austin and Jacobson, *How New York.*
66. Ibid., 6.

and fewer arrests for felonies. At the same time, the crime rate—and therefore actual commission of felonies—dropped. This drop in felony arrests is what contributed to the drop in the correctional population. The increase in misdemeanor arrests contributed to a small increase in the correctional population. However, taken together, these two shifts created a huge drop in the correctional population. This result demonstrates why local policies are just as vital to reducing mass incarceration as state legislation, and how every state could benefit from a strategy that incorporates both levels of reform.[67]

Escalated Stop and Frisk policing did not necessarily lead to recovery of more illegal weapons, as compared to when fewer Stop and Frisks were made.[68] Rather, the escalation led residents of targeted communities to believe that they were being racially profiled so that police officers could fill quotas and clear public spaces for the city's white residents.[69]

An Atmosphere of Intimidation and Fear

Critical activists have deemed the surveillance practices that have resulted in disproportionate arrests of Blacks as a form of "social control."[70] Nahal Zamani, an advocacy program manager for the Center for Constitutional Rights, argued that contrary to Jacobson's findings, "Stop and Frisk—which is one form of discriminatory policing—is about targeting marginalized communities because they're seen as elements that need to be controlled and out of sight."[71]

Zamani interviewed a series of neighborhood residents, all of whom described the culture of fear that developed under Guiliani and Boomberg's tenure:

> For young people in my neighborhood, getting stopped and frisked is a rite of passage. We expect the police to jump us at any moment. We

67. Ibid.
68. Center for Constitutional Rights, "Stop and Frisk," 4: "Despite the City's attempts to justify the program as aimed at confiscating illegal weapons, a 2010 expert report by Professor Jeffrey Fagan that CCR submitted to the court in *Floyd* found that the weapons and contraband yield from stops and frisks hovered around only 1.14%—a rate no greater than would be found by chance at random check points."
69. Ibid., 11: "Blacks and Latinos are treated more harshly than Whites, being more likely to be arrested instead of given a summons when compared to White people accused of the same crimes, and are also more likely to have force used against them by police. These dramatic disparities were reflected in the interviews conducted for this report, where the role of race in stops and frisks was acknowledged by virtually everyone."
70. Center for Constitutional Rights, "Stop and Frisk," 20: "Many people feel that the role of the police in their communities is to enforce social control and not to address genuine community needs."
71. Interview with Nahal Zamani, Advocacy and Program Manager, Center for Constitutional Rights Misconduct and Racial Justice Docket, March 2013.

know the rules: don't run and don't try to explain, because speaking up for yourself might get you arrested or worse. And we all feel the same way—degraded, harassed, violated and criminalized because we're black or Latino.[72]

Interviewees further described an environment so saturated with a hostile police presence that being stopped and harassed by police has become integrated into the fabric of daily life experience.[73] Many explained how they changed their clothing style and/or hairstyles, altered their routes or avoided walking on the street, and made a "habit of carrying around documents such as ID, mail, and pay stubs to provide police officers if stopped."[74] One interviewee noted:

It makes you anxious about just being, walking around and doing your daily thing while having a bunch of police always there, always present and stopping people that look like me. They say if you're a young Black male, you're more likely to be stopped. So, it's always this fear that "okay, this cop might stop me," for no reason, while I'm just sitting there in my neighborhood.[75]

Residents of disproportionately policed neighborhoods also noted the lack of accountability in incidents of police aggression:

In my complex I feel like we're under torment, like we're under like this big gang that's bullying all of us. To me, NYPD is the biggest gang in New York. They're worse than any gang, 'cause they could get away with stuff. When they're killing people and they don't get [any] kind of disciplinary action.[76]

---

72. Communities United for Police Reform, "CPR Members Testify at City Hall in Support of the Community Safety Act," ChangeTheNYPD.org, October 11, 2012, http://tinyurl.com/hok3jhj. In January 2013, Communities United for Police Reform, a campaign to end discriminatory policing practices in New York City, "launched the first Leadership Development Institute ('LDI') to build the capacity of directly affected communities to hold the NYPD accountable. The LDI trained almost 30 individual members from nine organizations to conduct Know Your Rights workshops in their communities." Communities United for Police Reform, "CPR Holds Leadership Development Institute," ChangeTheNYPD.org, February 4, 2013, http://tinyurl.com/j8yam7k. Participating organizations in the first "Know Your Rights" training included the Audre Lorde Project, Bronx Defenders, FIERCE, the Justice Committee, Make the Road NY, NAACP Legal Defense Fund, New York City Anti-Violence Project, Picture the Homeless, Streetwise and Safe, VOCAL NY, and Youth Ministries for Peace and Justice.
73. Center for Constitutional Rights, "Stop and Frisk," 17: "These policing practices have created a growing gulf between the NYPD and the communities they police, where people are treated as 'a permanent under-caste,' and are unable to go about their daily lives without repeated harassment by police."
74. Ibid., 7.
75. Ibid., 17.
76. Ibid., 21.

Indeed, in the experiences of some individuals who were stopped and frisked, police officers behaved like the criminals they sought to arrest. For example, Derrick Barnicot reported that as he walked with a bike he had just bought for his girlfriend, an officer stopped him and told him that if they received another stolen bike report, they would come after him. Barnicot testified: "I felt endangered. I've been mugged before and it felt like that."[77]

People who are stopped and frisked have argued that they are being used as a means to an end—to fill quotas—and brutally so.[78] Another victim of these tactics shared:

My jeans were ripped. I had bruises on my face. My whole face was swollen. I was sent to the precinct for disorderly conduct. I got out two days later. The charges were dismissed. At central booking, they threw out the charge. No charge. I felt like I couldn't defend myself, didn't know what to do. No witnesses there to see what was going on. I just wish someone was there to witness it. I felt like no one would believe me. I couldn't tell anyone. I kept it in till now. . . . I still am scared.[79]

The trauma enacted upon people who are stopped and frisked can be isolating, as noted above, as well as enraging and humiliating. Police officers have been known to sexually harass individuals during random Stop and Frisks.[80] Furthermore, in addition to (literally) warrantless intimidation and resultant feelings of fear, an arrest can trigger severe consequences even when it does not lead to a conviction. Arrests can create permanent criminal records that are easily located on the internet by employers, landlords, schools, credit agencies, licensing boards, and banks.[81] While the extent of collateral consequences is hard to quantify, anecdotal evidence illuminates the considerable hardships caused by arrests. For example, thirty-six-year-old transit worker Daryl George, who had never been arrested, was in the lobby of a Brooklyn building when the police entered and searched everyone.[82]

77. Ibid.
78. Interview with Nahal Zamani, March 2013.
79. Center for Constitutional Rights, "Stop and Frisk," 5.
80. Ibid., 12. The people who describe being sexually harassed are often transgender people who are perceived to be sex workers. "I'm paranoid, scared . . . 'cause if I'm walking on the street, I better rush to a public place and run away from them 'cause I know I can get arrested for just walking on the street. 'Cause if I'm walking with my friend, they just assume that I'm a prostitute, that I'm a sex worker, or just because I'm a Hispanic transgender woman, because of my gender, I can just get arrested." Ibid.
81. Harry G. Levine and Loren Siegel, "Million a Year: The Cost of New York City's Marijuana Possession Arrests," Drug Policy Alliance, March 2011, PDF, p. 1, http://tinyurl.com/zfhevbd.
82. Police Reform Organizing Project, "The Narratives Project," http://tinyurl.com/jeaulz7.

He had no contraband, but he was arrested alongside someone who did.[83] The charges were dismissed—but not before the Transit Authority suspended him and he lost five months of pay and benefits.[84]

The feelings of violation are pervasive among those who have been stopped and frisked. Joseph "Jazz" Hayden, a community activist who initiated a Campaign to End the New Jim Crow at the Riverside Church, has argued that the state's rejection of certain populations, along with middle-class flight, has contributed to an extensive youth culture in which community members are enraged at their treatment by police officers, but also view it as normal.[85]

Critical activists seek to disrupt the atmosphere of normality. The practice of stopping and frisking Black people and other marginalized individuals has been challenged in the court system and New York City Council chambers.[86] Advocates have protested Stop and Frisk practices in three separate lawsuits filed in federal court that allege racial profiling and violations of constitutional rights, including *Floyd v. City of New York*.[87] In two of the court cases, advocates charged the city with breaching constitutional rights by allowing police officers to stop and frisk residents and visitors of private apartment buildings.[88] In these cases, the plaintiffs alleged that residents, who were simply in the hallways, stairwells, or elevators of their own buildings, or in front of their buildings, were under siege by police officers.[89] As one person testified:

> I'll go into the building with the key and they're still stopping me, asking me what I'm doing in the building. . . . In the summertime, it's nice outside. Why can't I hang out in front of my building? [The NYPD] give[s] you a ticket for trespassing 'cause you're sitting on the bench that's in front of your building. I can't sit on the bench in front of my building? Why's the bench there?[90]

83. Ibid.
84. Ibid.
85. Interview with Joseph "Jazz" Hayden, Cofounder, Campaign to End the New Jim Crow, February 2013.
86. See generally *Ligon v. City of New York*, 925 F. Supp. 2d 478 (S.D.N.Y. 2013) (challenging NYPD Stop and Frisk practices); *Davis v. City of New York*, 902 F. Supp. 2d 405 (S.D.N.Y. 2012) (class action challenging Stop and Frisk practices).
87. Editorial, "Stop and Frisk, Part 3," *New York Times*, October 8, 2012, at A22 (discussing three federal cases related to *Davis v. City of New York* involving Stop and Frisk practices).
88. See *Ligon*: "On September 24, 2012, plaintiffs filed a motion for a preliminary injunction, seeking an order requiring the NYPD to create and implement new policies, training programs, and monitoring and supervisory procedures that specifically address the problem of unconstitutional trespass stops outside TAP buildings." See also *Davis*: "The lawsuit alleges that defendants' actions have resulted in a widespread pattern of unlawful stops, questioning, frisks, searches, and arrests of NYCHA residents and their invited guests."
89. Center for Constitutional Rights, "Stop and Frisk," 17: "The scale and scope of stop-and-frisk practices in communities of color have left many residents feeling that they are living under siege."

The phenomenon of entering buildings and randomly searching residents is amplified in the domain of public housing. A 2010 report documented that residents of the New York City Housing Authority (NYCHA) sites receive inordinate attention from the police.[91] Many public housing residents describe being constantly harassed when coming to and going from their apartments.[92] Officer Serrano recorded a lieutenant at roll call urging each officer to commit five "verticals"—sweeps of apartment buildings—in addition to other Stop and Frisk activities.[93] In spaces associated with moral mayhem and violence—that is, pollution—rank-and-file officers were encouraged to heavily police the premises.

The Moral Pollution of Possessing Pot

In 2011, the number one offense for which people were arrested in New York City was marijuana possession.[94] From 1997 through 2010, the NYPD made 536,000 arrests for exposing pot in public.[95] In 2011 alone, 50,684 persons were arrested for carrying small amounts of marijuana.[96] Black people made up more than 50 percent of youth arrested for possessing marijuana that was described by police as displayed in public view.[97] Although government health surveys found that young whites used marijuana at higher rates than young Black and Latino persons, the NYPD arrested Black and Latino youth for marijuana possession at a disproportionately higher rate than whites.[98]

Yet, possession of less than twenty-five grams of marijuana was not a crime under New York State law; rather, it is supposed to be treated like a traffic violation.[99] New York State's 1977 Marijuana Reform Act

---

90. Ibid., 18.
91. Ibid., 19.
92. Ibid., 6: "You shouldn't be held up in your apartment, if you have one. You shouldn't be afraid to come outside and go to the store to get a soda for fear that the police are going to stop you, and you're either going to get [an] expensive, a high-cost summons or you're going to get arrested."
93. Gonnerman, "Inside Officer Serrano's Hidden Camera."
94. Levine and Siegel, "Million a Year," 57.
95. Ibid.
96. Drug Policy Alliance, "Marijuana Arrests in NYC: Fiscally Irresponsible, Racially Biased and Unconstitutional," 2012, PDF, p. 1, http://tinyurl.com/z7mffse. These numbers are in stark contrast to the period prior to Rudolph Giuliani's mayoral administration. From 1978 until 1993, fewer than forty thousand people *total* were arrested for possession of marijuana. Levine and Siegel, "Million a Year," 3. Beginning with Giuliani's administration, the NYPD implemented Stop and Frisk policies, directly targeting communities that are predominantly inhabited by young Blacks and Latinos. By 2000, more than fifty thousand marijuana arrests began to be made *annually*.
97. Harry G. Levine, "New York City's Marijuana Arrest Crusade . . . Continues," September 2009, PDF, p. 4, http://tinyurl.com/ztz4b7w.
98. Ibid.

decriminalized simple possession of pot but did not decriminalize smoking or displaying it in public.[100] Therefore, if during a Stop and Frisk, an NYPD officer encountered marijuana and ordered the individual to disclose it, once the marijuana was in public view, the individual could be prosecuted for committing a crime.

Police officers, then, were performing illegal acts. In short, the instrumental arm deployed to regulate morality in society was itself acting against the law, by forcing people to reveal marijuana and consequently arresting them, often to meet internal quotas (also illegal). Professor Harry Levine has argued that individual officers and low-level commanders are part of a widespread system of surveillance, intimidation, and training that is not considered unjust by officials, but in fact, is implemented immorally:

> Narcotics and patrol police, their supervisors, and others within in [sic] the NYPD frequently benefit from the marijuana possession arrests. The arrests are relatively safe, easy, and provide training for new officers. The arrests gain overtime pay for patrol and narcotics police and their supervisors. The pot arrests allow officers to show productivity, which counts for promotions and choice assignments. Marijuana arrests enable the NYPD to obtain fingerprints, photographs and other data on many young people they would not otherwise have in their criminal justice databases.[101]

Levine noted that in 2009, the percentages of Blacks, Latinos, and whites who were frisked were "nearly identical to the percentages of each group that [were] arrested for possessing small amounts of marijuana."[102] In other words, disproportionate stopping and frisking of Blacks and Latinos is directly correlated with disproportionate arrests for display of marijuana. Levine's findings corroborated statistics compiled by the Police Reform Organizing Project, which noted:

> In recent years, the top ten precincts for marijuana arrests in New York City averaged 2,150 marijuana arrests for every 100,000 residents; the populations in those precincts are more than 90 percent nonwhite. The 10 precincts with the lowest rates of marijuana arrests averaged 67 out of 100,000 residents, and are more than 80 percent white.[103]

99. N.Y. Penal Law §221.05 (McKinney 2010) (punishing first offense of unlawful possession of marijuana with only a fine). Possession of marijuana in a public place is still a crime if the marijuana is burning or open to public view.
100. Ibid.
101. Levine, "Marijuana Arrest Crusade," 8.
102. Ibid.

Black youth were disproportionately targeted for offenses committed more often by white youth. But Black youth were constructed as morally polluted, and thus were treated as threats to the social order. Indeed, New York City–based officials and social justice advocates identify both policing reform and revised drug legislation as necessary for racial equality.[104] During his tenure, Bloomberg distinguished himself from conservative politicians who staunchly supported Stop and Frisk practices as part of a zero-tolerance approach to drug use. But he continued to support policies that entrapped Black youth in city databases. On the one hand, Bloomberg signaled his support for decriminalizing marijuana policies during the 2012 legislative session when Governor Mario Cuomo announced his support for legislative reform.[105] In September 2012, Police Commissioner Raymond Kelly issued a memorandum clarifying that the police were not to arrest people who take small amounts of marijuana out of their pockets after being stopped.[106] In February 2013, Bloomberg announced that people arrested for marijuana possession would no longer spend the night in jail—if they had a valid identification card and if there were no outstanding warrants for their arrests. Yet, people that were stopped for possessing pot would still be arrested, fingerprinted, and entered into the New York City criminal justice database.[107]

Strident moral opposition to marijuana possession came from upstate conservatives. For conservatives, Stop and Frisk practices fostered important social norms. Conservative state representatives from predominantly white, rural, upstate districts opposed Stop and Frisk reform as legislative action that would sanction drug use, a practice that would lead to personal debilitation and social decay.[108] In 2012, Senate Majority Leader Dean Skelos stated that "being able to walk around with 10 joints in each ear and it would only be a violation—I think that's wrong."[109] John J. Flanagan, a Long Island Republican,

103. Police Reform Organization Project, "New York City's Failure: Harsh, Unjust Police Tactics," June 2011, PDF, p. 4–5, http://tinyurl.com/jesjbn5.

104. See Drug Policy Alliance, "Marijuana Arrests in NYC," 2 (highlighting the economic costs of and the racial bias inherent in enforcing New York marijuana laws).

105. Thomas Kaplan, "Bloomberg Backs Plan to Limit Arrests for Marijunana," *New York* Times, June 4, 2012, at NY Region.

106. Ibid.

107. Michael M. Grynbaum and Michael Barbaro, "From Bloomberg, a Warning of Life After Bloomberg," *New York Times*, February 15, 2013, at A21.

108. Dan Collins, "GOP Bump on the Road to Stop-and-Frisk Reform," *Huffington Post*, June 22, 2012, http://tinyurl.com/zwww3r7 (reporting on Republican opposition to a proposed New York State law that would decriminalize the open display of small amounts of marijuana so that police could not arrest individuals possessing marijuana during Stop and Frisks when they turn out their pockets).

argued that "marijuana still is a gateway drug to so many other much more dangerous things."[110] Conservative Party Chairman Mike Long concurred:

> I don't see any difference between a small amount or a large amount, I think [marijuana] is still an illegal substance that is not good for society. I think we shouldn't be saying to our young people that if this law passes, it's OK, you're only going to get a violation, it's not a big deal, it's just a ticket. It's like jaywalking. It's *not* like jaywalking, it's clearly more serious. It's addictive, it starts some people on a road of life into darkness, and it destroys too many families. I feel very strongly about it. I think that maybe my personal position is a little bit more moral than some people have, but I think that those of us in public life have an obligation, whether the tide is going against us, to stand up for what you believe in very strongly, and not move, not budge.[111]

Long also linked drugs—including marijuana—to violent crime.[112] Therefore, in his view, Stop and Frisk policing practices deterred people from using a "gateway drug" to mayhem.[113] Long further described the Stop and Frisk practices as a public safety measure that has "saved lives" and taken guns off of the street.[114] Criminalizing people who are in possession of a "harmful" substance such as marijuana functions as part of public safety.[115] In short, "people who don't want to spend a night in jail don't have marijuana on them."[116] For Long, to possess an illegal drug is to commit a morally polluting act.

Whereas conservatives have seen current Stop and Frisk policies as a means for promoting individual moral character, critics of the policies have seen decriminalization as a struggle for racial justice and consequently the promotion of a different kind of moral society.[117] In critics' eyes, decriminalization would aid in dismantling a cultural

---

109. James King, "Senate Majority Leader Dean Skelos (Unintentionally) Explains Why 'Public View' Weed Law Makes No Sense," *Village Voice* Blogs, June 7, 2012, http://tinyurl.com/z7emea2.

110. Thomas Kaplan and John Eligon, "Divide in Albany Kills Proposal on Marijuana," *New York Times* (June 19, 2012).

111. Interview with Mike Long, Chairman, New York State Conservative Party, March 2013.

112. Ibid.

113. Ibid.

114. Ibid.

115. Ibid.

116. Ibid.

117. See Kaplan and Eligon: "Mr. Cuomo, a Democrat, said: 'You have old folks like me who say, "Whoa, the decriminalization of marijuana: What are you saying? Everyone is going to walk around smoking marijuana, and that's O.K.?" So I think the Senate got a lot of blowback, pardon the pun.'"; see also Kaplan: "Mr. Cuomo, a Democrat, framed the issue as one of racial justice as well as common sense, saying that the police in New York City were wasting time, resources and good will making tens of thousands of unnecessary arrests."

and legal double standard in which young Black men are targeted and arrested.[118] Possessing marijuana "cannot be criminal behavior for one group of people and socially acceptable behavior for another group of people, where the dividing line is race," argued Assembly Member Hakeem Jeffries, a Brooklyn Democrat, in 2012.[119] Leroy Gadsden, president of a branch of the National Association for the Advancement of Colored People in Jamaica, Queens, stated:

> Some of our police officers are making race-based discretionary decisions on who they're going to arrest for low-level marijuana possession. Therefore, of course, if you're a young, black male, even a female, you're going to feel that you're being targeted when you notice that your white counterparts are not being arrested for the same thing.[120]

Gabriel Sayegh, co-founder of the Katal Center for Health, Equity, and Justice, framed the struggle to decriminalize marijuana in historical terms: "Drug policy has been used for over a hundred years to target and manage and in many ways neutralize communities, at specific times, for specific terms, for the maintenance of white supremacy."[121]

In the eyes of decriminalization activists, it was not morally defensible that racial disparities, fiscal waste, constitutional violations, and the lifelong impact on young people were borne most dramatically in communities of color in a clearly biased way.[122]

Advocates also highlighted immoral fiscal waste: New York City spent $75 million on marijuana arrests in 2013.[123] A single arrest cost the city on average between $1,000 and $2,000.[124] The message on the part of critical advocates, then, was not that marijuana was harmless but that greater social harms were enacted through fiscal waste and especially through the infringement on community members' constitutional rights.

There existed strident opposition to decriminalizing marijuana from members of community boards and older residents who witnessed drug dealing in their neighborhoods and who were concerned about rebellious youth.[125] However, advocates argued that, for the most part,

118. Interview with Gabriel Sayegh, New York State Policy Director, Drug Policy Alliance, February 2013.
119. Kaplan, "Bloomberg Backs Plan."
120. Ibid.
121. Interview with Gabriel Sayegh, New York State Policy Director, Drug Policy Alliance, February 2013.
122. Ibid.
123. Ibid.
124. Ibid.

people care less about the drug than they do its ill effects on their neighborhoods.[126] Community members were concerned with poverty, joblessness, failing schools, and violence.[127]

From 1993 to 2013, organizers against police brutality conducted research, trained directly affected members of communities, and organized protestors who were outraged by police profiling and brutality.[128] Organizers for Communities United for Police Reform declared that their movement was rooted in a philosophy of human rights that uplifts the inherent dignity of all persons and the right of every person to live a basic, fulfilling life.[129]

The coalition worked closely with media outlets. During the *Floyd* trial, the *New York Times* and WNYC, a local public radio station, covered Stop and Frisk practices extensively and established interactive maps detailing where most Stop and Frisk incidents took place.[130]

Communities United for Police Reform also proposed a four-pronged Community Safety Act bill in the New York City Council.[131] Two parts of the bill—protecting New Yorkers against discriminatory profiling by the NYPD and establishing an NYPD Inspector General Office—were passed in August 2013.[132]

Some members of the City Council responded to the outcry by speaking out repeatedly against Stop and Frisk practices in the mainstream press, holding two public forums in Brooklyn and Queens,[133] and organizing a community-wide hearing for the Community Safety Act.[134] Furthermore, the Police Reform Organizing Project sought to organize

125. Ibid.
126. Ibid.
127. Ibid.
128. CPR held a Leadership Development Institute. See note 73 of this chapter.
129. See Communities United for Police Reform, "Priorities for the New NYPD Inspector General: Promoting Safety, Dignity and Rights for all New Yorkers," ChangeTheNYPD.org, June 2014, PDF, http://tinyurl.com/zou2sju: "[Communities United for Police Reform] aim[s] to help build a lasting movement that promotes public safety and policing practices based on respect for the rights and dignity of all New Yorkers."
130. Matthew Bloch, Ford Fessenden, and Janet Roberts, "Stop, Question and Frisk in New York Neighborhoods," *New York Times*, July 11, 2010, http://tinyurl.com/hk8mt8f.
131. Communities United for Police Reform, "Support the Community Safety Act: Legislation to Combat Discriminatory Policing and Hold the NYPD Accountable," ChangeTheNYPD.org, PDF, http://tinyurl.com/jjbr8gj.
132. Ibid.
133. Karen Clements ("NY City Council Hears Testimonies Against NYPD Stop, Question & Frisk," Examiner.com, October 25, 2012, http://www.examiner.com/article/ny-city-council-hears-testimonies-against-nypd-stop-question-frisk [site discontinued]) notes that the two New York City Council Civil Rights Committee Hearings on the NYPD's Stop and Frisk practices took place on Tuesday, October 23, 2012, in Brooklyn and Wednesday, October 24, 2012, in Queens.
134. Communities United for Police Reform, "NY City Council to Hold Hearing on Community Safety Act," ChangeTheNYPD.org, October 1, 2012, http://tinyurl.com/jv7mlor.

clergy.[135] A February 2013 Declaration of the Interfaith Coalition for Police Reform stated:

> We, the undersigned, as leaders of the faith community, share a commitment to human rights, public safety, and the dignity of every member of our society. Because of these commitments, we feel compelled to speak out against the harsh, ineffective, and unjust Stop-and-Frisk policy, and to call for reform of unfair police practices including quota systems; profiling on the basis of race, gender identity, sexual orientation, and religious identity; and the resulting abusive tactics conducted by the New York City Police Department. We believe that the widespread harassment of already marginalized citizens of our city, especially African-American and Latino young men, immigrant Muslim communities, and the LGBTQ community, is an affront to the sacredness of the spirit within each and every person.[136]

These organizing efforts, and sympathetic official responses, garnered broad support, and consequently gained small successes in redefining Black bodies that were associated with moral pollution. With the number of Stop and Frisks at nearly seven hundred thousand in 2011, the numerous campaigns and coalitions sought to implement multiple strategies for confronting police practices of brutalizing Black bodies and controlling Black spaces.[137] They furthermore shifted public opinion that justified stop and frisk policing. Critical activists humanized impoverished Black New Yorkers: testimonies, documents, sympathetic media stories, and visible protests shifted public fear of the morally polluted Black youth to the aggressive white police officer. In this way, critical activists effectively shifted racialized pollution boundaries: unchecked police officers who stopped and frisked passersby were constructed as threatening, and Black youth were associated with victimhood.

---

135. Police Reform Organizing Project, "Interfaith Coalition," February 21, 2013, http://tinyurl.com/jdurght.
136. Ibid. The statement was signed by Imam Al-Hajj 'Abdur-Rashid, The Mosque of Islamic Brotherhood; Revered Rubén Austria, missionary pastor for the Promised Land Evangelical Covenant Church in the Bronx; Reverend Derrick Boykin, associate minister at Walker Memorial Baptist Church; Reverend Pat Bumgardner, senior pastor of Metropolitan Community Church of New York; Rabbi Jill Jacobs, executive director for T'ruah: The Rabbinic Call for Human Rights; and Dr. Anne Klaeysen, leader of the New York Society for Ethical Culture and Humanist Chaplain at Columbia University and New York University Paul Decoster, lay minister for the United Church of Christ for All Souls Bethlehem Church; Rev. Dr. Edgard Francisco Danielsen-Morales, Assistant Pastor for Congregational Life, Metropolitan Community Church of New York; Katherine Henderson, president of Auburn Theological Seminary; Raquel Irizarry, lay minister for the United Church of Christ for All Souls Bethlehem Church; Rev. Tom Martinez, All Souls Bethlehem Church; Pastor Joseph Tolton, associate pastor, social justice at the Rivers of Rehoboth Church.
137. NYCLU, "Stop-and-Frisk 2011," 3.

At the same time, the strategies employed by critical activists did not lead to mass uprisings. The outrage harnessed in grassroots organizing remained sporadic and isolated, and while New Yorkers broadly participated in occasional rallies and marches, the majority of strategies were confined to the legislative and courtroom spheres. Thus, while the anti-Stop-and-Frisk movement created awareness and drew sympathy, and indeed, successfully redefined police officers as immorally violent, a mass movement that would reconstruct the images of Black people and Black spaces lay dormant. The anti-Stop-and-Frisk movement made important gains in challenging racialized pollution boundaries, but ultimately did not inspire a nationwide confrontation of violent policing and the US penal system.

Conclusion: Bodies, Spaces, and Police Hostility in New York City

Between 1993 and 2013, NYPD officers violently maintained a symbolic line between polluted Black bodies, dangerous spaces, and moral white society. Black youth were stopped and frisked because their very bodies demarcated them as threats to the moral order and expendable in the social body. Indeed, it is not what they *did* but rather the moral pollution represented by their bodies that mattered. The routine operations of NYPD officers appeared so strikingly brutal that they gained the attention of middle class New Yorkers. Furthermore, as they carried out routine operations, NYPD officers garnered nationwide disapproval after executing several unarmed Black men, among them Amadou Diallo, Patrick Dorismond, Sean Bell, and in 2014, Eric Garner.

One year after the *Floyd* trial concluded, the NYPD again found itself in the national spotlight. The police murder of Eric Garner, a forty-three-year-old father of six, was recorded on a cell phone video and immediately went viral. Garner suffered from multiple health problems, including asthma and sleep apnea, both of which impacted his ability to breathe. On July 17, 2014, two NYPD officers approached Garner, who was unemployed and sometimes sold loose cigarettes in front of a convenience store to help make ends meet. The cell phone video recorded by Garner's friend Ramsey Orta depicts two police officers arguing with Garner. A third officer in plainclothes, Daniel Pantaleo, moves behind Garner and puts him in a chokehold, throwing him to the ground. As he is held in the chokehold lying on the ground, Garner says eleven times: "*I can't breathe.*" He falls unconscious. Minutes later, he is dead.

Garner's murder illuminates the link between routine stops and the uncalled for brutality that is central to a hostile police culture. Supervisors as well as rank-and-file officers identify dark bodies as dangerous and morally polluting. The hostility expressed by the NYPD perpetuates the boundaries between people accepted as safe versus those identified as threatening to the social order. Garner was not a physical threat; indeed, he had trouble walking to the corner due to his health problems. Yet, he was a Black man standing in an impoverished community. In defending himself, Garner attempted to challenge the symbolic social boundaries that the police maintain under the threat of violence and death.

Garner's murder occurred *after* the NYPD began scaling back stops. As the NYPD accelerated new strategies under Commissioner Bill Bratton, the number of stops reported by cops fell 97 percent, from a high of 685,700 in 2011 to 22,900 in 2015. Although stops *and* crime rates fell to record lows,[138] Garner's death shows that police aggression and brutality remain the norm in many communities. Indeed, this is the salience of the Movement for Black Lives. Critical activists in New York City protested Garner's murder, but it was not until the execution of Michael Brown on August 9, 2014, in Ferguson, Missouri, that a national movement to make police hostility and violence visible arose. As members of marginalized communities formed the vanguard of a new racial justice movement that drew its inspiration from political prisoners, the Black Panther Party, and the Black radical tradition, the plight of Black New Yorkers became part of a national narrative. No longer was there a clear dichotomy between the Black inner city and the white communities that formed a ring around the urban core. The moral stigma attached to Black bodies and neighborhoods permeated every region of the United States, including the suburbs. In the next chapter, I examine the Black Lives Matter movement and its ongoing challenge to racialized pollution boundaries in US society.

138. The murder count stood at 536 in 2010 and at 352 in 2015. There were 1,471 shooting incidents in 2010 (1,773 victims). By 2015, shootings had dropped to 1,130 (1,339 victims). Editorial, "We Were Wrong: Ending Stop and Frisk Did Not End Stopping Crime," *Daily News*, August 8, 2016, http://tinyurl.com/z7dqnfh.

Brittany Ferrell, co-founder of Millennial Activists United, protests the murder of Michael Brown in Ferguson. Credit: Heather Wilson/PICO Network

Alexis Templeton, Brittany Ferrell, and other protestors confront the police during a nightly stand off. Credit: Heather Wilson/PICO Network

The Rev. Renita Lamkin (left) and protestor march on the streets of Ferguson. Credit: Heather Wilson/PICO Network

People from across Saint Louis take to the streets and protests expand throughout the city in response to an off-duty police officer shooting another young man—Vonderrit Meyer on October 8, 2014. Credit: Heather Wilson/PICO Network

The Rev. Traci Blackmon, senior pastor of Christ the King UCC, leads a protest march. Credit: Lawrence Bryant/St. Louis American

Rev. Osagyefo Sekou, organizer for the Fellowship of Reconciliation (FOR), and fellow clergy protest police killings of black men in Ferguson. Credit: FOR Archives

Dr. Cornel West (left), Rev. Starsky Wilson, pastor of St. John's UCC, and Rahiel Tesfamariam protest on Moral Monday, August 10, 2015. Credit: Wiley Price/St. Louis American

Tory Russell (Hands Up United, front left), Bishop John Selders (Moral Monday CT, left with collar), Rev. Julie Taylor (center), Bree Newsome (with bullhorn), and other Moral Monday protestors march in Ferguson to mark the one-year anniversary of Michael Brown's murder. Credit: Ethan Vesely-Flad/Fellowship of Reconciliation

Dr. Cornel West and the Rev. Osagyefo Sekou climb over police barricades during a 2015 Moral Monday protest. Credit: Heather Wilson/PICO Network

Anthony Grimes, co-founder of the Denver Freedom Riders, speaks out against racism and xenophobia. Credit: Anthony Grimes/Fellowship of Reconciliation

5

———

Confronting Pollution: Protest as the Performance of Purity in the Black Lives Matter Movement

Introduction

In the Black Lives Matter movement (BLM),[1] the criminalized Black body takes center stage. By asserting the importance of skin color in an ostensibly colorblind society, BLM engages constructs of racialized social pollution on multiple fronts. The movement brings historical constructs of Blackness into contemporary consciousness. Organizers challenge universal concepts of rights and dignity by analyzing how those concepts are racialized. Grassroots protestors uplift images of bodies and privilege confrontational street activism that disrupts common practices, such as commuting and shopping. People of all ages create social media conversations that run parallel to mainstream media and interrupt the narratives of corporate media without relying on

1. Following other scholars and activists, I distinguish between #BlackLivesMatter, the hashtag; Black Lives Matter Network, the nationwide, chapter-based organization; and BLM, a decentralized movement consisting of individual activists as well as affiliate organizations that emphasize the importance of Black lives. See Bill Fletcher, "From Hashtag to Strategy: The Growing Pains of Black Lives Matter," *In These Times*, September 23, 2015.

those same outlets. Chapters and individuals operate under decentralized leadership in a process that sometimes causes friction yet consistently advances a narrative about the worth of Black lives. Spokespeople privilege intersectionality and queer identity, insisting that racism needs to be addressed in tandem with sexism, classism, and homophobia. BLM, in a departure from the civil rights movement of the 1950s and '60s, challenges symbolic constructs of racialized social pollution by insisting that multiple identities are simultaneously marginalized and ostracized. Therefore, not only skin color but also disparaging constructs of gender, class, and sexuality must be acknowledged and confronted within and outside of Black communities.

BLM, like recent grassroots movements such as Occupy Wall Street and the Arab Spring, relies on social media as well as street protests to confront racialized constructs of social pollution that are institutionalized in policing forces and prisons, as well as schools, housing, and health care systems. Furthermore, street protestors employ chants and nonviolent direct action while refusing the "respectability politics" of the civil rights movement.[2] The emphasis on "interrupting business as usual" uplifts consciousness raising as a primary goal and liberationist rhetoric that asserts radical social change.

History/Herstory of the Black Lives Matter Movement

On social media in July 2013, #BlackLivesMatter became a rallying cry. A seventeen-year-old Black teenager, Trayvon Martin, was shot to death in Sanford, Florida. A six-person jury subsequently acquitted the killer, George Zimmerman, a twenty-eight-year-old white, Latino man. The acquittal struck a deep chord. From the same city in which Oscar Grant, an eighteen-year-old Black youth, had been killed by a white officer in 2009, Alicia Garza posted an impassioned response to the verdict on her Facebook account:

2. "Respectability politics" refers to a belief in the idea that proper dress and speech will garner respect from officials and will guard against harassment by the police. See Brittney Cooper, "Misconceptions about the Black Lives Matter Movement," *Cosmopolitan*, September 8, 2015. Marc Lamont Hill borrows the term "respectability politics" from Evelyn Brooks Higginbotham to expand his claim. Hill (*Nobody: Casualties of America's War on the Vulnerable, from Ferguson to Flint and Beyond* [New York: Atria, 2016], 28) writes: "[Michael] Brown's story highlights how respectability politics around who deserves public support and protection within the Black community, as well as the expansion of the market-driven punishment state, creates an environment where constitutional affordances like due process and protection from cruel and unusual punishment are reflexively denied to those considered part of the 'criminal class.'" For many observers, Hill writes, the accusation that Brown stole cigarillos compromised his moral authority, and thus he was unworthy of respect.

I continue to be surprised at how little Black lives matter. And I will continue that. Stop giving up on black life . . . black people. I love you. I love us. Our lives matter.[3]

Garza's friend Patrisse Khan-Cullors amended Garza's last three words to "Black Lives Matter." Soon thereafter, a New York City–based immigration-rights organizer, Opal Tometi, created the Facebook and Twitter platform #BlackLivesMatter.

The phrase "Black Lives Matter" did not expand beyond a small circle of activists until a year later, in August 2014, when Michael Brown, an eighteen-year-old resident of Ferguson, Missouri, was shot by a white police officer while walking down a street. Brown lived in Canfield Apartments, subsidized housing units in the small suburb of Ferguson. He had recently graduated from Normandy High School, which had lost accreditation in 2012. He intended to enroll in a local college to study a trade.[4] As Marc Lamont Hill writes in *Nobody: Casualties of America's War on the Vulnerable from Ferguson to Flint and Beyond*, Brown was not a traditional hero.[5] But to residents of Canfield Apartments, Brown mattered.

For activists broadly, Brown's socially marginalized status and violent execution at the hands of a white police officer illuminated enduring institutionalized racism. Officials' rhetoric and policies verified a world view in which Black male bodies represent internal moral pollution. Activists fought against both this symbolic construct and the character assassination conducted after Brown's death. Indeed, the Black Lives Matter movement privileges the people who are outside of "respectability politics," who are marginalized *within* Black communities due to their gender and poverty, as well as their sexuality and gender expression. In short, the Black Lives Matter movement makes visible the dignity of those who are outside of mainstream social norms and economic structures.

Brown's murder occurred on the heels of the killing of Eric Garner, a forty-three-year-old father of six, who was strangled to death on Staten Island by a white police officer on July 17, 2014. Daniel Pantaleo put Garner into a fatal chokehold after Garner sold loose cigarettes out-

3. Quoted in Jelani Cobb, "The Matter of Black Lives," *The New Yorker*, March 14, 2016.
4. Hill, *Nobody*, 1–3. The day on which he was murdered by police officer Darren Wilson, Brown had purportedly stolen cigarillos from a local convenience store in order to use the papers for rolling marijuana blunts. The friend who was with him at the time acknowledged that Brown smoked marijuana.
5. Ibid., 1–3.

side of a convenience store. Activists protesting the murders of Brown and Garner employed the phrase "Black Lives Matter" to emphasize racist policing practices and the brutality embedded in daily interactions between police officers and Black men. Street protests, followed by nationwide outrage in the acquittal of both officers, sparked a racial justice movement that became the longest street protest since the Montgomery Bus Boycott of 1955. Indeed, these mass demonstrations mark the first mass protest of the symbolic construct of the polluted Black body since the civil rights and Black Power movements.

Philosophies and Strategies in the Black Lives Matter Movement

The nationwide, decentralized movement known as Black Lives Matter—with multiple (sometimes competing) ideological frameworks, strategies, structures, and demands—embraces the ideal of an organic, grassroots initiative that springs from the communities that are most directly impacted by disproportionate policing. The different ideological frameworks guiding various actions have roots in historic Black freedom struggles: should Black people, who were denied personhood and rights, seek to influence the state, or should Black people seek alternative mechanisms for self-governance outside of the state?[6] Garza, for example, draws from Black liberation activists such as Assata Shakur and Angela Davis to critique racism, capitalism, sexism, and homophobia as interlocking spheres of oppression within a racist society. Indeed, Garza, as an intellectual descendant of self-identified Black radicals, identifies multiple spheres of social pollution: not only racialized peoples but also those who are marginalized due to class, gender, and sexual identities are uplifted and made visible. It is only through analyses of the origins of racist thinking and institutions, and through disparate yet connected grassroots movements, that communities of color can deconstruct and diminish state power and subsequently govern themselves.

> What we are dealing with right now is a disease that has plagued America since its inception. Convicting a few cops isn't going to deal with that disease. We've been trying hard this year to be clear that state violence is bigger than police terrorism. Although police terrorism plays a specific role on behalf of the state, it is not the totality of what state violence looks like or feels like in our communities. We've been shifting the narrative to talk

6. Keeanga-Yamahtta Taylor references the ideological splits in the Black Lives Matter movement in her book *From #BlackLivesMatter to Black Liberation* (Chicago: Haymarket, 2016), 174.

about state violence being structural racism. Given that, what we are lifting up here is that we need a bigger vision than just Band-Aid reforms—we need to move towards a transformative vision that touches on what's at the root of the problems we are facing.[7]

In a 2015 interview with *The Nation*, Garza explicitly identified a contradiction between insisting on the importance of Black lives and continuing to resource police departments to police in "better" ways.[8] In other words, policing reform and the "unapologetic Blackness" that is central to the Black Lives Matter movement are incompatible.[9] Garza argued that community members must understand the origins of police forces in order to critique contemporary policing practices, for police forces were established to explicitly target racialized, socially threatening dark bodies.

> Right now we have a really harmful set-up where the police police themselves. They act as judge, jury and executioner, usurping democracy. . . . I'm not sure that the way that we can have policing where black lives matter because the institution of policing is rooted in the legacy of catching slaves. But what we can do in the interim is make sure that police departments don't get tax dollars for tanks, for bazookas, for flash grenades and things like that. We can make sure that police departments that have been shown to exercise a pattern and a practice of discriminatory and quite frankly racist policing don't get resources to do that. . . . The other thing we can do immediately is insist on more oversight over police departments—oversight that is accountable to the communities the police purport to serve. What this looks like is civilian review boards that actually have teeth. In the worst cases, review boards are still constructed by the police. People who are not going to raise questions or rock the boat are handpicked to play a role.[10]

Garza identifies movement building as first a transformation in grass-

7. Mychal Denzel Smith, "A Q&A with Alicia Garza: Co-Founder of #BlackLivesMatter," *The Nation*, March 24, 2015.
8. This argument, while not explicitly attributed to Michel Foucault, can be seen in *Discipline and Punish: The Birth of the Prison* (New York: Vintage, 1977), in which Foucault argues that the point of punishment in modernity is to punish in better ways.
9. Smith, "Q&A with Co-Founder Alicia Garza." The phrase "unapologetic Blackness" was coined by the organization Black Youth Project 100. See L'lerret Ailith, "BYP100 in Defense of Black Rage and Black Resistance," Black Youth Project 100, July 8, 2016, http://tinyurl.com/hq7herb.
10. Smith, "Q&A with Co-Founder Alicia Garza." In a 2016 interview with "The Guardian," Garza named practical actions that officials can take, such as "defunding police departments with a track record of violence, introducing a national training standard for officers, and mandating psychiatric testing." See Elle Hunt, "Alicia Garza on the Beauty and the Burdens of Black Lives Matter," The Guardian, September 2, 2016. https://www.theguardian.com/us-news/2016/sep/02/alicia-garza-on-the-beauty-and-the-burden-of-black-lives-matter.

roots consciousness and second, a change in immediate laws and leadership. Her critique of policing, then, follows an ideological stance founded upon critical reflections on historic patterns of racism and commitment to community accountability. The struggle must be fought on ideological, indeed symbolic, terms rather than pragmatic, short-term proposals. She does not, then, propose that police units receive taxpayer dollars to purchase body cameras for police officers.

> When we sit and think about what the world needs to looks like in order for black lives to actually matter, there is a debate: what is going to make our communities safe, how do we deal with harm, how do we solve problems that come up in our communities? . . . The point to me is to be able to dig into these questions as opposed to being prescriptive about what the answers are.[11]

The cofounders of #BlackLivesMatter critique policing; furthermore, they uplift the importance of queer—including transgender and gender nonconforming—identity. Indeed, the cofounders have embraced multiple overlapping socially stigmatized identities and reconstructed the image of the socially polluted body into a socially powerful symbol. They have institutionalized their symbolic approach by creating a decentralized network of twenty-six local chapters throughout the United States that adopt thirteen core principles, initiate actions, and hold events. In *New Yorker* staff writer Jelani Cobb's assessment:

> Garza, Cullors, and Tometi advocate a horizontal ethic of organizing, which favors democratic inclusion at the grassroots level. Black Lives Matter emerged as a modern extension of Ella Baker's thinking—a preference for ten thousand candles rather than a single spotlight. In a way, they created the context and the movement created itself. . . . For Garza, the assurance that black lives matter is as much a reminder directed at black people as it is a revelation aimed at whites. . . . As society at large has devalued black lives, the African-American community is guilty of devaluing lives based on gender and sexuality.[12]

Indeed, the Black Lives Matter Network website, which spells out the three founders' principles for initiating a Black Lives Matter chapter, states that gender identity must be privileged alongside racial identity. Black women must be able to act, free from the sexism, misogyny, and

11. Ibid.
12. Cobb, "The Matter of Black Lives."

male-centeredness that plagued previous racial justice social movements, such as the civil rights movement. Furthermore:

> Black Lives Matter is an ideological and political intervention in a world where Black lives are systematically and intentionally targeted for demise. It is an affirmation of Black folks' contributions to this society, our humanity, and our resilience in the face of deadly oppression. . . . We are committed to embracing and making space for trans brothers and sisters to participate and lead. We are committed to being self-reflexive and doing the work required to dismantle cis-gender privilege and uplift Black trans folk, especially Black trans women who continue to be disproportionately impacted by trans-antagonistic violence.[13]

In short, the #BlackLivesMatter founders critique the historical roots of racism, capitalism, sexism, and gender norms, and argue that pragmatic solutions cannot be enacted upon a rotted base without replicating the decay. Symbolic reconstruction of marginalized persons and practical alternatives to the state are key to movement building.

A number of affiliated organizations and activists nationally advocate for immediate, pragmatic policy solutions to disproportionate policing, even while recognizing that policy can fall short of the social transformation for which Black activists are calling.[14] The Movement for Black Lives policy table, consisting of fifty national racial justice organizations, stated in August 2016:

> We believe in elevating the experiences and leadership of the most marginalized Black people, including but not limited to those who are women, queer, trans, femmes, gender nonconforming, Muslim, formerly and currently incarcerated, cash poor and working class, differently-abled, undocumented, and immigrant. We are intentional about amplifying the particular experience of state and gendered violence that Black queer, trans, gender nonconforming, women and intersex people face. There can be no liberation for all Black people if we do not center and fight for those who have been marginalized. It is our hope that by working together to create and amplify a shared agenda, we can continue to move towards a world in which the full humanity and dignity of all people is recognized.[15]

The symbolic image of the upstanding Black leader, then, is challenged by a new generation of activists who embrace those bodies that have been constructed as polluted even within Black communities. The sig-

---

13. "Guiding Principles," Black Lives Matter, http://tinyurl.com/hdrslsh.
14. Ibid.
15. "Platform," The Movement for Black Lives, http://tinyurl.com/zhmrv5v.

nificance of this approach shatters older generations' adherence to common notions of respectability and morality. Indeed, policy proposals emerge from BLM activists' embrace of rejected, polluted identities within Black communities. The Black Lives Matter Policy Table proposed six overarching transformative changes in a multilayered platform during the Democratic National Convention. It includes:

> 1. End the War on Black People. 2. Reparations. 3. Invest in education, health, and safety of Black people. 4. Economic Justice. 5. Community control. 6. Political power.[16]

Because many affiliate organizations and campaigns operate under the broad umbrella "Black Lives Matter," there is significant disparity in philosophies of social change. Other theories and strategies have arisen, some of which contrast with the #BlackLivesMatter founders' approach. DeRay Mckesson, a high-profile activist who was involved in anti-police-brutality protests in Ferguson after Michael Brown's murder, has run for mayor in Baltimore and has earned public praise from elected leaders such as President Obama. Mckesson and his colleagues Johnetta Elzie, Brittany Packnett, and Sam Sinyangwe have focused on pragmatic solutions rather than ideological tenets to end police brutality. In August 2015, the group founded "Campaign Zero" to propose immediate solutions to disproportionate policing and police killings.

Campaign Zero proposes a series of policy platforms to end aggression by police officers by reforming legislation, as well as community demands, policy recommendations from research organizations, and the President's Task Force on 21st Century Policing.[17] Importantly, the website describing "The Problem" of police violence and "The Solutions" to police violence does not explicitly mention disproportionate policing against Black people. Rather, the founders of Campaign Zero indicate that police violence is fundamentally a result of poor public policies and practices that lead to police brutality. Consequently, Campaign Zero advocates suggest that the problem of police violence is about incompetent training rather than embedded racism in US society. Indeed, the leadership emphasizes the material conditions experienced by disproportionately policed communities. The leadership proposes ten points that incorporate existing laws from various states to "end police violence in America."[18]

16. Ibid.
17. https://www.joincampaignzero.org/solutions/#solutionsoverview.
18. "Vision," Campaign Zero, http://tinyurl.com/hr8ulsk.

The ten points include:

(1) End broken windows policing; (2) Community oversight; (3) Limit use of force; (4) Independently investigate and prosecute; (5) Community representation; (6) Body cameras/film the police; (7) Training; (8) End for-profit policing; (9) Demilitarization; (10) Fair police union contracts.[19]

Campaign Zero advocates, among other tenets, that more Black people should be hired as police officers,[20] that more funds should be available for departments to purchase body cameras, and that officers should receive better training. They suggest, in effect, that policing can be fixed with policy changes and better practices without challenging the image of the polluted Black body in society.

The proposal that police officers wear body cameras is particularly contentious within the broader BLM movement, as many activists fear that increased surveillance will lead to increased data collecting on communities' most vulnerable populations. The Don't Shoot Coalition, consisting of nearly fifty St. Louis area organizations convened in the aftermath of the shooting death of Michael Brown, critiqued a set of policy recommendations put forth by the Ferguson Commission, including the proposal to use body cameras. The Don't Shoot Coalition lobbies for needed policing reforms; similarly to other policy coalitions, it focuses on pragmatic solutions rather than engaging in historical constructs of moral pollution. The Coalition states:

> Body cameras have been touted as a potential solution to concerns about policing in communities of color, but in reality, the implementation involves many complexities, as we see playing out in cities like Los Angeles and Denver. Cameras have the potential to provide documentation that protects the public against police misconduct and also affords accountability for officer actions. However, problem areas that we need policies to address include officer discretion to turn off the cameras, citizens' and especially victims' privacy rights, public and press access to recorded incidents and practices for preserving recordings. In addition, law enforcement will want to consider the impact on police investigative practices and the dangers and benefits of using body camera footage for police supervision and training, among other issues.[21]

19. "Solutions," Campaign Zero, http://tinyurl.com/z64rt9q.
20. The campaign does not address the fact that Black police officers also kill Black people without cause. See the context of Keith Lamont Scott's murder in Charlotte, North Carolina, on September 21, 2016, in which Scott was shot to death by a Black police officer while exiting his vehicle.
21. Denise D. Lieberman and Michael T. McPhearson to Francis Slay, Lewis Reed, and Darlene Green, September 16, 2015, PDF, http://tinyurl.com/jd4eg2j.

While Campaign Zero departs from many allied anti-police-brutality organizations, on other policy matters Campaign Zero is aligned with BLM activist and policy groups. The campaign argues that the profit motive in policing hinders effective policing, and therefore quotas for tickets, fees, and fines that are levied against residents, and revenue gained in the drug war should be abolished. Indeed, the analysis of revenue gained by police officials remains pertinent in Ferguson and surrounding police departments, where a Department of Justice investigative team found that garnering revenue for city coffers drove harsh policing and court practices.[22]

The language of Campaign Zero's policy platform is decidedly race-neutral and aimed at policy makers. However, the founders also established a website, MappingPoliceViolence.org, that is aimed at community activists. It states: "Use this tool to hold Police Chiefs and Mayors accountable for ending police violence in your city."[23] MappingPoliceViolence.org provides geographical and numerical data on killings by police, including the number of Black people killed by police between 2013 and 2016. MappingPoliceViolence.org similarly suggests that police violence against Black people is a result of inept training in certain locales. "Black people are 3x more likely to be killed by police than white people; 30% of black victims were unarmed in 2015, compared to 19% of white victims. *Where you live matters: black people are 7x more likely to be killed by police in Oklahoma than Georgia.*"[24] The founders also argue—as do scholars who study the War on Drugs—that rates of crime do not correlate with police killing people. For example, the founders point out that Newark, New Jersey, with a 52 percent Black population and a murder rate of 40 per 100,000 residents, has not had a murder by police officers since 2013. Conversely, St. Louis, Missouri, with a 47 percent Black population and a slightly lower murder rate (38 per 100,000 residents), saw sixteen Black people shot and killed by St. Louis Metro police between 2013 and August 2016.[25]

Campaign Zero/Mapping Police Violence leaders, then, emphasize that practical solutions in existing institutions can resolve the gross patterns of police violence that result in Black deaths and that trigger

22. United States Department of Justice Civil Rights Division, "Investigation of the Ferguson Police Department," March 4, 2015, PDF, http://tinyurl.com/zhywh7r.
23. "Police Accountability Tool," Mapping Police Violence, accessed August 24, 2016, http://tinyurl.com/gmxcyr9.
24. "Police Violence Map," Mapping Police Violence, accessed August 24, 2016, http://tinyurl.com/j8n74rv.
25. Ibid.

the grievances of BLM activists. The focus on practical solutions led by the state, rather than engagement with the historical roots of symbolic Black pollution, illuminates two divergent ideological approaches in the broader Black Lives Matter movement. At the same time, there is a consistent emphasis on the criminalized Black body as well as on raising consciousness about racism. Two of the founders who use Twitter prolifically to assert a pro-Black message—Mckesson and Elzie—state that the movement is simultaneously focused on solutions and on changing consciousness. Mckesson wrote: "There are people who choose to put their bodies on the line, saying we will physically confront the system, that you know we will no longer be silent with our bodies, but this fight will also be a hearts and minds fight as well, and the power of Twitter is the power of the story."[26]

Mckesson frequently tweets: "I love my blackness, and yours."[27] In an op-ed on the one-year anniversary of Michael Brown's killing, Mckesson wrote:

> I am often asked what it is like to be on the "front line." But I do not use the term "front line" to describe us, the protestors. Because everywhere in America, wherever we are, our blackness puts us in close proximity to police violence. Some of us have chosen a more immediate proximity, as we use our bodies to confront and disrupt corrupt state practices. But every black person is in closer proximity to police violence than we sometimes choose to acknowledge: in many ways, we are all on the "front line"—whether we want to be or not. We did not discover injustice, nor did we invent resistance last August. Being black in America means that we exist in a legacy and tradition of protest, a legacy and tradition as old as this America. And, in many ways, August is the month of our discontent. This August, we remember Mike Brown. But we also remember the Watts Rebellion, and the trauma of Katrina—three distinct periods of resistance prompted or exacerbated by police violence. Resistance, for so many of us, is duty, not choice.[28]

In short, an emphasis on Black bodies roots the work of Campaign Zero/Mapping Police Violence activists, despite their use of race-neutral policy language. Other organizations affiliated with BLM—Ferguson-based organizations, as well as Black Youth Project 100, Cleveland Action, Ohio Student Association, Million Hoodies Movement for

26. Brent McDonald and John Woo, "They Helped Make Twitter Matter in Ferguson Protests," *The New York Times*, August 10, 2015.
27. Ibid.
28. DeRay Mckesson, "Ferguson and Beyond: How a New Civil Rights Movement Began—and Won't End," *The Guardian*, August 9, 2015.

Justice, Project South, Southerners on New Ground—advocate an inter-sectional approach to promoting Black identity. The broad grassroots struggle against pollution boundaries includes not only people marginalized due to Blackness but also those bodies that are deemed morally polluted due to their class, gender, and sexuality.

Strategically, Black Lives Matter activists are united in some pragmatic approaches: they advocate for civilian oversight of police unions and resist racist oppression by using social media and engaging in mass street protests. In short, they employ similar strategies in the struggle against racialized, gendered, and sexual pollution boundaries. When female activists nationwide pointed out that Black men had become the focal point in the movement to combat police brutality, organizers created the hashtag #SayHerName and mobilized around Sandra Bland, Rekia Boyd, and violence against Black transgender women.[29] They effectively used social media, including Facebook, Twitter, and Tumblr, to focus on gender-based violence in the war against Black people.

Ferguson: From Social Media to Street Protest

The killing of Michael Brown on August 9, 2014, was the proverbial spark that lit the powder keg of outrage felt by Black youth who were systemically marginalized and brutalized in the routine practices of police, municipal courts, and local jail officials. The Department of Justice report on Ferguson, released in March 2015, found that the city of Ferguson sought to generate revenue rather than promote public safety. Police officers violated the First and Fourth Amendments of the Constitution, while supervisors encouraged unconstitutional stops, frisks, tickets, warrants, and arrests. Excessive force and persistent racial bias on the part of police officers and city officials resulted in a pattern of daily oppression for residents of Ferguson. Furthermore:

> [The DOJ] investigation has uncovered substantial evidence that the court's procedures are constitutionally deficient and function to impede a person's ability to challenge or resolve a municipal charge, resulting in unnecessarily prolonged cases and an increased likelihood of running afoul of court requirements. At the same time, the court imposes severe penalties when a defendant fails to meet court requirements, including added fines and fees and arrest warrants that are unnecessary and run

29. Rahiel Tesfamariam, "Why the Modern Civil Rights Movement Keeps Religious Leaders at Arm's Length," *The Washington Post*, September 18, 2015.

counter to public safety. These practices both reflect and reinforce an approach to law enforcement in Ferguson that violates the Constitution and undermines police legitimacy and community trust.[30]

Not only were court procedures deficient and exploitative, but routine policing practices unjustly harmed residents. Anecdotal evidence sheds light on patterns of abuse. A police officer accused a Black man, who was sitting in a parked car after a basketball game, of pedophilia and charged him with eight counts of violating Ferguson's municipal code. In yet another situation, police officers viciously addressed a man who was attempting to assist a loved one:

> In one instance from May 2014, for example, a man rushed to the scene of a car accident involving his girlfriend, who was badly injured and bleeding profusely when he arrived. He approached and tried to calm her. When officers arrived they treated him rudely, according to the man, telling him to move away from his girlfriend, which he did not want to do. They then immediately proceeded to handcuff and arrest him, which, officers assert, he resisted. EMS and other officers were not on the scene during this arrest, so the accident victim remained unattended, bleeding from her injuries, while officers were arresting the boyfriend. Officers charged the man with five municipal code violations (Resisting Arrest, Disorderly Conduct, Assault on an Officer, Obstructing Government Operations, and Failure to Comply) and had his vehicle towed and impounded.[31]

In another incident, police officers charged a Black woman who had parked her car illegally in 2007 with two citations and a $151 fine plus fees. The court subsequently charged her with seven Failure to Appear offenses, each of which imposed new fines and fees, totaling more than $1,000.[32]

The Department of Justice Report on Ferguson further describes how officers disproportionately used excessive force—including electronic control weapons, stun guns, and dogs—against Black Ferguson residents.

> Statistical analysis shows that African Americans are more likely to be searched but less likely to have contraband found on them; more likely to receive a citation following a stop and more likely to receive multiple citations at once; more likely to be arrested; more likely to have force used

30. United States Department of Justice Civil Rights Division, "Investigation of the Ferguson Police Department," March 4, 2015, PDF, p. 42, http://tinyurl.com/zhywh7r.
31. Ibid., 81–82.
32. Ibid., 4.

against them; more likely to have their case last longer and require more encounters with the municipal court; more likely to have an arrest warrant issued against them by the municipal court; and more likely to be arrested solely on the basis of an outstanding warrant.[33]

Residents of Ferguson were constructed as morally polluted, and were targeted, harassed, and exploited by city officials. Furthermore, residents of Ferguson were not alone in suffering a city administration that focused on generating revenue at their expense. Indeed, the practice is pervasive in St. Louis County. Keeanga-Yamahtta Taylor, in her text *From #BlackLivesMatter to Black Liberation*, states:

> According to a report from Better Together, a nonprofit group, Ferguson does not even rank among the top twenty municipalities in St. Louis County that rely on fees and fines as the central source of their operating budgets. The small city of Edmundson, five miles away, brings in nearly $600 a year for every resident in court fines, more than six times the amount in Ferguson. In the nearby town of Bel-Ridge, a traffic light was rigged so that police could change it as people entered the intersection, boosting their city budget by 16 percent.[34]

It was in Ferguson, however, that young people rose up and resisted the racialized pollution boundaries that were most fully expressed in the contemptuous approaches of white police officers toward Black residents and in unrelenting municipal court practices. The St. Louis-based Organization for Black Struggle (OBS), which has mentored Black youth activists, is one of numerous activist organizations and collec-

33. Ibid., 71. "African Americans experience disparate impact in nearly every aspect of Ferguson's law enforcement system. Despite making up 67% of the population, African Americans accounted for 85% of FPD's traffic stops, 90% of FPD's citations, and 93% of FPD's arrests from 2012 to 2014. Other statistical disparities, set forth in detail below, show that in Ferguson: African Americans are 2.07 times more likely to be searched during a vehicular stop but are 26% less likely to have contraband found on them during a search. They are 2.00 times more likely to receive a citation and 2.37 times more likely to be arrested following a vehicular stop. African Americans have force used against them at disproportionately high rates, accounting for 88% of all cases from 2010 to August 2014 in which an FPD officer reported using force. In all 14 uses of force involving a canine bite for which we have information about the race of the person bitten, the person was African American. African Americans are more likely to receive multiple citations during a single incident, receiving four or more citations on 73 occasions between October 2012 and July 2014, whereas non-African Americans received four or more citations only twice during that period. African Americans account for 95% of Manner of Walking charges; 94% of all Fail to Comply charges; 92% of all Resisting Arrest charges; 92% of all Peace Disturbance charges; and 89% of all Failure to Obey charges. African Americans are 68% less likely than others to have their cases dismissed by the Municipal Judge, and in 2013 African Americans accounted for 92% of cases in which an arrest warrant was issued. African Americans account for 96% of known arrests made exclusively because of an outstanding municipal warrant." See pp. 62-63.

34. Taylor, *From #BlackLivesMatter*, 127.

tives that have called for resistance, accountability, and new leadership. These organized groups include Hands Up United, The Lost Voices, Millennial Activists United, Tribe X, Ferguson Action, Ground Level Support, and the Don't Shoot Coalition.[35]

For these protestors, social media has facilitated immediate organizing against police brutality. Twitter, Facebook, Tumblr, Instagram, and YouTube are strategic implements to shift symbolic boundaries of racialized social pollution: outrage at police violence, alongside new constructs, narratives, and images of Black people are posted, discussed, and confronted in a virtual world. Provocative images and videos of police violence are viewed instantly, inciting outraged responses and mass mobilization.[36]

The #BlackLivesMatter hashtag set the stage for grassroots movement building but was not in widespread use until July 2015. A 2016 media analysis report, *Beyond the Hashtags*, concluded that #BlackLivesMatter was used only forty-eight times in June 2014 and in 398 tweets in July 2014. Indeed, #BlackLivesMatter did not become a popular hashtag until August 9, 2014, when Michael Brown was killed by Darren Wilson. After Brown's murder, the number of #BlackLivesMatter tweets skyrocketed to 52,288.[37] Newly created hashtags, such as #Ferguson and #HandsUpDontShoot, quickly appeared. Anthropologists Yarimar Bonilla and Jonathan Rosa note that "during the initial week of [Ferguson] protests, over 3.6 million posts appeared on Twitter documenting and reflecting on the emerging details surrounding Michael Brown's death; by the end of the month, '#Ferguson' had appeared more than eight million times on the Twitter platform."[38] The Black Lives Matter hashtag and other Ferguson-related hashtags became a popular rallying cry against the hostile, routine practices that associated exploited Black bodies with pollution.

Indeed, Twitter emerged as an effective tool to challenge racialized constructs of moral pollution and racialized pollution boundaries.[39] As

---

35. http://www.handsupunited.org; http://www.thelostvoices.org; http://fundersforjustice.org/mil lennial-activists-united/; https://www.facebook.com/TribeX.STL/posts/334215746755808; http://fergusonaction.com; https://twitter.com/gls_ferguson?lang=en; https://www.facebook.com/dontshootstl/.

36. Bijan Stephen, "Social Media Helps Black Lives Matter Fight the Power," *Wired*, October 2015.

37. Deen Freelon, Charlton D. McIlwain, and Meredith Clark, *Beyond the Hashtags: #Ferguson, #Black-LivesMatter, and the Online Struggle for Offline Justice*, Center for Media and Social Impact, American University, February 2016, PDF, p. 9, http://tinyurl.com/zqz9yrk.

38. Yarimar Bonilla and Jonathan Rosa, "#Ferguson: Digital Protest, Hashtag Ethnography, and the Racial Politics of Social Media in the United States," *American Ethnologist* 42, no. 1 (January 2015): 1–2.

39. The "Beyond the Hastags" report, as well as Bonilla and Rosa's "#Ferguson," provide qualitative

in the days after the execution of Michael Brown, Twitter use escalated after the non-indictment of Darren Wilson on November 25, 2014. Within a few hours of the grand jury's decision, more than 3.5 million tweets appeared under the hashtag #FergusonDecision.[40] The social media communities collectively known as "Black Twitter" have allowed users nationally to participate in a racial justice conversation outside of mainstream venues and thus to combat racialized constructs of polluted Black bodies. *Beyond the Hashtags* authors found that social media posts by activists were essential for drawing attention to Michael Brown's story, in large part because protestors could critique police murders without relying on corporate media. While some conservatives denounced the protests on social media, the vast majority of posts uplifted the BLM narrative of unjust police violence against Black people.[41] Twitter educated people, drew attention to racist constructs of sexualized Black bodies—including transgender women—and provided a platform to advocate for institutionalized police reforms.

Social media scholars argue that social media uniquely benefits communities associated with pollution, and even social media that is deemed disembodied activism provides a space for activists to contest images of polluted Black bodies.[42]

> #Ferguson did what many of these other tools [such as transistor radios and email] did: It allowed a message to get out, called global attention to a small corner of the world, and attempted to bring visibility and accountability to repressive forces. . . . The use of hashtags such as #Hands UpDontShoot, #IfTheyGunnedMeDown, and #NoAngel speak to the long history of inaccurate and unfair portrayal of African Americans within mainstream media and to the systematic profiling and victim blaming suffered by racialized bodies.[43]

Although it exists in a virtual, seemingly disembodied sphere, social

---

and quantitative data to support this claim. The percentage of people of African descent who use Twitter (22 percent) is much higher than that of white users in the United States (16 percent). Bonilla and Rosa, 6. Furthermore, Bonilla and Rosa state that "the news surrounding Michael Brown's death dominated Twitter much more than Facebook. Facebook moved too slowly for the eventfulness of Ferguson. For the denizens of #Ferguson, the posts on Facebook were "yesterday's news—always already superseded by the latest round of tweets." See ibid., 8.

40. Ibid., 11. See also Alexandra Olteanu, Ingmar Weber, and Daniel Garcia-Perez, "Characterizing the Demographics Behind the #BlackLivesMatter Movement," Cornell University, December 17, 2015, http://arxiv.org/abs/1512.05671.

41. Freelon, McIlwain, and Clark, *Beyond the Hashtags*, 5. The report found that "black youth discussed police brutality frequently on Twitter, but in ways that differed substantially from how activists discussed it." Ibid.

42. Ibid., 8.

43. Bonilla and Rosa, "#Ferguson," 7, 9.

media has become a site for reenvisioning, revaluing, and reconstructing the image of the polluted Black body. Social media users post texts as well as images to contest images of Black moral corruption. Bonilla and Rosa describe the pushback against descriptions of Michael Brown as a "criminal" and "thug." Following an article in the *New York Times* that described Brown as "no angel," social media users created a #NoAngel hashtag and refuted the suggestion that only well-behaved teenagers deserved to be treated fairly by police officers. One person tweeted, "I am #NoAngel, so I guess I deserve to be murdered too. Yep, perfectly acceptable to gun down a person if they aren't a Saint."[44]

Indeed, it is in this process of creating new, confrontational symbols that BLM activists push against boundaries of racialized social pollution and create narratives that strategically contest constructed interpretations of Black criminality. Like Twitter, Facebook offers a digital space in which users can reconstruct the image of the polluted Black body.

After Trayvon Martin was killed in 2012, activists used Facebook images to protest his murder. Thousands of activists posted photographs of themselves wearing sweatshirts with hoods and holding cans of soda and bags of Skittles. The embodied act of donning a hoodie—a racialized symbol when connected to a Black body—pushed against symbolic boundaries of social pollution. Bonilla and Rosa argue: "Hoodies are only signs of criminal behavior when they are contextualized in relation to particular racialized bodies."[45] Similarly, holding candy and soda—items that George Zimmerman construed as weapons—became a symbolic act of resistance to the pervasive constructs of Black criminalization.

White BLM activists have used their bodies creatively to confront racialized social pollution. In one instance, a group of white Lutheran clergy submitted photos of themselves to a Florida police department when the #UseMeInstead social media campaign took off in January 2015.[46] These mostly white clergy wore collars and vestments in the submitted photos; in so doing, they announced that they, too, should be considered threatening to the mainstream social structure.

Social media activism has effectively pushed against racialized boundaries of social pollution in large part due to its seamless interac-

---

44. Ibid., 9.
45. Ibid., 8.
46. Leah Gunning Francis, *Ferguson and Faith: Sparking Leadership and Awakening Community* (St. Louis: Chalice, 2015), 159.

tion with street and campus protests. While some activists have begun to bemoan the shortcomings of platforms such as Twitter—which they argue can replace embodied activism[47]—many protestors engage in both social media and street marches. Demonstrators held up their hands to mimic Brown, after eyewitnesses stated that he held his hands in the air moments before he was killed. On November 30, 2014, five African American St. Louis Rams players ran out onto the football field with their hands up in the air, indicating their solidarity with the BLM movement. To protest the non-indictment of Wilson, throughout the country protestors held "die ins" for four-and-a-half minutes to symbolize the four-and-a-half hours that Michael Brown lay in the middle of the street in Ferguson. These actions pushed against racialized social boundaries by referencing, adopting, and refuting the constructed threat of the polluted Black body.

Confronting Boundaries of Pollution: Street and Campus Activism

On the night after Michael Brown's murder, protestors took to the streets.[48] It was August 10, 2014. They held a vigil in front of the Ferguson Police Department to demand that the officer who shot Michael Brown be fired and held accountable for murder.[49] The demonstration escalated when some protestors smashed cars and looted local stores. The following day, the FBI opened an investigation into Michael Brown's killing; that evening, riot police fired tear gas and rubber bullets at the protestors. The street challenge to constructs of the polluted Black body and racist police hostility turned violent as armed guards with militarized weapons and vehicles met demonstrators.[50]

Four days later, on August 15, the police released a video purporting to show Michael Brown stealing cigars from a local convenience store on the morning of his murder.[51] Police officials constructed Brown as a polluted Black body, a common criminal, thus justifying his murder

47. Kate Aronoff, Q&A with Elijah Armstrong, "Inside the Dream Defenders' Social Media Blackout," *Waging Nonviolence*, September 30, 2015. The Dream Defenders did not use social media for three months. Armstrong states: "After a while, it seems like social media can overshadow the work that's being done on the ground because it's not uplifted in the same light or held in the same regard. The on-the-ground work is the most important work we do, and we got caught up a little bit in social media. For the most part, though, I think we've done a good job of connecting the work that we do on social media to our base, and we make sure that it's staying in line with that."

48. http://stlouis.cbslocal.com/2014/08/12/timeline-the-death-of-michael-brown-and-unrest-in-ferguson/.

49. http://www.voanews.com/a/michael-brown-shooting/2530351.html?layout=1.

50. Ibid.

by suggesting that, as a hoodlum, he deserved to be killed. It was not Brown's action of stealing cigarillos, however, that attracted Darren Wilson's attention—Wilson did not connect Brown to the theft[52]—but rather, it was Brown as a young Black man, walking down the street: a symbol of the polluted Black body. Protestors interpreted the release of the video as character assassination of Brown: the criminalization of a polluted Black male body.[53] The protestors' increased anger led to heightened clashes with the police. On August 16, the Missouri governor declared a state of emergency and imposed a curfew on Ferguson. On August 18, the National Guard arrived with tanks and machine guns to quell the "enemy forces" and "adversaries."[54] Protestors encountered "MRAPS, LRADs, full body armor, assault weapons, grenade launchers and a complement of other military toys from the Pentagon's 1033 program."[55]

The Ferguson uprising shifted the assertion that Black Lives Matter from a social media conversation to a nationwide social movement. Previous street protests to contest disproportionate police brutality against Black people had occurred. An anti-Stop-and-Frisk coalition had led marches and trainings, proposed legislation, and sued the city of New York for police brutality against Latino and Black residents (see chapter 4). In the wake of the acquittal of George Zimmerman's killing of Trayvon Martin, the Dream Defenders camped in protest for thirty-one days in the office of Governor Rick Scott. The majority-Black organization embodied protest in the state of Florida.

After Michael Brown was killed in August 2014, a street movement erupted in Ferguson. Night after night, protestors put their bodies on the street. Clergy held vigils and prayed publicly. While the polluted Black body was constructed as lazy or violent, the nonviolent demonstrations offered new images of Blackness. Police officers responded with tear gas, billy clubs, and rubber bullets. The protestors remained. Police officers repeatedly pointed guns at protestors and journalists and charged at them.[56] They wore full SWAT gear and drove heavily

51. http://www.usatoday.com/story/news/usanow/2014/08/15/ferguson-missouri-police-michael-brown-shooting/14098369/.
52. http://www.dailykos.com/story/2014/10/28/1339820/-What-Mike-Brown-did-and-did-not-do-inside-of-the-Ferguson-convenience-store.
53. Bonilla and Rosa, 6.
54. See Barbara Starr and Wesley Bruer, "Missouri National Guard's Term for Ferguson Protesters: 'Enemy Forces,'" *CNN Politics*, April 17, 2015, http://tinyurl.com/jlvahmv.
55. Jamala Rogers, *Ferguson is America: Roots of Rebellion* (St. Louis: Mira Digital Publishing, 2015), Kindle location 1742–43.
56. https://www.nytimes.com/2014/08/19/us/ferguson-missouri-protests.html; http://www.newsweek.com/journalists-arrested-assaulted-and-teargassed-ferguson-264610. Riot police aimed

militarized vehicles. The protestors held their ground and refused to disperse: they asserted new boundaries between pollution and purity by asserting rectitude and honor.

Protestors demonstrated in front of the Ferguson police station every night for more than a year. In the wake of Darren Wilson's grand jury acquittal on November 25, 2014, activists heightened their nightly protests outside of the Ferguson police station and nationwide.[57] During the day, they disrupted traffic and shopping in urban and suburban areas:[58] there could be no business as usual while Black bodies were criminalized, constructed as polluted, and exploited for municipal gain. The protestors performed sit-ins and die-ins, and occupied police stations: they used their bodies to challenge public spaces in which they were expected to be deferential, passive, and intimidated. Rather, the protestors asserted a new public authority. *"Whose Streets? Our Streets!"* They were arrested and charged with crimes. Still, their Black bodies protested and claimed public space that had once been racialized as white.

The street protests spread to college campuses.[59] Students demonstrated in public spaces such as libraries and cafeterias. They disrupted public events. They employed social media and physical protests simultaneously, sharing images, videos, and strategies as they put their bodies in visible spaces. By challenging ostensibly neutral spaces, these students illuminated the history of racism in institutions of higher education and the contemporary contexts of white power in classrooms and administrations. In so doing, they challenged racialized pollution boundaries in elite settings.

Student activism on college campuses expanded to include demands on senior administrators: to hire more faculty of color, to teach the perspectives of socially marginalized people in the classroom, and to recognize micro- and macroaggressions against students and faculty of color.[60] They reconstructed the polluted Black body and asserted the

guns at credentialed journalists as well as protestors who were on the ground with their hands in the air.

57. https://www.nytimes.com/2014/11/25/us/ferguson-darren-wilson-shooting-michael-brown-grand-jury.html.

58. https://www.rt.com/usa/208887-thousands-protest-decision-ferguson/.

59. http://www.truth-out.org/news/item/36135-student-protest-the-black-lives-matter-movement-and-the-rise-of-the-corporate-university.

60. http://www.courant.com/education/hc-yale-racial-protest-1110-20151109-story.html; "The Africana student community of Oberlin College to the Oberlin College board of trustees, Marvin Krislov, Eric Estes and all other appropriate governing bodies of Oberlin College," January 2016, petition, http://tinyurl.com/j8ar2nu. As a result of their attempts to push social boundaries, students of color experienced attacks from white students. See "USC Upstate Student Demands

importance of placing Black voices in positions of authority. Students put forth analyses and made explicit demands. Students at Oberlin College wrote in January 2016:

> Oberlin College and Conservatory is an unethical institution. . . . In the 1830s, this school claimed a legacy of supporting its Black students. However, that legacy has amounted to nothing more than a public relations campaign initiated to benefit the image of the institution and not the Africana people it was set out for. Along the same lines stated by UNC Chapel Hill students in their 2015 document "A Collective Response to Anti-Blackness," you include Black and other students of color in the institution and mark them with the words "equity, inclusion, and diversity," when in fact this institution functions on the premises of imperialism, white supremacy, capitalism, ableism, and a cissexist heteropatriarchy.[61]

Among its demands for systemic change, the documents' authors called for an increase in Black students of African descent, an increase in Black administrators and faculty, safe spaces for Black students, changes to hegemonic curricula, and an end to gentrification and institutional complacency.[62]

Challenges to the polluted Black body reverberated during the 2016 Democratic primaries as well. Young activists demanded recognition of systemic racism from the Democratic Party elite.[63] BLM activists confronted Bernie Sanders publicly and attempted to disrupt Hillary Clinton events.[64] At the same time, when the Democratic Party endorsed the BLM platform, movement leadership explicitly rejected the approval.[65] They argued that social change could occur only by consciousness raising, mass demonstrations, and community accountability—not by representational politics, elite leadership, and elected figureheads.

Indeed, for BLM protestors, "militant, direct action, nonviolent protest" that did not ask for acceptance or a place at the table but rather demanded accountability and community leadership, shaped a

Change after Black Lives Matter Posters Damaged," *Fox Carolina*, December 17, 2015, http://tinyurl.com/j8uynbr.

61. "The Africana student community of Oberlin College to the Oberlin College board of trustees."
62. Ibid.
63. Bill Fletcher, "From Hashtag to Strategy."
64. http://www.mintpressnews.com/clinton-campaign-shuts-down-black-lives-matter-protest/208592/.
65. http://www.huffingtonpost.com/entry/black-lives-matter-dnc_us_55e48104e4b0c818f6188cab; http://thehill.com/blogs/ballot-box/presidential-races/252303-black-lives-matter-rejects-show-of-support-from-the-dnc; http://www.mediaite.com/online/blacklivesmatter-rejects-dnc-resolution-of-support/.

nationwide activist approach. Protestors sought to put Black bodies in public spaces to challenge racialized geographical boundaries. The practice of bodily protest started to shift notions of who belonged in the street—pure, white, unthreatening bodies—and who did not—criminalized Black people such as Michael Brown. Social media abetted the Ferguson uprising and consequent demonstrations, but the protestors' use of their dark bodies to claim the street, to resist dispersion even in the face of militarized vehicles, tear gas, and rubber bullets, was essential for initiating a shift in historically racialized pollution boundaries. With their dark bodies, the protestors confronted agents of state violence, held the line, and claimed public space. Their refusal to flee in the threat of state violence pushed forward powerful images of Black bodily defiance, resistance, and resurrection.

Conclusion

The Black Lives Matter movement challenges pollution boundaries on multiple levels: not only do protestors reconstruct the image of the polluted Black body, they also address the construct of immorality in gendered and sexualized bodies. Demonstrators employ a range of strategies and tactics to shift pollution boundaries: the use of social media and the engagement of street protests have placed the reconstructed symbol of the Black body at center stage. Regardless of identity or circumstances, the Black body is worthy of protection from state violence.

Indeed, BLM protestors have disrupted unquestioned notions of colorblindness and universal rights by stating unequivocally that Black people are oppressed and by asserting unapologetically that Black lives are worthy of protection, fairness, and economic well-being. In a racialized society that has historically and systemically denied Black people opportunities for fair-wage employment, decent housing, quality education, and equal treatment under the law, the Black Lives Matter movement is redrawing the lines of racial pollution. In this movement, white government officials and police officers that sustain racist practices have assumed the taint association with pollution. The protestors have become associated with purity, clarity, stamina, dedication, and a sustained call to justice.

6

———

Seeing Jesus in Michael Brown: New Theological Constructions of Blackness

Introduction

Members of the clergy and the Black church have been largely peripheral to the Black Lives Matter (BLM) movement. However, a few prominent activists self-identify as Christian, and several liberationist clergy have been at the forefront of the Ferguson protests. Sermons by and interviews with these liberationist clergy offer an important reconstruction of Blackness and, consequently, an important challenge within the broader BLM movement. A Christian narrative that inverts traditional notions of power reinforces rather than contradicts the central assertion of the Black Lives Matter movement.

Clergymembers offer important symbolic reconstructions of Blackness: they challenge historical images of Blackness as physical representations of inner immorality and pollution. For clergy in the BLM movement, the criminalized body of Michael Brown and the crucified body of Jesus convey a theological assertion: criminalized Black youth, who are associated with moral pollution, are crucified as Jesus was two thousand years ago. Furthermore, as followers of Jesus, clergypersons are called to challenge racial injustice. Several clergypersons in the St.

Louis area identify Michael Brown as Jesus of Nazareth: born in desperate conditions, living among oppressed peoples, crucified by state violence, and resurrected in the Social Gospel.

Generational Differences between Clergy and Young Activists

In their theological reconstructions of Blackness, liberationist clergy have adopted elder roles in a movement primarily led by young activists. While not every supportive minister has been welcomed—Black, male ministers who are deemed opportunistic, such as Al Sharpton, have been publicly booed by activists who state, "This ain't yo mama's civil rights movement"[1]—BLM activists embrace liberationist clergy whose theology challenges images of Black criminalization and, thus, enduring pollution boundaries.

The BLM movement differs starkly from the civil rights movement of the 1950s and '60s.

> The front lines of the fight for civil rights are no longer "manned" by the traditional leaders of the black community: well-dressed, respectable clergymen. From Emmanuel AME Church's historic fight against slavery in Charleston, S.C. to the Rev. Martin Luther King's leadership in the 1960s, the church was the control center in black America's struggle for civil rights for generations. Its authority infused the civil rights movement with traditional values—hierarchical leadership, respectability politics and the guiding principles of reconciliation and nonviolence. Today's movement has dismissed these criteria, operating without centralized leadership and accepting as many straight women and LGBTQ people on the frontlines as straight men.[2]

Indeed, many Black, male clergy take a strong stance against LGBTQ rights and thus reject the leadership of a street movement led by self-identified queer young people. Thus, while many Black clergy push against racialized pollution boundaries, these same leaders adhere to sexualized pollution boundaries, thus perpetuating a generational divide. BLM activists' queer-friendly, non-Christian political commitments have led many clergy in the St. Louis region to shun the protests in Ferguson. Reverend Traci Blackmon, a United Church of Christ pastor in a suburb adjoined to Ferguson, acknowledges that Black

1. "Tef Poe - War Cry (2014)," YouTube video, 4:57, posted by "postmeback," January 11, 2015, http://tinyurl.com/z57u92g. See also Rahiel Tesfamariam, "Why the Modern Civil Rights Movement Keeps Religious Leaders at Arm's Length," *The Washington Post*, September 18, 2015.
2. Tesfamariam, "Modern Civil Rights Movement."

churches in the St. Louis region tend to be conservative and that the majority of social justice–oriented pastors are white.

The phenomenon of generational tensions between youth and Black clergy is broader than the St. Louis region. Black church leaders nationally accept the hierarchical leadership and the "respectability politics" integral to mainstream institutions, both of which BLM activists have staunchly rejected. Black clergy are often focused on fostering institutional involvement in longstanding civil rights organizations such as the NAACP. Many clergy believe that incremental legal challenges, such as court case rulings, are an effective strategy for social change. Furthermore, rising through traditional institutional mechanisms, such as graduating from high school, getting a college degree, and finding a stable job, are seen as mitigating the corrosive effects of racism. For many middle-class Black clergy, people of African descent should seek to be included within the boundaries of mainstream society rather than accept the label of ostracized and rejected outcast. Thus, Black clergy members are often seen as adopting the status quo: the pollution boundaries that perpetuate racism, classism, and homophobia.

In short, many of the clergy in the St. Louis region resist following youth leadership due to generational and ideological differences.[3] Activist BLM leaders have rejected an incremental, organizational approach that upholds racialized pollution boundaries in US society. BLM activists resist the social norms that deem their very identities—young, Black, queer, impoverished—as threats to the church and to the social order.

Even as there exist generational, philosophical, theological, and strategic divides, Black liberationist churches and liberal white churches have served important purposes: Family members of Black youth who are killed by police officers have been affiliated with prominent clergy and the church. The family members of Trayvon Martin, Michael Brown, Eric Garner, and other victims of police brutality have held prayer meetings and services in churches, and have responded to overtures from clerical leadership. Furthermore, several BLM activists have incorporated liberation theology into their protests: Brittany Packnett of Campaign Zero/Mapping Police Violence regularly tweets Scripture. Bree Newsome, who took down the flag in the South Carolina state capitol after nine Black church members were killed by a white supremacist, publicly self-identifies as Christian and acknowl-

3. Interview with Reverend Osagyefo Sekou, nondenominational pastor and former field organizer with the Fellowship of Reconciliation, January 2015.

edges that she quoted Scripture from the Hebrew Bible as she transgressed state laws. Asked to explain her theological justification for taking down the flag, Newsome stated that she envisioned herself as David defeating Goliath in the name of God.[4] Marissa Johnson, who interrupted presidential candidate Bernie Sanders on stage in Seattle during the Democratic primaries, self-identifies as an evangelical Christian.[5]

Black Liberation Theology and the Black Lives Matter Movement

Indeed, for a handful of prominent BLM activists, Black liberation theology inspires and sustains confrontational activism. James H. Cone, the founder of Black liberation theology, writes: "Living in a world of white oppressors, blacks have no time for a neutral God. The brutalities are too great and the pain too severe."[6] God intends for the liberation and freedom of individual minds and oppressed communities, thus Black people must be allowed to live in social conditions that foster freedom of body, mind, and heart. Cone elaborates:

> The black theologian must reject any conception of God which stifles black self-determination by picturing God as a God of all peoples. Either God is identified with the oppressed to the point that their experience becomes God's experience, or God is a God of racism. . . . The blackness of God means that God has made the oppressed condition God's own condition. This is the essence of the Biblical revelation. By electing Israelite slaves as the people of God and by becoming the Oppressed One in Jesus Christ, the human race is made to understand that God is known where human beings experience humiliation and suffering. . . . Liberation is not an afterthought, but the very essence of divine activity.[7]

In the contemporary United States, liberationist clergy argue, Jesus of Nazareth chose "the least of these": impoverished, unemployed, queer, Black youth. This interpretation of Jesus is central to Black liberation theology, which draws both from the Black nationalism of Malcolm X and the liberal Christian theology of Martin Luther King Jr. Black nationalism emphasizes Black pride, dignity, self-determination, and

4. https://www.democracynow.org/2015/7/2/exclusive_extended_interview_with_bree_newsome.
5. Nina Shapiro, "Marissa Johnson Part of a New, Disruptive Generation of Activists," *The Seattle Times*, August 15, 2015.
6. James H. Cone, *A Black Theology of Liberation* (Maryknoll, NY: Orbis, 1970), 63–64.
7. Ibid.

beauty. King's theological approach to the Bible emphasized the God-given humanity of all people, especially the poor and dispossessed.

The aspiration to spiritual freedom requires acknowledgement of the desperate social conditions that many Black people navigate on a daily basis. Historical and contemporary contexts of slavery, Jim Crow segregation, housing segregation, school segregation, job and wage discrimination, racial profiling, and disproportionate policing practices that result in heavy fines and incarceration have resulted in trauma. Generational poverty, familial instability, violence, and subjugation to a violent penal system regulate the movements of Black people. Jamala Rogers, in her 2015 book *Ferguson Is America: Roots of Rebellion*, describes the economic context that fueled the August 2014 uprising:

> St. Louis' 20 percentage point gap between the unemployment rate of African Americans and white Americans is the largest of any city in America, according to the Census. Black poverty is viewed as part of state violence and it's no coincidence that black workers have taken to the street in support of black life.[8]

Thus, Black liberation theology seeks to illuminate the full thrust of institutional and cultural racism while advocating for the intellectual and spiritual potential of Black people. Young activists and clergy embrace the tenets of liberation theology and the model of Jesus of Nazareth as a poor Jew who challenged pollution boundaries in his day: he healed the sick and demon possessed, dined with outcasts, called women into his circle of disciples, and challenged authority figures. Furthermore, Jesus of Nazareth as the Christ embodied God, chose to suffer, and willingly challenged oppression. Jesus was oppressed; he took the side of the oppressed.

Leah Gunning Francis, author of *Ferguson and Faith*, asserts: "For these clergy, to stand with the oppressed is to stand with God; to correct injustices in the world . . . is to work with God."[9] Many of the clergy in Ferguson believe that to be human is to be created in the image of God, and whenever one's humanity is distorted or discounted, it is an affront to God.[10] Thus, those who are constructed as polluted—young

---

8. Jamala Rogers, *Ferguson Is America: Roots of Rebellion* (St. Louis: Mira Digital Publishing, 2015), Kindle location 853–59.
9. Leah Gunning Francis, *Ferguson and Faith: Sparking Leadership and Awakening Community* (St. Louis: Chalice, 2015), 91.
10. Ibid., 156.

Black queer people and individuals with criminal convictions—are, in the eyes of God, pure.

For liberationist clergy, as for BLM protestors, always at stake is the oppressed body: the body of Jesus, the body of Michael Brown, and the bodies of Black people nationwide who have been murdered by police officers. Four themes emerge in clergy responses to Michael Brown's killing: Jesus's birth, ministry, crucifixion, and resurrection.

The Birth of Jesus as Protest

Theologians active in the BLM movement interpret the birth of Jesus as protest against first-century pollution boundaries. The Gospel of Matthew narrates Jesus's birth in a stable, surrounded by animals, "because there was no room in the inn." The Reverend Osagyefo Sekou, an ordained elder in the Church of God in Christ, theologizes the poverty and pain of Jesus's birth as significant for BLM:

> I understand the gospel of Jesus as a story about God choosing to become flesh in the body of an unwed teenage mother among an unimportant people in an unimportant part of the world. Jesus—a Palestinian Jewish peasant living under Roman occupation—is the salvation of the world. God as flesh was a subject of an empire.[11]

Similarly, the Reverend Traci Blackmon, senior minister of Christ the King UCC, interprets the meaning of Christ's birth as a political confrontation between impoverished, polluted Jews and wealthy, elite Romans:

> In the birth of Christ during the Roman Empire, high militarization, Mary and Joseph are in the midst of a system that they are forced to comply with. [Jesus, as God incarnate] could have been born in wealth and royalty. But God chose to manifest Godself among the poor and marginalized in society. Not even to just the poor and marginalized, but a poor brown woman, in an Afrosemitic context, among this Roman Empire, in poverty—in such abject poverty that it is highlighted that there is not even a place for him to lie his head. And I think that if you can be born anywhere that you want to be born, which I believe about Christ, and you choose to be born among the lowly, not among the high, that the birth in and of itself is an act of protest. That you would choose to associate yourself by privilege of who you are, elevates those who are not elevated any other kind of way. So for me, that's an act of protest, which contin-

11. Sekou, January interview.

ues throughout Christ's life and reign. . . . I can read the story [of Jesus of Nazareth] into all oppression, but if you take this situation and read the story, you know that after the birth of Jesus, Herod mandates that all children are killed because he is trying to get to Jesus. There is a slaughter of innocence that happens from the Empire in this text, these casualties are an attempt to keep this child from rising, because the story has already been prophesied, has already been told. That story is very much rooted in the killing, the assassination, of men of color. . . . I think that [the killing of Mike Brown] too is a manifestation of fear, at a systemic institutional level, and so we choose to kill that which we fear, which we cannot control. And the Black male in our society has been categorized and depicted as someone to be feared. And so I believe that even in the killing of Mike Brown, if you listen to the interview with Darren Wilson, he does not call him anything human. He calls him the incredible hulk. He calls him a demon.[12]

Fear of certain bodies that cannot be controlled, as Herod feared Jesus at his birth, illuminates broader social practices in which identified groups are subjugated, even killed with impunity, so those in power can sustain their positions. Indeed, liberationist clergy draw multiple parallels between the circumstances of Jesus of Nazareth's birth and the condition of Black people, especially Black youth, in a society premised on white norms and institutions. The white bodily norm is contrasted with the morally polluted Black body. Despite the fact that Darren Wilson and Michael Brown were the same height, 6'4", Wilson observed in Brown an "angry" and "aggressive" menacing threat that justified murder.[13]

The conditions of Christ's birth, then, illuminate the narrative of liberation theology: those who are socially unimportant and feared are, in God's eyes, chosen to save all of humankind. Those who are politically dispossessed have the capacity to be spiritually powerful: the saviors of the world. In privileging the status of the powerless, Christians have the opportunity to meet God.

12. Interview with Reverend Traci Blackmon, Pastor, Christ the King United Church of Christ, Florissant, Missouri, January 2015. In Darren Wilson's Grand Jury testimony, Wilson who was 6'4" referred to Michael Brown, who was also 6'4," as the "incredible hulk," and a "demon." See http://time.com/3605346/darren-wilson-michael-brown-demon/.
13. See http://time.com/3605346/darren-wilson-michael-brown-demon/.

The Ministry of Jesus as Protest

The narrative of Jesus of Nazareth—a poor Jew, a carpenter, a dispossessed Palestinian—is central to liberation theology and to the act of contesting racialized constructs of pollution. Liberation theologians identify Jesus as a nonviolent revolutionary who organized the poor in the face of occupation.[14] Gustavo Gutiérrez, a Latin American priest who penned the first text on liberation theology in 1968, wrote:

> But the poor person does not exist as an inescapable fact of destiny. His or her existence is not politically neutral, and it is not ethically innocent. The poor are a by-product of the system in which we live and for which we are responsible. They are marginalized by our social and cultural world. They are the oppressed, exploited proletariat, robbed of the fruit of their labor and despoiled of their humanity. Hence the poverty of the poor is not a call to generous relief action, but a demand that we go and build a different social order.[15]

Gutiérrez, a Roman Catholic priest who lived in the slums of Peru, took a vow of poverty that required him to "walk with and be committed to the poor." To do so, he stated, was to encounter God, who is simultaneously revealed and hidden in impoverished, oppressed people. Gutiérrez drew from Matthew 25:31–40:

> When the Son of Man comes in his glory, and all the angels with him, then he will sit on his glorious throne. Before him will be gathered all the nations, and he will separate people one from another as a shepherd separates the sheep from the goats. And he will place the sheep on his right, but the goats on the left. Then the King will say to those on his right, "Come, you who are blessed by my Father, inherit the kingdom prepared for you from the foundation of the world. For I was hungry and you gave me food, I was thirsty and you gave me drink, I was a stranger and you welcomed me, I was naked and you clothed me, I was sick and you visited me, I was in prison and you came to me." Then the righteous will answer him, saying, "Lord, when did we see you hungry and feed you, or thirsty and give you drink? And when did we see you a stranger and welcome you, or naked and clothe you? And when did we see you sick or in prison and visit you?" And the King will answer them, "Truly, I say to you, as you did it to one of the least of these my brothers, you did it to me."

14. Reverend Osagyefo Sekou, "The Gospel Is Not a Neutral Term: An Interview with Reverend Sekou," *Medium*, October 24, 2014, http://tinyurl.com/jzvocey.
15. Gustavo Gutiérrez, *A Theology of Liberation* (Maryknoll, NY: Orbis, 1973).

In the first century, Jesus of Nazareth uplifted those whose bodies were deemed polluted: bleeding and invalid people, lepers, demon-possessed men, and women. In this way, Jesus reached out to the "least of these." Blackmon reflects:

> I believe very strongly that there is a God, who is a God of justice and of equity. . . . I believe very strongly that the intent of the Bible is to point to that Jesus, to the Jesus who is the God of the oppressed . . . a Black Jesus that is representative of those who are marginalized and who are targeted and who are oppressed in every way. And I've *always* believed that about Jesus.[16]

Clergy on the frontlines of the Ferguson protest assert that to self-identify as Christian is fundamentally a political act that pushes against racialized pollution boundaries, as Jesus himself challenged the marginalization of those who were deemed polluted. Furthermore, to carry one's body into protest wearing a clerical collar is to proclaim affinity with polluted bodies. Clergy, then, challenge symbolic constructs of pollution by donning elite symbols, embracing polluted bodies, and facing police violence on the frontlines. These liberationist clergy have elevated Christian symbols to rebuke state-inflicted pollution boundaries: at the vanguard, kneeling and praying, taking communion, and reading names of those killed by police officers, they have used symbolic power to challenge the material power of the police. Reverend Sekou recounts clergy activism in the nights after Michael Brown was killed:

> During their nightly protest at the Ferguson Police station, local clergy came out to support them and bear witness in solidarity. Clergy knelt and prayed in front of a garrison of police repenting for our silence and supporting the young folks who we followed to the space of resistance and place of injustice. After our spontaneous prayer meeting, young folks asked us to step aside as they stood in the middle of the street willing to risk arrest. The line of police wielding long brown wooden batons and donning riot gear marched lock step toward the young folks in the street. Something got a hold of me. I darted out in between the youth activists and advancing police. I knelt and prayed. I was promptly surrounded by police, snatched up and placed in a blood stained police van but the youth would not back down. For almost two hours the youth sat down in the middle of the street and refused to leave until I was released. Captain Ron Johnson was ushered from his home, and came out to negotiate with the

---

16. Blackmon interview.

youth. And they were not having it. I was eventually released from the police van.

On Moral Monday as a part of Ferguson October, a group of faith leaders were arrested as we prayed and called on the police to repent for being part of an evil system of policing. As an act of resistance we created a memorial for the Mike Browns of America. Rev. Charles Burton, a local pastor and activist, laid down on the soaked ground. His body was traced with chalk and candles lit. Pastors and Rabbis read the unarmed names of those killed by the police. Clergy positioned themselves along the police line to take confession. We, then, advanced towards the entrance of the police station. Police placed batons against a few of our throats, swung wildly at others, but we prayed, raised our voices in song and worship. We moved again to enter the police station and many were thrown to the ground and arrested. Seventeen of us were charged with assault against a law enforcement officer, along with the blanket charge of disturbance of the peace (ironically, given the ever-present chant of "No justice, no peace"). A total of forty-three people face charges from that morning alone.[17]

Clergy who have put their bodies on the line in nonviolent direct action see themselves as following the ministry of Jesus, who peacefully confronted state violence and execution. On an August 2014 night of violent reprisals from police officers, Reverend Renita Lamkin was shot with a rubber bullet. Yet for Lamkin, the agony of taking a rubber bullet was a mark of discipleship. She stated: "I'm following the teachings and practices of Christ. And what did Christ tell me to do? He taught me to go where people were being johnned and outcast and put aside, and hear people that other people were telling to be quiet, to touch the people that other people said can't be touched."[18]

To self-identify as Christian, then, is to confront racialized pollution boundaries with one's body. Following the Black liberation theology of James H. Cone, Reverend Sekou states: "First and foremost, the gospel is not a neutral term. . . . It is motivation to resist oppression. Thus we must resist in the way in which Jesus resisted. We must be present with the least of these as he called and be willing to go to the cross as he did."[19]

Liberationist clergy have identified young protestors as carrying out the liberationist ethic of Jesus of Nazareth, despite the fact that many

17. Sekou, January interview.
18. Interview with Reverend Renita Lamkin, Pastor, St. John's African Methodist Episcopal Church, January 2015.
19. Sekou, January interview.

of the youth resist the institutional church. The youth are adopting powerful symbolic rituals and preaching—through nonviolent direct actions, demonstrations, marches, chants, die-ins, sit-ins, and vigils.[20] God is present in the youth:

> For we have seen you in [the youth's] faces, O God. We have seen you when they scream and they yell and they are angry. We have seen the very face of God in them. We have seen that God has tattoos on God's face and that God sags God's pants and that God loves us so much that God is willing to stand in front of tanks and tear gas and bear witness to a truth that they will not bow down. And so, for them, we pray and we say, "Thank you, thank you, thank you for these young people who have made us all a little more courageous, who have made us all a little more angry, and who have made us all a little more considerate that we must do our work with deep, abiding love."[21]

These clergy see Jesus in Michael Brown because Michael Brown symbolizes the polluted Black body, the very body embraced by Jesus of Nazareth. The lack of quality public education—Brown lived in the sole unincorporated school district in the state of Missouri—and disproportionate criminalization result in significant poverty, institutionalization, and hopelessness in the St. Louis area.[22] Dietra Wise Baker, a chaplain for the St. Louis County juvenile detention center, stated: "For all intents and purposes, in the context that I serve in every day, Mike's body is still on the ground."[23]

Fellow clergy in the St. Louis area echo Baker's theological interpretation. The length of time that Brown lay in the street, along with the character assassination initiated by officials after his death, sparked outrage and defiance. The conditions further illuminated the desperate conditions underlying the chant: "We have nothing to lose but our chains." In the wake of the August 2014 protests, Blackmon, along with the Reverend Starsky Wilson, pastor of St. John's United Church of Christ in St. Louis, joined the Ferguson Commission to propose solutions to the issues surrounding poverty, early childhood care, education, and transportation in Ferguson.[24] Wilson, cochair of the Ferguson Commission, reflected: "What if Mike Brown is our Jesus Christ? What

20. Reverend Starsky Wilson, "Politics of Jesus" (sermon, St. John's United Church of Christ, St. Louis, MO, August 31, 2014).
21. Francis, *Ferguson and Faith*, 155.
22. Blackmon interview.
23. Francis, *Ferguson and Faith*, 92.
24. "Rev. Starsky Wilson: Faith in Ferguson," YouTube video, 13:29, from the 2015 Samuel DeWitt Proctor Conference, posted by "KineticsLive," February 19, 2015, http://tinyurl.com/zoy9kc3.

if Mike Brown was the thing that pushed us to the point of doing God's true work that's needed to be done?"[25] For these clergy, the fundamental act of challenging racialized constructs of moral pollution, of uplifting the people marginalized and outcast due to their bodies and their social status, is the work of Jesus.

Baker, too, saw the Ferguson protests as a call to the community, particularly the church, to address the broader systemic injustice in Ferguson and the broader St. Louis area. "We're always talking about doing something, but something about this movement forced us to be the hands and feet for the Christians and for Jesus."[26]

Clergy nationwide drew on the analogy of Michael Brown and Jesus. Valerie Bridgeman, a visiting associate professor of homiletics and Hebrew Bible at Methodist Theological School in Ohio, reflected:

> These Ferguson citizens screamed in the face of police who trained their military-grade weapons on the crowds. Wounded. And Michael Brown became the symbol of a community's rejection, of black communities—not just in Ferguson, but throughout the country—being despised. . . . Michael was crushed and bore the punishment for being black in the USA for us all. . . . We are left to ask of God, "Why are the Michaels of our communities bearing all our iniquities?"[27]

Liberationist clergy have made explicit connections between the political tenor of Jesus's times and the oppression experienced by Black youth who are constructed as polluted today. Marginalized groups—of women and queer youth, of young people like Michael Brown who are raised in communities with unincorporated school districts, without access to affordable transportation—are linked to the polluted groups of Jesus's time. Social elites determine how persons without status access institutional benefits. On the Sunday after Michael Brown was killed, Reverend Wilson preached:

> The extreme poverty of Jesus's time feels like the poverty of our time, with a chasm between the haves and have nots, the people who got and those who get forgotten. . . . We call it the poverty tax, like the lack of access to healthy foods, the overticketing for driving while Black, and the higher taxes for gas in the "hood." There were three warrants for arrest for every

---

25. Francis, *Ferguson and Faith*, 133.
26. Ibid., 164.
27. Reverend Dr. Eric D. Barreto, Billy Honor, Valerie Bridgeman, Greg Carey, Dr. Karyn L. Wiseman, and Brian Bantum, "Preaching Reflections on Michael Brown and Ferguson," *Huffington Post*, August 15, 2014, http://tinyurl.com/jjckzla.

household in Ferguson. When we say "poverty tax" we're talking about ticketing that targets people disproportionately and has them under the burden of warrants.[28]

For the clergy, then, the youth were enacting a biblical vision: God was with the young people in the streets who would not back down.[29] A prophetic action was taking place: God chose polluted Black youth; God stood against militarized police with tanks and machine guns; God's people would prevail. The youth were a persecuted people, akin to the Israelites fleeing the Egyptian army in Exodus and the Jews who were disempowered under Roman occupation. Michael Brown represented Jesus the Christ; furthermore, by protesting his death, the Black youth in Ferguson represented the meaning of Christ. The call to action to Christians nationwide stated explicitly:

> Just get on the streets. Come be on the streets. Come at least once. Get on the streets. I'm telling you you're going to meet Jesus there. Jesus [is] on the street and you're going to be transformed if you come to the street.[30]

Crucifixion on the Cross: State Violence against Black People

The four Gospels illuminate the events that led to the crucifixion of Jesus: a poor Jewish carpenter from rural Palestine who assumed rabbinic leadership and publicly criticized authority figures. One of his disciples betrayed him. After the disciple gave Jesus over to Jewish authorities, the Roman Empire executed him. That Jesus was killed by the state holds particular salience for BLM liberationist clergy: Jesus's execution represents the state-sanctioned violence against polluted Black people who are killed by police officers. The cross upon which Jesus hung is akin to the specter of police brutality as well as the daily, sanctioned actions by police officers and courts that disproportionately penalize, marginalize, and profit from the struggles of poor Black people.[31]

Indeed, liberationist clergy regularly name those known to have been killed by acts of violent aggression: Amadou Diallo, Sean Bell, Trayvon Martin, Walter Scott, Jermaine Reid, Phillip White, Eric Garner, Freddie Gray, Aiyana Jones, Sandra Bland, Kimani Gray, John Craw-

28. Wilson, "Politics of Jesus."
29. Sekou, January interview.
30. Francis, *Ferguson and Faith*, 93.
31. Wilson, "Politics of Jesus."

ford III, Michael Brown, Miriam Carey, Sharonda Coleman-Singleton, Tommy Yancy, and Jordan Baker, among others.[32] In 2015, police killed at least 346 Black people in the United States.[33]

Theologically, state violence against Black people is represented by the crucifixion of Jesus, which is often portrayed as a fierce dichotomy between the forces of good and evil, purity and pollution, heaven and hell. Clergy have analogized this battle to the confrontation between protestors and state police in Ferguson after Michael Brown was killed. While many scholars have problematized the association of whiteness with goodness,[34] the color dynamics in theologies of Ferguson are inverted: the predominantly Black protestors are associated with goodness, and the predominantly white police officers are associated with evil. Reverend Lamkin theologized the street battle as a confrontation between the loving presence of God and a chaotic spirit: "In the spirit I could imagine that there was a line of warring angels that stood between the people and the police and kept people at bay and kept the police at bay."[35]

For Lamkin, the protestors embodied love in an evil space, similar to Jesus in a corrupt society. God-given vitality fueled the courage and determination to confront oppression. "When I see the uprising in the streets, I see people saying 'my life has value, and dammit, I'm going to live.' And they're fighting for their life, literally. They're fighting for the right to be fully alive."[36]

Jamala Rogers, cofounder of the Organization for Black Struggle, wrote in 2016 that as state data on racial profiling became more accurate, the statistics on racial profiling got worse, "bearing out the fact that black people were disproportionately being stopped for no good reason other than the color of their skin. These disparities were supposed to trigger an effort by local police departments to address the over-representation. It never did."[37]

Subsequent reports on conditions in Ferguson reveal the magnitude

32. The song "Hell You Talmbout," by Janelle Monáe, names these victims. See "HELL YOU TALM-BOUT-Janelle Monáe, Deep Cotton, St. Beauty, Jidenna, Roman Gian Arthur, George 2.0," YouTube video, 6:38, posted by "Easy Squeeze," August 14, 2015, http://tinyurl.com/pxotjc4. For a complete list of unarmed victims in 2014 and 2015, see "Unarmed Victims," Mapping Police Violence, accessed August 12, 2016. http://tinyurl.com/jbnqe7j.
33. https://mappingpoliceviolence.org.
34. For a searing critique of how racism is embedded in language, see Frantz Fanon, *Black Skin, White Masks* (New York: Grove, 1952), chapter 5.
35. Lamkin interview. Lamkin is the white mother of two Black teenagers and a pastor of an African Methodist Episcopal church.
36. Ibid.
37. Rogers, *Ferguson Is America*, Kindle location 959–62.

of state-inflicted suffering. A March 2015 Department of Justice report illuminated a racist, white power structure in a city that was nearly 70 percent Black: In addition to all-white city officials, the Ferguson police department had only three Black officers at the time of Michael Brown's murder. The report asserted Ferguson law enforcement efforts were focused on generating revenue and thus violated the law and undermined community trust, especially among African Americans.[38] Police engaged in unconstitutional, even criminal, practices of excessive force, such as the use of dogs on children and illegal uses of stun guns. Furthermore, police officers conducted unconstitutional stops and arrests of neighborhood residents and schoolchildren. They served arbitrary warrants for arrest: in the year 2013, approximately nine thousand warrants were issued for over thirty-two thousand offenses, primarily to African American residents of Ferguson. In addition to racially biased and harsh policing practices, the municipal court imposed unduly harsh penalties for missed payments and appearances. Indeed, the DOJ report describes the unfair, punitive approach of the municipal court to deriving as much revenue as possible from the impoverished Black residents of Ferguson. The DOJ concluded that law enforcement and municipal court practices "disproportionately harm Ferguson's African American residents and are driven in part by racial bias."[39]

A 2015 report by the Ferguson Commission further illuminated racial disparities in the St. Louis region:

> For thousands of St. Louisans, the status quo is killing them. The status quo means living in a food desert, with no grocery stores for miles around; sending your children to underperforming schools that get fewer resources but dole out more punishments; driving in fear of a court system that will put you in jail for failure to pay a traffic ticket.[40]

The Ferguson Commission's report touched upon some of the identified problems; the Don't Shoot Coalition, comprised of St. Louis–area grassroots organizations, acknowledged the Commission's analysis and called for further recommendations.[41]

---

38. United States Department of Justice Civil Rights Division, "Investigation of the Ferguson Police Department," March 4, 2015, PDF, http://tinyurl.com/zhywh7r.
39. Ibid., 64.
40. Ferguson Commission, "The Process of Change," *Forward through Ferguson: A Path toward Racial Equity*, October 14, 2015, PDF, http://tinyurl.com/htcvfjs.
41. Don't Shoot Coalition, "Comments in Response to Ferguson Commission Recommendations Relating to Police Practices," September 16, 2015, PDF, p. 1, http://tinyurl.com/jlkxhax: the Don't

Protestors in Ferguson shed light on these practices of disproportionate penalization of Black people and the poor public policies that
lacked public accountability. Their unwillingness to support a corrupt,
racist system was hailed as prophetic by clergy members who had
themselves become social elites with a liberationist analysis. As the
youth protested, these clergy, some of whom addressed health disparities and childhood poverty in their daily work, saw with greater clarity the magnitude of state-inflicted suffering. BLM protestors revealed
institutional failures and state violence through a new lens. Like Jesus
of Nazareth, they challenged the status quo and insisted on the importance of people who have been constructed as polluted outcasts. They
embodied a risen Christ.

Indeed, state violence against Black people would not be the last
word. Cone theologizes: "The cross places God in the midst of a crucified people, in the midst of people who are hung, shot, burned, and
tortured."[42] Yet the cross, which represents state-sanctioned terror,
"inverts the world's value system with the good news and hope that
hope comes by way of defeat, that suffering and death do not have the
last word, that the last shall be first and the first last."[43] Reverend Wilson preached:

> The cross was God's critique with powerless love snatching defeat, snatch-
> ing victory from defeat. This is the remix. God takes the track of public
> terror and execution and intimidation, scratches the intimidation, mod-
> ulates the input, samples the creative reinterpretation, and turns the
> prophetic terror into prophetic calls to action. It sounds familiar. This is
> the remix. God takes the killing of a young Black man in the street and the
> strand of blood that goes down Canfield. He wipes away the blood, lifts up
> the eyes, doesn't make us sorrowful, but makes us happy to push a move-
> ment on today. This is the remix. God desired for us to be a new people, to
> go from personal pain to public protest.[44]

The inversion of traditional social values—acquiescence, obedience,
professionalism, self-security—becomes a hindrance, even a liability, in

Shoot Coalition "has advocated in its calls to pass the Fair and Impartial Policing Act. The Commission could have backed specific proposals to fix the faults in data collection, add pedestrian
stops and add some specific carrots and sticks to ensure departmental improvements." They also
believe the proposed policies need to go further and include making community policing the primary philosophy, implementing civilian oversight, banning tear gas at protests, implementing
structural changes, improving hiring and training, and thoughtfully addressing the use of body
cameras.
42. James H. Cone, *The Cross and the Lynching Tree* (Maryknoll, NY: Orbis, 2011), 26.
43. Wilson, "Politics of Jesus."
44. Ibid.

this interpretation of the cross. Jesus's crucifixion calls self-identified Christians to negate social norms that differentiate between pure and polluted people and to adopt radical interpretations of salvific purity. To bear the cross, then, is to embrace those polluted bodies that are dark, tattooed, pierced, gender nonconforming, and representative of illness; it is to look directly at state-inflicted violence in all of its dimensions. It is to claim the polluted and reject the socially pure. The acts of stripping away appearances, embracing suffering, and standing against state violence lead to the resurrection.

> So this is an anti-establishment stance that manifests through love, abundant love, which ends up conquering even death. So Jesus lives this life of protest for 33 years, and then he is crucified. And he's crucified—and I take the text of liberal preachers—so you can say that Christ too hung for 4 ½ hours. . . . And he hangs with a sign that identifies him as king of the Jews, which could also be interpreted as his "hands up" sign. And yet, the ultimate protest against that becomes the Resurrection.[45]

Resurrection: Sustained Protest in the Streets

Young protestors in front of the Ferguson police station, night after night, facing down officers with batons, tear gas, and rubber bullets, collectively created a new Black body that lifted up the slain body of Michael Brown and did not allow his murder to go unforgotten. Rather, these Black protestors, many of whom were young and queer, resurrected a fierce spirit of resistance and unwillingness to let the status quo maintain racialized pollution boundaries. In their brown skin and confrontational stances, in their raised fists and angry hip-hop chants, in their constant vigilance and presence, they represented moral purity: a resurrected Christ, an unwillingness for death, oppression, and injustice to remain the last word.

In the Gospel of Luke, a resurrected Jesus joins the disciples as they walk to Emmaus. The eyes and hearts of the disciples are opened as they listen to Christ. In the Ferguson uprising that erupted in August 2014, clergy argued, the eyes of Black people nationwide were opened: Twitter and Facebook facilitated an urgent conviction that racialized pollution boundaries—racial profiling, economic deprivation, and substandard schools and housing—would not be tolerated. When army tanks, machine guns, and tear gas were deployed against nonviolent

45. Blackmon interview.

protestors who were deemed "enemies," the eyes of mainstream America were opened. There existed resurrection in the statement that Black lives, constructed as morally polluted, matter. Oppression would not be the final word.

Liberationist clergy preach that the resurrection of Jesus the Christ is experienced in the sustained struggle for justice for the morally polluted members of society. In the BLM movement, as protestors have challenged racialized pollution boundaries—as they have occupied streets and police stations, marched, engaged in social media conversations, and formed infrastructure for long-term organizing—they have performed purity. Reverend Wilson states:

> Jesus's politics are real, revolutionary, radical, and our Christian roots. So what we must ask at a time that looks like Jesus's time: how might we push his politics in our day, which looks so much like his day? How did this poor, marginalized, oppressed, revolutionary cat from the other side of the tracks start the greatest movement for social change that the world has ever seen? . . . To say that Black lives actually matter is to make a prophetic alternative statement, to say that we will have a movement, we will lead a movement, that is not just men in front, not just at the mic, we will proclaim the power of the sisters and the various folk: that is prophetic, it is giving a glimpse of the picture that we desire to have come forth. This has always been God's way to build a movement and proclaim God's politics. For wandering Hebrews, he cast a vision for a promised land. For Galileans, the kingdom of heaven. For a persecuted people, the vision of the ekklesia, a community that shared all that they had, so that everyone's needs got met. And for a divided western world, a vision of beloved community that is a vision of a multiracial community where peace and justice is the governing ethic. To boost the politics of Jesus, we must magnify this picture of people made in the image and likeness of God.[46]

Jesus of Nazareth, the chosen Christ, was resurrected three days after crucifixion. Central to the narrative in Luke is the uplifting of polluted members of society: those who are chosen to hear God's message most directly. Reverend Sekou points to the Scripture in the Gospel of Luke 24:6–11:

> "He is not here; he has risen! Remember how he told you, while he was still with you in Galilee: 'The Son of Man must be delivered over to the hands of sinners, be crucified and on the third day be raised again.'" Then

46. Wilson, "Politics of Jesus."

they remembered his words. When they came back from the tomb, they told all these things to the Eleven and to all the others. It was Mary Magdalene, Joanna, Mary the mother of James, and the others with them who told this to the apostles. But they did not believe the women, because their words seemed to them like nonsense.

Reverend Sekou asks: "Who's the first to proclaim that Jesus has risen? The unauthorized. The sisters. The Gospel begins by those who are not authorized to engage in religious leadership. The disciples, the men, they're hiding."[47] Indeed, in the resurrection, elite members of society are bypassed. Marginalized, polluted persons are chosen to meet the angels.

In short, those who are deemed socially polluted are the intuitive receivers of the message of resurrection: death is not the last word; there is hope in sustained struggle. Liberationist clergy participating in BLM have privileged the bodies, experiences, and needs of BLM youth. They have sought to offer mentoring, regenerative spaces, and healing rituals even outside of the Christian tradition.

Clergy have also embodied their commitment to the Black Lives Matter movement in ways that illuminate their symbolic revision of pollution and purity. They have worn clerical collars to indicate that the church is on the side of protest, performed sacramental liturgy in the streets by creating altars, and provided welcome tables. "That image that we set the table in the streets and everybody is at that table, that's the kingdom of God. That's the reign of God."[48] They seek to symbolize God's presence in the midst of righteous protest against racialized pollution boundaries that are sustained by racism, poverty, and policing. God is on the side of the polluted; in fact, the polluted are most readily positioned to hear God.[49]

Conclusion: Protest as the Performance of Purity

Liberationist clergy understand their commitment to the Black Lives Matter movement as pushing against social boundaries that demarcate Black lives as inferior, polluted, and socially marginalized. To join the protestors is to reconstruct—indeed, resurrect—Black skin, hair, phenotype, and cultural expressions as symbolically pure. Clergy play an

47. Reverend Osagyefo Sekou, "What Mike Brown Still Means" (panel discussion, St. John's United Church of Christ, St. Louis, MO, August 9, 2015).
48. Francis, *Faith and Ferguson*, 118.
49. Ibid., 156.

important role in the symbolic reconstruction of Blackness, as clergy ritualize notions of purity and celebrate a Gospel message that privileges "the least of these." Liberationist clergy interpret the dimensions of Jesus's life—birth, ministry, crucifixion, and resurrection—in the context of Black oppression. These clergy challenge policing and imprisonment practices by claiming divine presence in the Black bodies that are constructed as polluted and disproportionately criminalized. God is present in the midst of suffering. Jesus, as God embodied, was persecuted as a member of an occupied territory within the Roman Empire and chose to minister to the polluted members of his community. Thus, to follow Jesus in a contemporary setting is to embrace the Black bodies that are demarcated as polluted. To walk with Jesus is to redefine the racially polluted outcast as chosen by God. To resurrect Jesus is to engage in sustained protest, to mentor and care for weary activists, and to institutionalize racially just practices that acknowledge historical and contemporary racism and hold officials accountable.

To sustain racial justice protest is to perform purity in a context in which marginalized Black people are constructed as polluted. The Black Lives Matter movement, in all of its dimensions, has directly and strategically pushed against racialized pollution boundaries by insisting on the importance of Black lives, including Black bodies that are marginalized *within* Black communities. BLM protestors, then, perform symbolic acts of purity on multiple fronts: by privileging queer, including transgender, leadership; by engaging in new social media strategies as well as historic embodied demonstrations; and by reconstructing the image of Christ in the slain body of Michael Brown and the fierce street protests that erupted after his execution.

The last shall be first and the first, last. Those who have been constructed as polluted are pure in heart, indeed, chosen by God, and in their protests against racialized pollution boundaries, and in their hard work building institutions of accountability, Black Lives Matter protestors perform their purity again and again.

7

Conclusion: Reconstructing the Image of the Polluted Black Body

Constructing the Image of the Polluted Black Body

Societies draw symbolic boundaries between the polluted and the pure. In the United States, authorities identify these boundaries as moral boundaries and use penal policies and practices to enforce them. The rhetoric of willful evil and the employment of punishment apparatuses to distinguish between the polluted and the pure is a central aspect of the contemporary penal state. A less obvious dimension of the penal state is the process of constructing members of historically oppressed racial groups as immoral bodies that need to be controlled and contained. These dark bodies are associated with weakness and wantonness—dependency on welfare, drugs, and violence. They are distinguished from white moral bodies, which, in the eyes of conservative thinkers, are associated with self-discipline, self-denial, and obedience to authority. Whereas people who are seen as moral move about freely, people associated with immorality are subjected to policing forces and rigid systems of discipline.

These rigid systems include mandatory minimum drug laws and long sentences—sometimes life sentences—for petty crimes. They consist of rural prisons—in predominantly white communities—that function to contain the danger represented by Black bodies. They operate as sophisticated apparatuses that chase and remove the "pollution" that offends the dominant collective consciousness.

The association of dark skin with moral pollution has a long history—much longer than most criminal justice scholars and critical activists acknowledge. It stretches back to thirteenth-century moral geography, religious interpretations of dark-skinned people during the age of exploration, the establishment of colonies in which Black people were enslaved, and Enlightenment projects of scientific investigation and moral philosophy. Whites defined Blacks as degraded beings who were incapable of achieving salvation; whites thought of themselves as embodiments of saving grace. They believed that God ordained differences in position within society and that the fixed values in the moral universe decreed that some should rule and some should serve. Even when Enlightenment principles of reason replaced biblical revelation as the guiding ethos by which to shape society, European intellectuals and the Founding Fathers of the United States embraced a myth of Anglo-Saxon purity and freedom. They believed that whites had special capacities for liberty that were culturally and providentially definitive of their race. Conversely, they believed Blacks to be inferior in physical beauty as well as mental capacity.

Notions of Black immorality fueled widespread fear as newly formed Northern states passed laws to emancipate slaves. Even abolitionists expressed the conviction that intemperance, indolence, and crime prevailed among free Black people. Northern whites of different political stripes generally believed that Black degradation was a result of environment and that Black persons could embody moral character. A growing movement led by religious leaders sought to establish penal institutions that would instill "good moral character"—whether by rehabilitative approaches or by brute force—in those convicted of crimes. From the beginning, Black defendants were incarcerated at rates far disproportionate to their population numbers. Even as officials espoused their desire to morally reform convicts, these penal institutions resembled the institution of slavery in ways that were not generally acknowledged by penitentiary advocates. Prison and plantation authorities forced those seen as morally degenerate to labor without payment in harsh conditions. They isolated their subjects from the general population by confining them to a fixed habitat. They relied on the whip and other slavekeeping devices such as iron masks to enforce discipline.

After the Civil War, Southern state penal systems also mirrored the institution of slavery. In the South, Black people were constructed as inferior by nature: their criminality was innate, part of the divine design. Whereas the institution of chattel slavery had controlled the danger of moral pollution posed by Black bodies, now Black Codes and state penal systems would force Black Southerners to stay at the bottom of the social hierarchy, return to work on plantations, and labor under long sentences for emerging industries such as coal, lumber, and the railroad. Prisoners died in drastic numbers, officials contended, because the average Black convict was inherently immoral: prone to debasement and degeneracy. In officials' minds, inner decay, not the brutal conditions, led to high rates of mortality.

Dominant cultural beliefs in Black criminality reemerged as the nonviolent civil rights movement of the mid-twentieth century faded and some impoverished Black communities embraced the rhetoric of the Black Power movement as a means for social change. Many participated in urban rebellions and riots. Representations of irredeemable Black males who chose violence of their own accord replaced images of the rehabilitated white male criminal in popular media. Portrayals of violent Black revolutionaries and crack addicts—"social dynamite" and "social junk"—dominated television screens. The Willie Horton ads in the 1988 presidential campaign stroked latent fears of the Black male rapist. Media outlets in the 1990s publicized nightly parades of Black bodies in the clutches of police officers.

Mass Imprisonment to Reify Pollution Boundaries

The system of warehousing people associated with moral pollution relies on images, archetypes, and symbols: a "criminal" is a threat to the social order. A heightened consciousness of crime, and of poor people with dark skin, has gradually become institutionalized and routinized in everyday life.[1]

The US penal system is, in fact, a new form of controlling Black people that is preceded by slavery, northern penitentiaries, postbellum penal systems, and legal segregation.[2] Like these former systems of

---

1. Garland, *Culture of Control*, 139–65.
2. Davis, "From the Convict Lease System to the SuperMax Prison"; Loïc Wacquant, "Deadly Symbiosis: When Ghetto and Prison Meet and Mesh," *Punishment & Society* 3, no. 95 (2001); Alexander, *The New Jim Crow*. Two Christian ethicists, James Samuel Logan and Mark L. Taylor, also offer an

social control, mass incarceration serves an "extra-penological function of the criminal justice system as instrument for the management
of dispossessed and dishonored groups."[3] At the heart of the new form
of racial control is an unchanging racial ideology that defines the basic
economic, political, and cultural structures of US society. It is "stun-
ningly comprehensive" in its multifaceted functions:[4] it operates as a
way to manage rising inequality and surplus populations;[5] it subju-
gates Black people through social divisions as well as legal statutes; it
is perpetuated by cultural representations that normalize the presence
of Black people in prison.

The economic element capitalizes on market dynamics, but more
directly controls Black, urban, poor people who face few opportunities
for gainful employment. Economic crises in the seventies and neoliberal economic restructuring in the eighties went hand-in-hand with
law-and-order policies and the War on Drugs,[6] further marginalizing
unemployed Black adults who make up what William Julius Wilson
and other sociologists term an "underclass."[7] The Reagan administration's economic policies, favoring corporations and wealthy individuals, underpinned a broad federal policy effort to "replace social
welfare with social control" while buttressing a racialized subtext of
the exploitative "welfare queen."[8] This economic function continues
today; indeed, sociologist Bruce Western demonstrates that "class
inequality increased dramatically from 1983 to 2001, and that by the
early twenty-first century the chances of imprisonment were more
closely linked to race and school failure than at any other time in the
previous twenty years."[9] Furthermore, as impoverished Black people
are locked out of wage-labor job markets and sent to prison, official
unemployment statistics fail to acknowledge real rates of joblessness.[10]

analysis in this trajectory of thought. See Logan, *Good Punishment? Christian Moral Practice and U.S.
Imprisonment* (Grand Rapids: Eerdmans, 2008) and Taylor, *The Executed God: The Way of the Cross in
Lockdown America* (Minneapolis: Fortress, 2001).

3. Wacquant, "Deadly Symbiosis," 95.
4. Alexander, 4.
5. Parenti, xii; Wacquant, 105.
6. For more on neoliberal economic policies as they related to incarceration, see Loïc Wacquant, *Punishing the Poor* and Parenti, 29–44.
7. William Julius Wilson, *When Work Disappears: The New World of the Urban Poor* (New York: Vintage,
1997); see also Wacquant, *Punishing the Poor.*
8. Beckett, 10.
9. Western, 78–79.
10. Ibid., 87.

The political function of mass imprisonment has coalesced with the economic function of racial control by capitalizing on working-class white anxiety. It operates in "Quality of Life" policing policies, in which poor people are racially profiled, rounded up by police officers, and detained for minor charges, such as loitering. It is furthered by the War on Drugs launched by the Reagan administration in 1982, resulting in a pattern in which ninety percent of people incarcerated for drug crimes are Black—although numerous studies have shown that whites and Blacks use and sell drugs at equivalent rates[11]—and in skyrocketing incarceration rates, in which nearly half of all people in prison are Black. It mirrors pre–civil rights discrimination in the form of widespread, state-based post-incarceration policies that bar people with felony convictions from gaining occupational licenses and from voting, thus rolling back the civil rights legislation enacted in 1964 and 1965.

Civil rights attorney Michelle Alexander thus summarizes the function of mass incarceration:

> The current system of control permanently locks a huge percentage of the African American community out of the mainstream society and economy. The system operates through our criminal justice institutions, but it functions more like a caste system than a system of crime control. Viewed from this perspective, the so-called underclass is better understood as an *undercaste*—a lower caste of individuals who are permanently barred by law and custom from mainstream society. Although this new system of racialized social control purports to be colorblind, it creates and maintains racial hierarchy much as earlier systems of control did. Like Jim Crow (and slavery), mass incarceration operates as a tightly networked system of laws, policies, customs, and institutions that operate collectively to ensure the subordinate status of a group defined largely by race.[12]

Functionally, mass incarceration operates in the minute details of the daily lives of Black people living in impoverished communities—pre-incarceration, during lockdown, and after prison. Pre- and post-prison, as impoverished Black people come from and return to what Loic Wacquant describes as the "hyperghetto," their role is, for the most part, to be contained.[13] With the loss of economic opportunities in the central city and with the simultaneous rise of punitive state

11. Alexander, 6-7; Human Rights Watch, "Cruel and Degrading," October 2006; Human Rights Watch, "Decades of Disparity," May 2009; Human Rights Watch, "Targeting Blacks: Drug Law Enforcement and Race in the United States," May 2008.
12. Alexander, 13.
13. Wacquant, "Deadly Symbiosis," 105.

institutions, the "hyperghetto" is more like a carceral setting than a community.[14] Public housing residents are under constant surveillance. Police officers—not security agents—exercise authority in public schools. In this way, the "hyperghetto" performs the same function as what Jonathan Simon terms "the waste management prison,"[15] which seeks not to rehabilitate, but rather, to subdue and contain whole populations that are associated with moral pollution.

The customary aspects of mass incarceration are sustained through cultural representations. Indeed, constructions of black immorality reside in images, archetypes, and anxieties.[16] The very image of the Black body today is connoted with moral pollution—that is, laziness and violence—in the same societal trajectory that perpetuated Black intellectual, spiritual, and cultural inferiority during slavery and in the aftermath of emancipation.

Whereas whites were valued for their capacity for reflection and their contributions to the nation-state as citizens, Black people were valued for the function of their bodies. In the twentieth century, after the success of the Republican law-and-order movement, the prevailing images of Black moral pollution in popular media tropes have morphed into the present-day image of the Black criminal.

Indeed, these images reinforce what Angela Y. Davis identifies as the generalized equation of "criminal" or "prisoner" with a Black male body.[17] The perpetuation of racism at every level of our society can be seen in the popular imagination viewing those populations in prison as public enemies.[18] Thus the images of the Black "welfare mother" and the dangerous hoodlum are "vituperated as the loathsome embodiment of their abject desecration, the 'dark side' of the 'American dream' of affluence and opportunity for all believed to flow from morality anchored in conjugality and work."[19] In short, between Black people represented as lazy, violent criminals and white people associated with hard work and economic mobility is a boundary between constructions of moral pollution and purity.[20]

The penal system thus institutionalizes racialized pollution boundaries, in that it perpetuates associations of Blackness and criminality.[21]

14. Ibid., 103.
15. Jonathan Simon, *How the War on Crime Transformed American Democracy and Created a Culture of Fear* (New York: Oxford, 2007), 141–75.
16. Garland, 135.
17. Davis, "From the Convict Lease System to the Super-Max Prison," 70.
18. Ibid., 73.
19. Wacquant, "Deadly Symbiosis," 120.
20. Ibid.

It practically revives and officially solidifies the centuries-old association of Blackness with immoral character, criminality, and devious violence. It asserts that Black people will only work with the threat of force upon them. Finally, it reinvents exploitative patterns in which rural whites and private companies profit from moving Black bodies from "hyperghetto" communities to hyper-secure carceral facilities in economically depressed rural landscapes.

The prison as an institution that perpetuates racialized pollution boundaries is also seen starkly in the lives of people who have been imprisoned for felony convictions. Branded as felons, they must not only identify themselves on job applications but are also legally barred from obtaining certain kinds of employment—mainly trades that require occupational licenses—as well as living in public housing, and voting. Under parole supervision, they are forced to report to state agents who wield enormous power over their lives. This level of domination in the lives of poor Black people serves as a means to control the morally polluting aspects of their existence, buttressed by the constant threat of returning them to prison.

Symbolic Reconstructions of Blackness in Racial Justice Movements

Racial justice activists in the anti-Stop-and-Frisk movement and the Black Lives Matter movement challenge the symbolic function of the contemporary penal system. Through social media and street protests, through an assertion of constitutional and human rights, they successfully reconstruct the image of the Black body as brutalized but not brutal, as subjugated but not aggressive. These activists have flipped the dominant narrative of Blackness and violence in US society and illuminated that policing forces, not Black people, are shockingly violent. Moreover, agents of the state commit brutal acts with impunity. These activists, while lacking institutional mechanisms to dismantle pollution boundaries, nonetheless have effectively shifted symbolic pollution boundaries by associating images of moral pollution with state agents. In other words, they have successfully illuminated the practices of unwarranted police violence against Black bodies and refuted the dominant narrative that justifies disproportionate force against, arrest of, and incarceration of Black people. In so doing, they have

21. Wacquant refers to the prison as a "race-making" institution. See Wacquant, "Deadly Symbiosis," 95, 116–20.

humanized and legitimized the Black body and created a new narrative.

An extraordinary dimension of shifting pollution boundaries extends to female, impoverished, and queer—especially transgender—Black people. Indeed, uplifting persons marginalized *within* Black communities is a fundamental commitment in the assertion that Black lives matter. To this end, the Black Lives Matter movement has challenged not only racialized but also gendered and sexualized pollution boundaries.

To date, the Black bodies that have been at the center of protests have been victims of police violence. The Movement for Black Lives has made visible only one part of the penal system, that of policing. In order to fully end "the War on Black People,"[22] symbolic reconstructions of Black victims of police brutality must extend further, for the movement presents an opportunity to dismantle the symbolic constructs that uphold mass imprisonment and reentry barriers. The Black Lives Matter movement, in its fierce critique of racism, sexism, and homophobia, has a platform to illuminate how the image of the "felon" is constructed and racialized. It can furthermore actively deconstruct the "ex-felon" and the barriers that render formerly incarcerated persons second-class citizens. In short, there exists great potential to tackle the symbolic pillars that uphold the US penal system and to put formerly incarcerated persons at the forefront of the movement.

In 2017, this movement is still in nascent form. It has challenged eyewitnesses to hold police officers accountable for their brutality, as seen in the filming of the execution of Alton Sterling by Abdullah Muflahi in Baton Rouge on July 5, 2016. It has emboldened Black community members throughout the country, as seen in the live stream video of the murder of Philando Castile by his girlfriend, Diamond Reynolds, in a suburb of Minneapolis, on July 6, 2016. It has spawned a social media movement and grassroots protests in multitudinous forms. In short, the Movement for Black Lives has heightened the consciousness and the empowerment of Black people.

Scholars and activists argue that this new consciousness must be institutionalized in order to be fully effective. Jamala Rogers argues that "Hands up, don't shoot can be redefined to hands up, count me in to do the hard work for meaningful change in my community."[23]

---

22. This framework is employed by the Movement for Black Lives policy table. See "End the War on Black People," The Movement for Black Lives, accessed September 30, 2017, http://tinyurl.com/zk2rg3y.

Rogers adheres to the logic of Angela Y. Davis's abolitionist argument to develop grassroots democratic institutions:

> Positing decarceration as our overarching strategy, we would try to envision a continuum of alternatives to imprisonment—demilitarization of schools, revitalization of education at all levels, a health system that provides free physical and mental care to all, and a justice system based on reparation and reconciliation rather than retribution and vengeance. The creation of new institutions that lay claim to the space now occupied by the prison can eventually start to crowd out the prison so that it would inhabit increasingly smaller areas of our social and psychic landscape.[24]

Institution building, as a continuum of protest, is the next stage to cultivating power. R. L. Stephens, the founder of Orchestrated Pulse and an organizer in Minneapolis, argues that the political power in BLM "seems to be in the hands of the power brokers who are choosing select people to be the new faces of an emerging leadership class. Meanwhile, the Black masses are being left behind to suffer and die."[25] Consequently, the most relevant goal for the movement for Black lives is to build "real power at the ground level for marginalized people."

This political power cannot only be built amongst Black people, argues Keeanga-Yamahtta Taylor. "While it is true that when Black people get free, everyone gets free, Black people in American cannot 'get free' alone. In that sense, Black liberation is bound up with the project of human liberation and social transformation."[26] Thus, Taylor argues, multiracial, class-oriented organizing that unites impoverished and low-wage workers forges a path forward.

Building political power is critical, and must occur in symbolic *as well as* material processes, for as *Racial Purity and Dangerous Bodies* has demonstrated, the symbolic construct of the morally polluted Black body sustains penal power. Davis argues that as abolitionist alternatives "strive to disarticulate crime and punishment, race and punishment, gender and punishment, then our focus must not only rest on the prison system as an isolated institution but must also be directed at all the social relations that support the permanence of the prison."[27]

23. Jamala Rogers, *Ferguson Is America: Roots of Rebellion* (St. Louis: Mira Digital Publishing, 2015), Kindle location 1224–25.
24. Angela Y. Davis, *Are Prisons Obsolete* (New York: Seven Stories, 2003), 107–8.
25. Bill Fletcher Jr., "From Hashtag to Strategy: The Growing Pains of Black Lives Matter," *In These Times*, September 23, 2015, http://tinyurl.com/j2wdgjz.
26. Keeanga-Yamahtta Taylor, *From #BlackLivesMatter to Black Liberation* (Chicago: Haymarket, 2016), 194.
27. Davis, *Are Prisons Obsolete?*, 112.

This book contends that these social relations are mediated as much through images, signs, and symbolism as they are through economic and political institutions. Thus, as protestors work to shift dynamics of power, to disassociate Blackness from criminality, and to hold penal officials accountable, it is necessary to reconstruct images of Blackness, indeed, to redraw symbolic boundaries of purity and impurity. The role of protest, then, is enduring. As organizers build new democratic institutions, as Black people achieve political power on small and large platforms, it is crucial that critical BLM activists challenge prevailing images of incarcerated and formerly incarcerated persons. In the same process in which BLM protestors have shunned "respectability politics" and elevated gender nonconforming, transgender, and queer leaders, the BLM movement has the potential to highlight the value of incarcerated and formerly incarcerated persons, many of whom have served time because they are symbolically constructed as morally polluted, reside in spaces associated with moral pollution, are targeted by racist police officers, and lack the resources to challenge the charges against them. In redrawing the symbolic construct of morally polluted persons, BLM uplifts the potential for leadership of formerly incarcerated persons.

The potential for elevating formerly incarcerated persons is perhaps most clearly signified by Keith Lamont Scott, a forty-three-year-old Black man who was fatally shot by a police officer in Charlotte, North Carolina, on September 20, 2016. Scott, a father of seven, possessed multiple misdemeanor and felony convictions, and had served time in prison.

Yet, Scott's status as a formerly incarcerated person was insignificant to the Black communities in Charlotte that rose up to protest his murder. Not only did organizations such as Showing Up for Racial Justice (SURJ) and clergy coalitions rally to hold the police department and the city accountable, but also ordinary protestors, including formerly incarcerated persons, took to the streets. The people who were constructed as morally polluted—people who had committed offensive acts, but moreover, possessed offensive bodies—visibly challenged prevailing images of power and structures of accountability. It remained inconsequential that the murdered person had committed acts that located him outside of the sphere of moral purity. The protestors challenged the symbolic pollution boundaries that led to his killing. Nightly marches confronted the sophisticated apparatuses of the penal system. In their demonstrations, the activists created a new symbol: the moral Black body that is worthy of protection and justice.

Bibliography

Abramsky, Sasha. *American Furies: Crime, Punishment, and Vengeance in the Age of Mass Imprisonment*. Boston: Beacon, 2007.

Alexander, Michelle. *The New Jim Crow: Mass Incarceration in the Age of Colorblindness*. New York: New Press, 2010.

Allen, Francis A. *Decline of the Rehabilitative Ideal: Penal Policy and Social Purpose*. New Haven, CT: Yale University Press, 1981.

Aristotle. *Politics*. In *The Basic Works of Aristotle*, edited by Richard McKeon. New York: Modern Library, 2001.

Austin, James, and Michael Jacobson. *How New York City Reduced Mass Incarceration: A Model for Change?* Brennan Center for Justice. January 2013. PDF. http://tinyurl.com/hgb425w.

Ayers, Edward L. *Vengeance and Justice: Crime and Punishment in the 19th-Century American South*. New York: Oxford University Press, 1984.

Azurara, Gomes Eannes de. *The Chronicle of the Discovery and Conquest of Guinea*. Vol. 1. London: The Hakluyt Society, 1896.

Baca, Jimmy Santiago. *A Place to Stand*. New York: Grove, 2001.

Baldwin, Ebenezer. *Observations on the Physical, Intellectual, and Moral Qualities of Our Colored Population*. New Haven, CT: L. H. Young, 1834.

Balibar, Etienne. *Race, Nation, Class: Ambiguous Identities*. New York: Verso, 1988.

Barlow, Melissa Hickman. "Race and the Problem of Crime in 'Time' and 'Newsweek' Cover Stories, 1946 to 1995." *Social Justice* 25, no. 2 (1998): 149–83.

Bean, Alan. *Taking Out the Trash in Tulia, Texas*. Desoto, TX: Advanced Concept Design, 2010.

Beaumont, Gustave de, and Alexis de Tocqueville. *On the Penitentiary System in the United States and Its Application in France*. Philadelphia: Carey, Lea & Blanchard, 1833.

Beckett, Katherine. *Making Crime Pay: Law and Order in Contemporary American Politics*. New York: Oxford University Press, 1997.

Beckett, Katherine, Kris Nyrop, and Lori Pfingst. "Race, Drugs, and Policing: Understanding Disparities in Drug Delivery Arrests." *Criminology* 44, no. 1 (February 2006): 105–37.

Bennett, William J., John DiIulio, and John P. Walters. *Body Count: Moral Poverty . . . and How to Win America's War Against Crime and Drugs*. New York: Simon & Schuster, 1996.

Bernasconi, Robert. "Kant as an Unfamiliar Source of Racism." In *Philosophers on Race: Critical Essays*, edited by Julie K. Ward and Tommy L. Lott, 145–66. Oxford: Blackwell, 2002.

_____. "Who Invented the Concept of Race? Kant's Role in the Enlightenment Construction of Race." In *Race*, edited by Robert Bernasconi, 11–36. Malden, MA: Blackwell, 2001.

Bernstein, Dan, with Hyejung Kim. "Under Custody Report: Profile of Incarcerated Offender Population Under Custody on January 1, 2012." State of New York Department of Corrections and Community Supervision. December 2012. PDF. http://tinyurl.com/z7jkmr6.

Blackmon, Douglas A. *Slavery by Another Name: The Re-Enslavement of Black People in America from the Civil War to World War II*. New York: Doubleday, 2008.

Blackstone, William. *Analysis of the Laws of England*. Oxford: Clarendon, 1756.

Blakeslee, Nate. *Tulia: Race, Cocaine, and Corruption in a Small Texas Town*. New York: Public Affairs, 2005.

Bobo, Lawrence, James R. Kluegel, and Ryan A. Smith. "Laissez-Faire Racism: The Crystallization of a 'Kinder, Gentler' Anti Black Ideology." In *Racial Attitudes in the 1990s: Continuity and Change*, edited by Steven A. Tuch and Jack K. Martin, 15–43. Westport, CT: Praeger, 1997.

Bonilla, Yarimar, and Jonathan Rosa. "#Ferguson: Digital Protest, Hashtag Ethnography, and the Racial Politics of Social Media in the United States." *American Ethnologist* 42, no. 1 (February 2015): 4–17.

Bright, Stephen B. "Discrimination, Death, and Denial: The Tolerance of Racial Discrimination in Infliction of the Death Penalty." In *From Lynch Mobs to the Killing State: Race and the Death Penalty in America*, edited by Charles J. Ogletree Jr. and Austin Sarat, 211–59. New York: New York University Press, 2006.

Buffon, Comte de. *A Natural History, General and Particular*. In *Race and the Enlightenment: A Reader*, edited by Emmanuel Chukwudi Eze. Malden, MA: Blackwell, 1997.

Bulkeley, Peter, *The Gospel Covenant; Or, The Covenant of Grace Opened*. London: Matthew Simmons, 1651.

Burton-Rose, Daniel, Dan Pens, and Paul Wright, eds. *The Celling of America: An Inside Look at the U.S. Prison Industry*. Monroe, ME: Common Courage, 1998.

Button, James W. *Black Violence: Political Impact of the 1960s Riots*. Princeton, NJ: Princeton University Press, 1978.

Calvin, John. *Institutes of the Christian Religion, Vols. 1 & 2*. Edited by John T. McNeil. Translated by Ford Lewis Battles. Philadelphia: Westminster, 1960.

Carrasco, Ben. "Assessing the CCPOA's Political Influence and Its Impact on Efforts to Reform the California Corrections System." California Sentencing and Corrections Policy Series. Stanford Criminal Justice Center, working paper, January 27, 2006.

Carson, E. Ann, and William J. Sabol. "Prisoners in 2011." Bureau of Justice Statistics. December 17, 2012. http://tinyurl.com/j74rhuf.

Carter, J. Kameron. *Race: A Theological Account*. New York: Oxford University Press, 2008.

Cartwright, Samuel. *Essays, being inductions drawn from the Baconian philosophy proving the truth of the Bible and the justice and benevolence of the decree dooming Canaan to be servant of servants*. Vidalia [LA], 1843.

Center for Constitutional Rights. "New York's Highest Court to Hear Challenges to Discriminatory Prison Telephone Charges." CCRJustice.org. October 23, 2007. http://tinyurl.com/z5ulkpw.

———. "Stop and Frisk: The Human Impact." July 2012. PDF. http://tinyurl.com/zw3l4va.

Chambliss, William, "Policing the Ghetto Underclass: The Politics of Law and Law Enforcement." *Social Problems* 41, no. 2 (1994).

Christianson, Scott. *With Liberty for Some: 500 Years of Imprisonment in America*. Boston: Northeastern University Press, 1998.

Clay, Henry. "An Address Delivered to the Colonization Society of Kentucky, at Frankfurt, December 17, 1829, by the Hon, Henry Clay, at the Request of the Board of Managers." *African Repository and Colonial Journal* 6, no. 1 (March 1830): 1–26.

Cohen, William. *At Freedom's Edge: Black Mobility and the Southern White Quest for Racial Control, 1861-1915*. Baton Rouge: Louisiana State University Press, 1991.

Colfax, Richard H. *Evidence Against the Views of the Abolitionists, Consisting of Physical and Moral Proofs of the Natural Inferiority of Negroes*. New York: James T. M. Bleakley, 1833.

Colton, Calvin. *Colonization and Abolition Contrasted*. Philadelphia: H. Hooker, 1839.

Cone, James H. *A Black Theology of Liberation*. Maryknoll, NY: Orbis, 1970.

———. *The Cross and the Lynching Tree*. Maryknoll, NY: Orbis, 2011.

Conover, Ted. *Newjack: Guarding Sing Sing*. New York: Vintage, 2001.

Cotton, John. "A Coppie of the Liberties of the Massachusetts Colonie in New England." In *Puritan Political Ideas: 1558-1794*, edited by Edmund S. Morgan, 177–202. Indianapolis: Bobbs-Merrill, 1965.

Daniels, Ron. "The Crisis of Police Brutality and Misconduct in America: The Causes and the Cure." In *Police Brutality: An Anthology*, edited by Jill Nelson, 240. New York: W. W. Norton, 2001.

Davis, Angela Y. *Are Prisons Obsolete?* New York: Seven Stories, 2003.

_____. "From the Convict Lease System to the Super-Max Prison." In *States of Confinement: Policing, Detention, and Prisons*, edited by Joy James, 60–74. New York: St. Martin's, 2000.

Davis, David Brion. *The Problem of Slavery in Western Culture*. Ithaca, NY: Cornell University Press, 1966.

Dew, Thomas R. *Review of the Debate of the Virginia Legislature of 1831 and 1832*. Richmond, VA: T. W. White, 1983.

Documents of the New York State Assembly. 62nd Session. *Report of the Committee on State Prisons, in Relation to the Mount-Pleasant Prison*. Vol. 6, no. 335. 1839.

Documents of the New York State Senate. *Testimony Taken by the Committee Appointed by the Senate, to Investigate the Affairs of the Auburn and Mount-Pleasant State Prisons*. Vol. 2, no. 48. 1840.

Donziger, Steven R., ed. *The Real War on Crime: The Report of the National Criminal Justice Commission*. New York: HarperPerennial, 1996.

Douglas, Mary. *Purity and Danger: An Analysis of the Concepts of Pollution and Taboo*. New York: Routledge, 2000.

Douglas, Kelly Brown. *Stand Your Ground: Black Bodies and the Justice of God*. Maryknoll, NY: Orbis, 2015.

Drayton, William. *The South Vindicated from the Treason and Fanaticism of the Northern Abolitionists*. Philadelphia: H. Manly, 1836.

Drug Policy Alliance. "Marijuana Arrests in NYC: Fiscally Irresponsible, Racially Biased and Unconstitutional." 2012. PDF. http://tinyurl.com/z7mffse.

Durkheim, Emile. *The Division of Labor in Society*. Translated by W. D. Halls. New York: Free Press, 1984.

Dyer, Joel. *The Perpetual Prisoner Machine: How America Profits from Crime*. Boulder, CO: Westview, 2000.

Edsall, Thomas Byrne, and Mary D. Edsall. *Chain Reaction: The Impact of Race, Rights, and Taxes*. New York: W. W. Norton, 1992.

Entman, Robert M., and Andrew Rojecki. *The Black Image in the White Mind: Media and Race in America*. Chicago: University of Chicago Press, 2010.

Erisman, Wendy, and Jeanne Bayer Contardo. *Learning to Reduce Recidivism: A*

50-State Analysis of Postsecondary Correctional Education Policy. Washington, DC: Institute for Higher Education Policy, 2005.

Erzen, Tanya. "Turnstile Jumpers and Broken Windows: Policing Disorder in New York City." In *Zero Tolerance: Quality of Life and the New Police Brutality in New York City,* edited by Andrea McArdle and Tanya Erzen, 19–49. New York: New York University Press, 2001.

Estes, Matthew. *A Defence of Negro Slavery, as It Exists in the United States.* Montgomery: Press of the *Alabama Journal,* 1846.

Evans, M. Stanton. *The Future of Conservatism: From Taft to Reagan and Beyond.* New York: Holt, Rinehart & Winston, 1968.

Fanon, Frantz. *Black Skin, White Masks.* New York: Grove, 1952.

Fellner, Jamie. *Decades of Disparity: Drug Arrests and Race in the United States.* New York: Human Rights Watch, 2009.

_____. *Targeting Blacks: Drug Law Enforcement in the United States.* New York: Human Rights Watch, 2008.

Fine, Michelle, Maria Elena Torre, Kathy Boudin, Iris Bowen, Judith Clark, Donna Hylton, Migdalia Martinez, "Missy," Rosemarie A. Roberts, Pamela Smart, and Debora Upegui. "Changing Minds: The Impact of College in a Maximum-Security Prison." January 2001. PDF. http://tinyurl.com/ ze9hu6p.

Flamm, Michael W. *Law and Order: Street Crime, Civil Unrest, and the Crisis of Liberalism in the 1960s.* New York: Columbia University Press, 2005.

Floyd v. City of New York, 959 F. Supp. 2d (S.D.N.Y. 2013). http://tinyurl.com/ h6cpur2.

Foucault, Michel. *Discipline and Punish: The Birth of the Prison.* Translated by Alan Sheridan. New York: Random House, 1995.

Francis, Leah Gunning. *Ferguson and Faith: Sparking Leadership and Awakening Community.* St. Louis: Chalice, 2015.

Frederickson, George M. *The Black Image in the White Mind: The Debate on Afro-American Character and Destiny, 1817–1914.* Hanover, CT: Wesleyan University Press, 1971.

Freelon, Deen, Charlton D. McIlwain, and Meredith Clark. *Beyond the Hashtags: #Ferguson, #BlackLivesMatter, and the Online Struggle for Offline Justice.* Center for Media and Social Impact, American University. February 2016. PDF. http://tinyurl.com/zqz9yrk.

Garland, David. *Culture of Control: Crime and Social Order in Contemporary Society.* Chicago: University of Chicago Press, 2001.

_____. *Punishment and Modern Society: A Study in Social Theory.* Chicago: University of Chicago Press, 1990.

Garrison, William Lloyd. *Thoughts on African Colonization.* Boston: Garrison & Knapp, 1832.

Gest, Ted. *Crime and Politics: Big Government's Erratic Campaign for Law and Order.* New York: Oxford University Press, 2001.

Gilmore, Ruth Wilson. *Golden Gulag: Prisons, Surplus, Crisis, and Opposition in Globalizing California.* Berkeley: University of California Press, 2007.

Goldberg, David Theo. "Surplus Value: The Political Economy of Prisons and Policing." In *States of Confinement: Policing, Detention, and Prisons,* edited by Joy James, 205–21. New York: St. Martin's, 2000.

Gonnerman, Jennifer. "How the Lingering Effects of a Massive Drug Bust Devastated One Family in a Small Texas Town." *The Village Voice.* July 31, 2001.

_____. "Officer Serrano's Hidden Camera: The Stop-and-Frisk Trials of Pedro Serrano: NYPD Rat, NYPD Hero." *New York Magazine.* May 19, 2013.

Gottschalk, Marie. *The Prison and the Gallows: The Politics of Mass Incarceration in America.* New York: Cambridge University Press, 2006.

Green, John C. "Seeking a Place." In *Toward an Evangelical Public Policy: Political Strategies for the Health of the Nation,* edited by Ronald J. Sider and Diane Knippers, 15–34. Grand Rapids: Baker Books, 2005.

Greenberg, David F., and Valerie West. "State Prison Populations and Their Growth, 1971–1991." *Criminology* 39, no. 3 (August 2001): 615–54.

Greene, Judith. "Entrepreneurial Corrections: Incarceration as a Business Opportunity." In *Invisible Punishment: The Collateral Consequences of Mass Imprisonment,* edited by Marc Mauer and Meda Chesney-Lind, 95–112. New York: New Press, 2002.

Greene, Lorenzo Johnston. *The Negro in Colonial New England: 1620-1776.* New York: Columbia University Press, 1942.

Gutiérrez, Gustavo. *A Theology of Liberation.* Maryknoll, NY: Orbis, 1973.

Hallinan, Joseph T. *Going Up the River: Travels in a Prison Nation.* New York: Random House, 2003.

Harper, Robert Goodloe. *A Letter from General Harper of Maryland, to Elias Caldwell, Secretary of the American Society for Colonizing Free People of Colour, in the United States, with their own consent.* Baltimore, 1818.

Haynes, Stephen R. *Noah's Curse: The Biblical Justification of American Slavery.* New York: Oxford University Press, 2002.

Herivel, Tara, and Paul Wright. *Prison Nation: The Warehousing of America's Poor.* New York: Routledge, 2003.

Herrnstein, Richard J., and Charles Murray. *The Bell Curve: Intelligence and Class Structure in American Life.* New York: Simon & Schuster, 1996.

Hildreth, Richard. *Despotism in America: An Inquiry into the Nature, Results, and*

Legal Basis of the Slave-Holding System in the United States. Boston: Whipple & Damrell, 1840.

Hindus, Michael Stephen. *Prison and Plantation: Crime, Justice, and Authority in Massachusetts and South Carolina, 1767-1878.* Chapel Hill: University of North Carolina Press, 1980.

Hirsch, Adam Jay. *The Rise of the Penitentiary: Prisons and Punishment in Early America.* New Haven, CT: Yale University Press, 1992.

Holifield, E. Brooks. *Theology in America: Christian Thought from the Age of the Puritans to the Civil War.* New Haven, CT: Yale University Press, 2003.

Huling, Tracy. "Building a Prison Economy in Rural America." In *Invisible Punishment: The Collateral Consequences of Mass Imprisonment,* edited by Marc Mauer and Meda Chesney-Lind, 197–213. New York: New Press, 2002.

Hurwitz, Jon, and Mark Peffley. "Public Perceptions of Race and Crime: The Role of Racial Stereotypes." *American Journal of Political Science* 41, no. 2 (April 1997): 375–401.

Ignatieff, Michael. *A Just Measure of Pain: The Penitentiary in the Industrial Revolution, 1750-1850.* New York: Penguin, 1978.

Jackson, George. *Soledad Brother: The Prison Letters of George Jackson.* New York: Bantam, 1970.

Jay, William. *Miscellaneous Writings on Slavery.* Cleveland, OH: Jewett, Proctor & Worthington, 1853.

Jefferson, Thomas. *Notes on the State of Virginia.* New York: Penguin, 1998.

_____. *The Papers of Thomas Jefferson.* Edited by Julian P. Boyd. Princeton, NJ: Princeton University Press, 1950.

Jenks, William. *Memoir of the Rev. Louis Dwight, Late Secretary of the Boston Prison Discipline Society.* Boston: T. R. Marvin, 1856.

Jennings, Willie James. *The Christian Imagination: Theology and the Origins of Race.* New Haven, CT: Yale University Press, 2010.

Jordan, Winthrop D. *White over Black: American Attitudes toward the Negro, 1550-1812.* Chapel Hill: University of North Carolina Press, 1968.

Kajstura, Aleks, and Peter Wagner. "Importing Constituents: Prisoners and Political Clout in California." The Prison Policy Initiative. March 2010. http://tinyurl.com/hlqdv65.

Kant, Immanuel. *Anthropology from a Pragmatic Point of View.* Edited and translated by Robert B. Louden. New York: Cambridge University Press, 2006.

_____. "Conjectures on the Beginning of Human History." In *Political Writings,* 221–34. Edited by H. S. Reiss. Translated by H. B. Nisbet. 2nd ed. New York: Cambridge University Press, 1991.

_____. "Of the Different Human Races." In *The Idea of Race,* edited by Robert Bernasconi and Tommy L. Lott, 8–22. Indianapolis: Hackett, 2000.

_____. "On the Use of Teleological Principles in Philosophy." In *Race*, edited by Robert Bernasconi. Malden, MA: Blackwell, 2001.

Ker, Leander. *Slavery Consistent with Christianity*. Baltimore: Sherwood, 1840.

King, Ryan S. "Disparity by Geography: The War on Drugs in America's Cities." The Sentencing Project. May 2008.

Koch, Adrienne. *The Philosophy of Thomas Jefferson*. New York: Columbia University Press, 1943.

Lafer, Gordon. "The Politics of Prison Labor: A Union Perspective." In *Prison Nation: The Warehousing of America's Poor*, edited by Tara Herivel and Paul Wright, 120–28. New York: Routledge, 2003.

_____. *Moral Politics: How Liberals and Conservatives Think*. Chicago: University of Chicago Press, 2002.

Larrimore, Mark. "Sublime Waste: Kant on the Destiny of the 'Races.'" In *Civilization and Oppression*, edited by Cheryl J. Misak, 99–125. Calgary: University of Calgary Press, 1999.

Lawrence, Sarah, and Jeremy Travis. "The New Landscape of Imprisonment: Mapping America's Prison Expansion." The Urban Institute. April 29, 2004.

Lee, Richard Henry. *The Letters of Richard Henry Lee*. Vol. 1. Edited by James Curtis Ballagh. New York: Da Capo, 1970.

Levine, Harry G. "New York City's Marijuana Arrest Crusade . . . Continues." September 2009. PDF. http://tinyurl.com/ztz4b7w.

Levine, Harry G., and Loren Sigel. "$75 Million a Year: The Cost of New York City's Marijuana Possession Arrests." Drug Policy Alliance. March 2011. PDF. http://tinyurl.com/zfhevbd.

Lewis, Orlando. *The Development of American Prisons and Prison Customs, 1776–1845, with Special Reference to Early Institutions in the State of New York*. Montclair, NJ: Patterson Smith, 1967.

Lewis, W. David. *From Newgate to Dannemora: The Rise of the Penitentiary in New York, 1796–1848*. Ithaca, NY: Cornell University Press, 1965.

Lichtenstein, Alex. *Twice the Work of Free Labor: The Political Economy of Convict Labor in the New South*. New York: Verso, 1996.

Linné, Carl von. *The System of Nature*. In *Race and the Enlightenment: A Reader*, edited by Emmanuel Chukwudi Eze. Malden, MA: Blackwell, 1997.

Lipton, Douglas, Robert Martinson, and Judith Wilks. *The Effectiveness of Correctional Treatment: A Survey of Treatment Evaluation Studies*. New York: Praeger, 1975.

Litwack, Leon F. *North of Slavery: The Negro in the Free States, 1790–1860*. Chicago: University of Chicago Press, 1961.

Locke, John. *Two Treatises of Government*. Edited by Peter Laslett. New York: Cambridge University Press, 1988.

Logan, James Samuel. *Good Punishment? Christian Moral Practice and U.S. Imprisonment.* Grand Rapids: Eerdmans, 2008.

Lomax, Adrien. "Prison Jobs and Free Market Unemployment." In *Prison Nation: The Warehousing of America's Poor,* edited by Tara Herivel and Paul Wright, 133–37. New York: Routledge, 2003.

Long, Charles H. *Significations, Signs, Symbols, and Images in the Interpretation of Religion.* Aurora, CO: Davies, 1999.

Lowndes, Joseph. *From the New Deal to the New Right: Race and the Southern Origins of Modern Conservatism.* New Haven, CT: Yale University Press, 2008.

Luther, Martin. *The Freedom of a Christian.* Philadelphia: Fortress, 1957.

Lynch, Mona. "Stereotypes, Prejudice, and Life-and-Death Decision Making: Lessons from Laypersons in an Experimental Setting." In *From Lynch Mobs to the Killing State: Race and the Death Penalty in America,* edited by Charles J. Ogletree Jr. and Austin Sarat, 182–209. New York: New York University Press, 2006.

Mancini, Matthew J. *One Dies, Get Another: Convict Leasing in the American South, 1866–1928.* Columbia: University of South Carolina Press, 1996.

Mann, Coramae Richey. *Unequal Justice: A Question of Color.* Bloomington: Indiana University Press, 1993.

Mann, Coramae Richey, Marjorie S. Zatz, and Nancy Rodriguez, eds. *Images of Color, Images of Crime.* 3rd ed. Los Angeles: Roxbury, 2006.

Manza, Jeff, and Christopher Uggen. *Locked Out: Felon Disenfranchisement and American Democracy.* New York: Oxford University Press: 2006.

Marshall, Thomas. "The Speech of Thomas Marshall, in the House of Delegates of Virginia, on the Abolition of Slavery, Delivered Friday, January 20, 1832. Richmond." *African Repository and Colonial Journal* 9, no. 11 (January 1834): 1–22.

Mather, Cotton. "The Negro Christianized: An Essay to Excite and Assist that Good Work, Instruction of Negro-Servants in Christianity (1706)." In *Against Slavery: An Abolitionist Reader,* edited by Mason Lowance, 18–20. New York: Penguin, 2000.

Mauer, Marc. "The Changing Racial Dynamics of the War on Drugs." The Sentencing Project. April 2009. PDF. http://tinyurl.com/hyns7du.

_____. "The Changing Racial Dynamics of Women's Incarceration." The Sentencing Project. February 27, 2013. http://tinyurl.com/hpbrxmh.

_____. *Race to Incarcerate.* New York: New Press, 1999.

Marc Mauer and Ryan King, "A 25 Year Quagmire: The War on Drugs and Its Impact on American Society," *The Sentencing Project* (Washington, DC, 2007),

McArdle, Andrea, and Tanya Erzen, eds. *Zero Tolerance: Quality of Life and the New Police Brutality in New York City.* New York: New York University Press, 2001.

215

Meiners, Erica R. *Right to Be Hostile: Schools, Prisons, and the Making of Public Enemies*. New York: Routledge, 2007.

Melossi, Dario, and Massimo Pavarini. *The Prison and the Factory: Origins of the Penitentiary System*. London: Macmillan, 1981.

Mendelberg, Tali. *The Race Card: Campaign Strategy, Implicit Messages, and the Norm of Equality*. Princeton, NJ: Princeton University Press, 2001.

Miller, Perry. *The New England Mind: From Colony to Province*. Cambridge, MA: Harvard University Press, 1967.

_____. *The New England Mind: The Seventeenth Century*. Cambridge, MA: Harvard University Press, 1939.

Miller, Perry, and Thomas H. Johnson, eds. *The Puritans: A Sourcebook of Their Writings*. Mineola, NY: Dover, 2001.

Mills, Charles W. *The Racial Contract*. Ithaca, NY: Cornell University Press, 1997.

Mitford, Jessica. *Kind and Usual Punishment: The Prison Business*. New York: Alfred A. Knopf, 1973.

Montesquieu, Baron de. *Spirit of the Laws*. Translated by Thomas Nugent. New York: D. Appleton, 1900.

Morone, James A. *Hellfire Nation: The Politics of Sin in American History*. New Haven, CT: Yale University Press, 2003.

Moss, Frank. "Persecution of Negroes by Roughs and Policemen, in the City of New York, August, 1900." In *Police Brutality: An Anthology*, edited by Jill Nelson, 60–87. New York: W. W. Norton, 2001.

Myers, Martha A. *Race, Labor, and Punishment in the New South*. Columbus: Ohio State University Press, 1998.

New York Civil Liberties Union (NYCLU). "Stop-and-Frisk 2011." May 9, 2012. PDF. http://tinyurl.com/j39q7tq.

Mae M. Ngai, *Impossible Subjects: Illegal Aliens and the Making of Modern America*. Princeton, NJ: Princeton University Press, 2004

Olteanu, Alexandra, Ingmar Weber, and Daniel Garcia-Perez. "Characterizing the Demographics Behind the #BlackLivesMatter Movement." Cornell University. December 17, 2015. http://arxiv.org/abs/1512.05671.

Omi, Michael, and Howard Winant. *Racial Formation in the United States: From the 1960s to the 1990s*. 2nd ed. New York: Routledge & Kegan Paul, 1986.

Oshinsky, David M. *"Worse Than Slavery": Parchman Farm and the Ordeal of Jim Crow Justice*. New York: Free Press, 1996.

Pager, Devah. *Marked: Race, Crime, and Finding Work in an Era of Mass Incarceration*. Chicago: University of Chicago Press, 2007.

Pager, Devah, and Bruce Western. "Race at Work." Paper presented at the New York City Commission on Human Rights conference "Race at Work—Realities of Race and Criminal Record in the NYC Job Market," Schomburg Center for Research in Black Culture, New York, December 9, 2005.

Parenti, Christian. *Lockdown America: Police and Prisons in the Age of Crisis.* New York: Verso, 1999.

Patterson, Orlando. *Slavery and Social Death: A Comparative Study.* Cambridge, MA: Harvard University Press, 1982.

Pens, Dan. "The California Prison Guards' Union: A Potent Political Interest Group." In *The Celling of America: An Inside Look at the U.S. Prison Industry,* edited by Daniel Burton-Rose, Dan Pens, and Paul Wright, 134–39. Monroe, ME: Common Courage, 1998.

_____. "Microsoft 'Outcells' Competition." In *The Celling of America: An Inside Look at the U.S. Prison Industry,* edited by Daniel Burton-Rose, Dan Pens, and Paul Wright, 114–21. Monroe, ME: Common Courage, 1998.

_____. "VitaPro Fraud in Texas." In *The Celling of America: An Inside Look at the U.S. Prison Industry,* edited by Daniel Burton-Rose, Dan Pens, and Paul Wright, 147–48. Monroe, ME: Common Courage, 1998.

Phillips, Kevin. *The Emerging Republican Majority.* Garden City, NY: Anchor, 1970.

Pinn, Anthony B. *Embodiment and the New Shape of Black Theological Thought.* New York: New York University Press, 2010.

"Platform." The Movement for Black Lives. http://tinyurl.com/zhmrv5v.

Plouffe, William C. "The Natural Law in the Minds of the Founding Fathers." *Vera Lex* 9, no. 1–2 (2008): 109–22.

Police Reform Organizing Project. "The Narratives Project." http://tinyurl.com/jeaulz7.

_____. "New York City's Failure: Harsh, Unjust Police Tactics." June 2011. PDF. http://tinyurl.com/jesjbn5.

Priest, Josiah. *Slavery, as it relates to the Negro, or African race: examined in the light of circumstances, history, and the Holy Scriptures: with an account of the origin of the black man's color, causes of his state of servitude and traces of his character as well as in ancient as in modern times: with strictures on abolitionism.* Albany, NY: C. Van Benthuysen, 1843.

Prison Discipline Society. *First Annual Report of the Board of Managers of the Prison Discipline Society, Boston, June 2, 1826.* 4th ed. Boston: T. R. Marvin, 1827.

Quadagno, Jill. *The Color of Welfare: How Racism Undermined the War on Poverty.* New York: Oxford University Press, 1994.

Rhodes, Lorna A. *Total Confinement: Madness and Reason in the Maximum Security Prison.* Berkeley: University of California Press, 2004.

Rivera, Luis N. *A Violent Evangelism: The Political and Religious Conquest of the Americas.* Louisville, KY: Westminster John Knox, 1992.

Roberts, Julian V., and Loretta J. Stalans. *Public Opinion, Crime, and Criminal Justice.* Boulder, CO: Westview, 1997.

Rogers, Jamala. *Ferguson Is America: Roots of Rebellion.* St. Louis: Mira Digital Publishing, 2015.

Ross, Andrew. "Areas A, B, and C: An Afterword." In *Zero Tolerance: Quality of Life and the New Police Brutality in New York City*, edited by Andrea McArdle and Tanya Erzen, 282–87. New York: New York University Press, 2001.

Rothman, David J. *Conscience and Convenience: The Asylum and Its Alternatives in Progressive America.* Boston: Little, Brown, 1980.

_____. *The Discovery of the Asylum: Social Order and Disorder in the New Republic.* Boston: Little, Brown, 1971.

Rusche, Georg, and Otto Kirchheimer. *Punishment and Social Structure.* New York: Columbia University Press, 1939.

Russell-Brown, Katheryn. *The Color of Crime.* 2nd ed. New York: New York University Press, 2008.

Sacks, Marcy. "'To Show Who was in Charge': Police Repression of New York City's Black Population at the Turn of the Twentieth Century." *Journal of Urban History* 31, no. 6 (2005): 799–819.

Saffin, John. "A Brief Candid Answer to a Late Printed Sheet, Entitled, *The Selling of Joseph* (1701)." In *Against Slavery: An Abolitionist Reader*, edited by Mason Lowance, 15–17. New York: Penguin, 2000.

Scheingold, Stuart A. *The Politics of Law and Order: Street Crime and Public Policy.* New York: Longman, 1984.

_____. *The Politics of Street Crime: Criminal Process and Cultural Obsession.* Philadelphia: Temple University Press, 1991.

Schmid, Muriel. "The Eye of God: Religious Beliefs and Punishment in Early Nineteenth-Century Prison Reform." *Theology Today* 59, no. 4 (January 2003): 546–58.

Sellin, Thorsten. *Slavery and the Penal System.* New York: Elsevier, 1976.

Sewall, Samuel. "The Selling of Joseph: A Memorial (1700)." In *Against Slavery: An Abolitionist Reader*, edited by Mason Lowance, 11–14. New York: Penguin, 2000.

Simon, Jonathan. *How the War on Crime Transformed American Democracy and Created a Culture of Fear.* New York: Oxford University Press, 2007.

Sloop, John M. *The Cultural Prison: Discourse, Prisoners, and Punishment.* Tuscaloosa: University of Alabama Press, 1996.

Smith, Rogers M. *Civic Ideals: Conflicting Visions of Citizenship in U.S. History.* New Haven, CT: Yale University Press, 1997.

Stout, Jeffrey. *Ethics after Babel: The Languages of Morals and Their Discontents.* Princeton, NJ: Princeton University Press, 2001.

Stroughton, William. "New England's True Interest." In *The Puritans: A Sourcebook of Their Writings*, edited by Perry Miller and Thomas H. Johnson, 243–45. Mineola, NY: Dover Publications, 2001.

Swanson, R. N. "The Pre-Reformation Church." In *The Reformation World*, edited by Andrew Pettegree, 9–30. London: Routledge, 2000.

Taylor, Keeanga-Yamahtta. *From #BlackLivesMatter to Black Liberation*. Chicago: Haymarket, 2016.

Taylor, Mark Lewis. *The Executed God: The Way of the Cross in Lockdown America*. Minneapolis: Fortress, 2001.

Terry v. Ohio, 392 U.S. 1, 88 S. Ct. 1868, 20 L. Ed. 2d 889 (1968).

Tonry, Michael. *Malign Neglect: Race, Crime, and Punishment in America*. New York: Oxford University Press, 1995.

———. *Thinking about Crime: Sense and Sensibilities in American Penal Culture*. New York: Oxford University Press, 2004.

Upchurch, Carl. *Convicted in the Womb: One Man's Journey from Prisoner to Peacemaker*. New York: Bantam, 1996.

United States Bureau of the Census. *Negro Population in the United States, 1790–1915*. New York: Arno, 1968.

United States Department of Justice. "Violent Crime Control and Law Enforcement Act of 1994." October 24, 1994. http://tinyurl.com/jas9j9p.

United States Department of Justice Civil Rights Division. "Investigation of the Ferguson Police Department." March 4, 2015. PDF. http://tinyurl.com/zhywh7r.

Wacquant, Loïc. "Deadly Symbiosis: When Ghetto and Prison Meet and Mesh." *Punishment and Society* 3, no. 1 (January 2001): 95–134.

———. *Punishing the Poor: The Neoliberal Government of Social Insecurity*. Durham, NC: Duke University Press, 2009.

Wagner, Peter, and Rose Heyer. "Importing Constituents: Prisoners and Political Clout in Texas." The Prison Policy Initiative. November 8, 2004. http://tinyurl.com/jyes8gy.

Wagner, Peter, Aleks Kajstura, Elena Lavarreda, Christian de Ocejo, and Sheila Vennell O'Rourke. "Fixing Prison-Based Gerrymandering after the 2010 Census: A 50 State Guide." The Prison Policy Initiative. March 2010. http://tinyurl.com/gwgy2rp.

Wagner, Peter, and Eric T. Lotke. "Prisoners of the Census: Counting Prisoners Where They Go, Not Where They Come From." *Pace Law Review* 24, no. 2 (2004): 587–608.

Weaver, Vesla Mae. "Frontlash: Race and the Development of Punitive Crime Strategy." *Studies in American Political Development* 21, no. 2 (Fall 2007): 230–65.

Weiser, Benjamin. "Officer's Lawsuit over Quotas Is Reinstated." *New York Times*. November 28, 2012.

West, Cornel. *Prophesy Deliverance! An Afro-American Revolutionary Christianity*. Philadelphia: Westminster, 1982.

_____. *Race Matters*. Boston: Beacon, 1993.

Western, Bruce. *Punishment and Inequality in America*. New York: Russell Sage Foundation, 2006.

Wey Gómez, Nicolás. *The Tropics of Empire: Why Columbus Sailed South to the Indies*. Cambridge, MA: MIT Press, 2008.

Wilson, James Q. *On Character: Essays*. Washington, DC: AEI, 1991.

_____. *Thinking about Crime*. New York: Basic Books, 1983.

Wilson, James Q., and Richard J. Herrnstein. *Crime and Human Nature*. New York: Simon & Schuster, 1985.

Wilson, Theodore Brantner. *The Black Codes of the South*. Tuscaloosa: University of Alabama Press, 1965.

Wilson, William Julius. *When Work Disappears: The New World of the Urban Poor*. New York: Vintage, 1997.

Witte, John, Jr. "How to Govern a City on a Hill: Puritan Contributions to American Constitutional Law and Liberty." In *God's Joust, God's Justice: Law and Religion in the Western Tradition*, 143–68. Grand Rapids: Eerdmans, 2006.

Wright, Paul. "Making Slave Labor Fly." In *Prison Nation: The Warehousing of America's Poor*, edited by Tara Herivel and Paul Wright, 112–19. New York: Routledge, 2003.

_____. "The Private Prison Industry." In *Prison Nation: The Warehousing of America's Poor*, edited by Tara Herivel and Paul Wright, 137. New York: Routledge, 2003.

_____. "Slaves of the State." In *The Celling of America: An Inside Look at the U.S. Prison Industry*, edited by Daniel Burton-Rose, Dan Pens, and Paul Wright, 102–6. Monroe, ME: Common Courage, 1998.

Young, Iris Marion. *Justice and the Politics of Difference*. Princeton, NJ: Princeton University Press, 1990.

Zimring, Franklin E., and Gordon Hawkins. *Crime Is Not the Problem: Lethal Violence in America*. New York: Oxford University Press, 1997.

Index